Quicken® 6
for
Windows®

Using
Quicken® 6 for Windows®

Linda A. Flanders

Using Quicken 6 for Windows

Copyright© 1996 by Que® Corporation

Library of Congress Catalog No.: 96-70777

ISBN: 07897-0996-1

98 97 96   6 5 4 3 2

Interpretation of the printing code: the rightmost double-digit number is the year of the book's printing; the rightmost single-digit number, the number of the book's printing. For example, a printing code of 96-1 shows that the first printing of the book occurred in 1996.

All terms mentioned in this book that are known to be trademarks or service marks have been appropriately capitalized. Que cannot attest to the accuracy of this information. Use of a term in this book should not be regarded as affecting the validity of any trademark or service mark.

Screen reproductions in this book were created using Capture from Mainstay, Camarillo, CA.

Composed in *ITC Century* and *ITC Highlander* by Que Corporation.

Credits

To my three favorite girls: Jade, Jordan, and Ali. Thanks for being patient and understanding so that I can do what I do. And always, to Scott, for your love, support, and commitment.

About the Author

Linda A. Flanders is a CPA and has worked in public accounting for Arthur Andersen & Co., and private accounting for Mayflower Group, Inc., where she specialized in taxation. She is the author of Que's *Using Quicken 5 for Windows, Using QuickBooks for Windows, Using Microsoft Money 2.0, Using TurboTax,* and various other books on financial software.

Acknowledgments

I'd like to thank Martha O'Sullivan for her cheerfulness while coordinating this project, Stephanie Gould for a great job with development, and Linda Seifert for her hard work, diligence, and dedication in editing this book.

We'd like to hear from you!

As part of our continuing effort to produce books of the highest possible quality, Que would like to hear your comments. To stay competitive, we *really* want you, as a computer book reader and user, to let us know what you like or dislike most about this book or other Que products.

You can mail comments, ideas, or suggestions for improving future editions to the address below, or send us a fax at (317) 581-4663. For the online inclined, Macmillan Computer Publishing has a forum on CompuServe (type **GO QUEBOOKS** at any prompt) through which our staff and authors are available for questions and comments. The address of our Internet site is **http://www.mcp.com/que** (World Wide Web).

In addition to exploring our forum, please feel free to contact me personally to discuss your opinions of this book: I'm **73602,2077** on CompuServe, and I'm **sgould@que.mcp.com** on the Internet.

Thanks in advance—your comments will help us to continue publishing the best books available on computer topics in today's market.

Stephanie Gould
Product Development Specialist
Que Corporation
201 W. 103rd Street
Indianapolis, Indiana 46290
USA

Contents at a Glance

Contents

Part III: Organizing Your Finances

Introduction

If you're like most people, you'd rather have a root canal than deal with your finances. Let's face it, financial management is one of those never-ending tasks that usually leaves you frustrated and depressed.

No matter how many hours you spend writing checks, balancing your checkbook, plugging away at your budget, or updating your investment portfolio, you're most certainly going to spend that many hours again next week or next month. It's kind of like dirty laundry; shortly after it's done, there's a new pile.

I'm sure that you'll find Quicken to be the answer. No, Quicken doesn't do your laundry for you, but it does make financial management a quick and easy process and a little bit fun, too. *Using Quicken 6 for Windows* provides the answers and solutions to making Quicken the financial package that solves all your needs.

What can Quicken do for me?

I've been using Quicken for the last eight years and have become quite dependent on my system to keep my finances in order. You may think because I'm a computer-book author that I learn and use all kinds of programs, and that's true. But the program that I choose to use after lots of analyzing and comparing is Quicken. Because I know the ins and outs of Quicken and other programs, I have a better-than-average feel for which programs work the way they're supposed to and save the most time. Quicken's the one. Quicken 6 for Windows really can help you gain control of your personal or business finances.

If you use the program in the simplest way, Quicken can maintain your check register for you by deducting payments and adding deposits to your checking account balance. No need for longhand math or burdensome calculators and you certainly won't have to worry about overdrawing your checking account because you made an arithmetic error. But the real value in Quicken lies in all the other great things it can do for you, like:

- Printing checks in just minutes

- Balancing your checkbook

- Reminding you to pay bills

- Accumulating data in the form of reports and graphs

- Keeping track of your cash and credit card expenditures

- Tracking your outstanding loans

- Budgeting your income and expenses

- Developing a plan to get out of debt

- Helping you gather your income tax information

- Updating security values in your investment portfolio

- Forecasting your cash flows

- Calculating college and retirement needs

- Storing your financial addresses

- Keeping your home inventory

- And much, much more

What's neat about Quicken is that you can do as little or as much as you want to do with it. At first, you may use just the basic features. As time goes on, you may want to ease into the rest as you become more comfortable with Quicken.

What do I need to use Quicken 6 for Windows?

Quicken 6 for Windows is developed for use with Microsoft Windows 95, or Windows 3.1. The screen shots throughout this book were shot in Windows 95. However, most of these screen shots will look the same in Windows 3.1. Any differences in functionality are pointed out throughout the book. Also, you will need equipment like a modem to use online banking or bill paying and a printer to print out checks and reports.

What's new in Quicken 6 for Windows?

 If you're already using an earlier version of Quicken, let me tell you what new things you can expect to do in this version:

- Develop a plan to get out of debt with the new Debt Reduction Planner. Learn how to use the Debt Reduction Planner in Chapter 22, "Getting Out of Debt."

- Uncover those hidden tax deductions that you may have missed with the Tax Deduction Finder. You'll find out how to use this new feature in Chapter 17, "Getting Ready for Tax Time."

- Do your online banking, bill paying, and update your security values all from one area in Quicken; the Online Banking & Investment Center. Online bill paying is covered in Chapter 25, "Making Online Payments," and online banking is explained in Chapter 26, "Doing Your Banking Online."

- Access the Quicken Web site and other financial Web sites with Quicken Live. Learn how to access these financial Web sites in Chapter 16, "Staying on Top of Your Investments."

- Update your investment portfolio with a new online quotes service that's free of charge for the first 12 months when you register your copy of Quicken. Chapter 16, "Staying on Top of Your Investments," shows you how to use online quotes to update your portfolio.

- Order a free credit report with Credit Check. Learn how to do this in Chapter 22, "Getting Out of Debt."

- Create two new EasyAnswer reports to tell you how much you paid to a payee for any time period and how much you spent on a category as a comparison from one time period to another. These new EasyAnswer reports are covered in Chapter 18, "Printing Reports."

- View a Billminder list of actions you need to take in Quicken whenever you start Windows. Using Billminder is explained in Chapter 10, "Scheduling Future Transactions."

- Get a warning from Quicken when you approach your credit limit in a credit card account. Learn about credit card limit warnings in Chapter 13, "Managing Your Credit Cards."

- Use the new Activity Bar at the bottom of the screen to access commonly used tasks in Quicken. In Chapter 2, "Learning the Quicken Ropes," you learn how to use the Activity Bar.

- Get help performing common tasks with the new How Do I? feature, which is covered in Chapter 2, "Learning the Quicken Ropes."

- Watch a video on how to complete a task with the Show Me feature found in key Help windows, also covered in Chapter 2, "Learning the Quicken Ropes."

- Get online financial advice from the experts with the new Advice button. Refer to Chapter 16, "Staying on Top of Your Investments," to find out how to get expert financial advice.

- See some real-life examples of how to use Quicken. Chapter 2, "Learning the Quicken Ropes," uncovers these examples.

- Organize your securities in reports and graphs by a preset list of asset classes. In Chapter 16, "Staying on Top of Your Investments," you see how to use asset classes.

- Display some of the EasyAnswer reports as graphs. Chapter 18, "Printing Reports," and Chapter 19, "Looking at Data Through Graphs," show you this new feature.

- Go online with Mutual Fund Finder to view mutual fund prospectuses for free. You see how to search for a mutual fund in Chapter 16, "Staying on Top of Your Investments."

- Sort transactions in registers by order of entry, date, amount, or check number. Chapter 5, "Introducing the Quicken Register," shows you how to sort transactions.

- Enter longer account names, descriptions, and memos. Various chapters throughout this book cover these new entry features.

- Use the right mouse button on any transaction to perform actions like memorizing, voiding, or scheduling. In Chapter 5, "Introducing the Quicken Register," you learn about this new mouse action.

- Display Quicken in all new color schemes. Chapter 24, "Making Quicken Work the Way You Want It To," tells you how to change color schemes in the program.

What makes this book different?

You don't need an advanced degree in computer science, accounting, or finance to read this book. If you can tell the difference between the left and right mouse buttons and between income and expenses, you've got all the technical background you need.

It's written in plain English, too. I promise not to bury you in detailed explanations and three-letter acronyms (TLAs). After all, you're not studying for a degree in computer science—you're trying to get your finances in order, with the help of an incredibly powerful program like Quicken.

With Quicken, there may be more than one way to do something. If you're planning to become a Quicken expert, you'd expect this book to give you step-by-step instructions for each of them. Not this book.

In this book, I focus on results. That means I'll tell you the best way to get each job done. There might be three other ways to do the same thing, but for most people, most of the time, the technique I describe is the one that will get results most quickly.

By the way, there's no quiz at the end of this book. Hope you're not disappointed.

How do I use this book?

This isn't a textbook. You don't have to start at page 1 and read all the way to the end. It's not a mystery novel, either, so if you want to skip to the last chapter first, be my guest.

You'll probably be surprised at some of the things that Quicken can do for you. That's why, if you have the time, it's worth flipping through the chapters, looking at the headings, and searching out the references to the things you need to do. The people who published this book went to a lot of trouble to make sure that those interesting ideas would leap off the page and catch your attention as you browse.

This book will come in especially handy when you're not sure where to begin. And if you get stuck, you'll probably find the way out in these pages.

How this book is put together

Some people will use every last feature in Quicken. Others will spend most of their time doing the same simple tasks over and over again. It doesn't matter which type you are—you'll find exactly what you're looking for. Look at this book as a tool to help you learn how Quicken 6 for Windows can help you manage your finances more effectively. The parts are divided into chapters that get into the specifics of the program. Inside each chapter, you'll find tips, hints, and plain-English instructions for getting your work done faster without having to ask what to do next.

Part I: Getting Started with Quicken

Here, you learn what Quicken looks like when you start it and how to do some of the more basic tasks with the program, like using the check register, writing checks, and balancing your checkbook. Find out where to get help and how to quit when your work is done.

Part II: Saving Time with Quicken

Want to really zip through your financial tasks? Come here to see all the neat shortcuts in Quicken that will make your life easier. See how mini-calendars, mini-calculators, and QuickFill help you fill fields with a click or a few keystrokes, while memorized and scheduled transactions help you fill in entire transactions.

Part III: Organizing Your Finances

Organization is what it's all about. Here, you'll learn how to be more organized than you ever thought possible. Once you're through this part, you'll be tracking your cash expenditures, be right on top of those credit cards, and be managing your debts. And don't forget about putting together a budget so that you know exactly where your hard-earned money is going.

Part IV: Analyzing Your Finances

Here's some good stuff that will help you quantify your financial situation and put it all in perspective. Managing your investments, printing reports, and creating graphs are what I talk about in this part. I also cover how to be ready, willing, and able at tax time.

Part V: Planning for the Future

"Live for today" may be your motto, but you've got to plan for the future if you hope to send those kids to college and retire while you can still punch the keys on your keyboard. Want to see your future cash flow? Want to see how much you need to sock away now to send little Ali to college? How about that investment you made last year; how's it doing now? Tired of being in debt? Develop a plan to get your head above water and get rid of your debts!

Part VI: Managing Quicken

You really should keep your Quicken system neat and tidy. Don't let old files hang around and clutter up your program. Come here to learn how to manage your Quicken files and prevent any accidental loss of data; backups and passwords are the key. Can you change the way Quicken works and looks? Sure you can. Go ahead, change the screen color, register size, iconbar, and lots more.

Part VII: Using Quicken's Online Features

Quicken's really keeping up with the times with its new online features. Do your banking and make payments online, without leaving the comfort (or discomfort) of your desk chair.

Special book elements

This book has a number of special elements and conventions to help you find information quickly—or skip stuff you don't want to read right now.

TIP **Tips either point out information often overlooked in the** documentation, or help you use your software more efficiently, like a shortcut. Some tips help you solve or avoid problems.

CAUTION **Cautions alert you to potentially dangerous consequences of a** procedure or practice, especially if it could cause serious or even disastrous results (such as loss or corruption of data).

Q&A ***What are Q&A notes?***

Cast in the form of questions and answers, these notes provide you with advice on ways to solve common problems.

 Plain English, please!

These notes explain the meanings of technical terms or computer jargon.

Throughout this book, a comma is used to separate the parts of a pull-down menu command. For example, to open another Quicken file, you'll choose File, Open. That means "Pull down the File menu, and choose Open from the list."

The underscore keys are hot keys and can be used as shortcuts.

New terms are in **bold**.

And if you see two keys separated by a plus sign as in Ctrl+X, that means to press and hold the first key, press the second key, then release both keys.

Sidebars are interesting nuggets of information

Sidebars provide interesting, nonessential reading, side-alley trips you can take when you're not at the computer or when you just want some relief from "doing stuff." Here you may find more technical details, funny stories, personal anecdotes, or interesting background information.

Part I: Getting Started with Quicken

1

Welcome to Quicken

● **In this chapter:**

- Can I start using Quicken at any time?

- How do I make the change from my system to Quicken?

- Okay, I'm ready to start Quicken

- I need to set up my checking account

- Time to stop working. How do I quit?

Quicken's timesaving features will make you wonder how you ever existed without it . . . . ⊙

You will quickly discover how easy Quicken is to use and then wonder why you waited so long to computerize your personal finances. What the microwave oven did for preparing dinner, Quicken does for managing finances. If you haven't used Quicken before, you may spend a little up-front time getting all of your information in the system, but after that, you're going to sail through all your financial tasks.

Your start date is important

So, you've decided to start using Quicken for your finances. Good for you! Now you need to give some thought to the best time to convert to Quicken. The day you convert is the day you stop using your old longhand methods and begin using Quicken.

So when are you going to take the plunge and put away your paper, pencil, and calculator? This is an important question. In the next few sections, I'll give you some things to think about. After that, I'll show you how to start your program and what you need to do to start Quicken 6 for Windows.

TIP　**If you're just going to use Quicken to help you maintain your** checkbook and print checks, the conversion date *is not* important. You can start using it at any time. But if you want Quicken to summarize your income and expenses, to help you with your budget, or to accumulate your tax deductions, you need a clean accounting cutoff point. From the cutoff date forward, Quicken handles all your financial information. Before the cutoff date, your manual system takes precedence.

Converting from your manual system to Quicken

Ideally, try to start using Quicken on January 1. This way you have a clean fiscal year start. From January 1 on you will have all your income and expenses recorded in one place. But realistically, this timing probably doesn't work. It may be June 15 and you're ready to start now! Well, that's okay, too. You can start Quicken anytime you want; just try to pick a natural cutoff date that makes switching from your manual system to Quicken easy. A natural cutoff date might be the ending date of your last bank statement or the first day of the month. If it is June 15, you could start on June 1 and enter those transactions that have transpired between June 1 and June 15, or you could wait until July 1 to start; whichever works best for you.

If you can't start at the beginning of the year, try starting at the beginning of a month. That way you can stop your manual records at the end of one month and start Quicken at the start of the next. Combining the two at the end of the year is then a breeze.

Avoiding common errors when converting to Quicken

Okay, you've decided that on March 1 you're going to switch from your manual system to Quicken. You're already looking forward to stepping off the financial paper trail, and you'll be glad you did! But you want to make sure all your tracks are covered, so you need to keep a few things in mind.

One error that you might make when you start using Quicken and stop using your manual system is you may record the same transaction twice. If March 1 is your start date, you'll want to start using Quicken from March 1 on. However, you might have already recorded a couple transactions in your manual checkbook register that are dated March 1. Don't record those in Quicken, too.

Also avoid the common pitfall of not recording a transaction in Quicken that's dated March 1 because you think it's already in your manual register.

A thorough review of your transactions is the only way to avoid these errors. Make sure that all of your check numbers are accounted for. If your manual system stops at check 1234, make sure that all checks up to that number are also recorded in your manual system. Then, start with check 1235 in Quicken.

I'm ready to start the program now

The kids are in bed, the coffee's on, your checkbook register is sitting next to your computer, and you're ready to get to work with Quicken. If you haven't installed Quicken on your computer, you need to do that first. If Quicken's already on your computer, all you need to do is start it. You'll start the program in one of two ways, depending on whether you are running Quicken in Windows 95 or Windows 3.1.

TIP **If you already have an earlier version of Quicken on your com-**
puter and you have created some files, you don't have to do much to start
using Quicken 6. When you install Quicken, the program looks for any
existing Quicken files and asks whether you want to convert them to the
new version. Select Yes to convert your old Quicken files and you're ready
to go in Quicken 6. When you start the program, Quicken 6 starts and
opens the last file that you worked in. To learn how to open a different file,
see Chapter 23.

Working in Windows 95

If you're running Windows 95, open the Start menu and choose Programs
(see Figure 1.1). Notice that your Programs menu will probably look different
than mine, but if you've installed Quicken 6 for Windows correctly, you
should see Quicken. Choose Quicken and then select Quicken 6 for Windows.

Fig. 1.1
When you click Start in
Windows 95 and then
select Programs, you
see a list of program
groups, or folders, from
your computer's hard
drive. Your Quicken 6
for Windows files are
located in the Quicken
program folder.

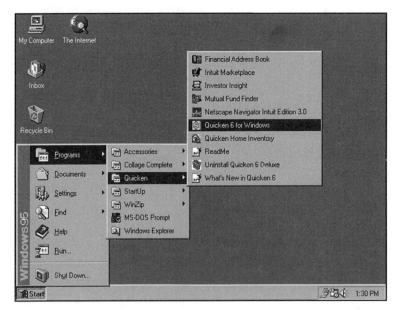

Working in Windows 3.1

For Windows 3.1 users, just double-click the Quicken icon from the Quicken
program group to start Quicken 6 for Windows.

I've never used Quicken before. What happens first?

If you've never used Quicken before, Quicken shows you the Quicken New User Setup window the first time that you start the program. Figure 1.2 shows you what your screen looks like the first time.

Fig. 1.2
Quicken shows you the New User Setup window if you've never used the program before. From here you will see a series of windows that help you get set up in Quicken.

Quicken displays a series of windows that help you walk through the things that you need to do to get Quicken set up the first time. Here's what will happen. First you'll answer some questions so that Quicken knows how you're going to organize transactions in your new Quicken file. Based on your response, Quicken will choose the categories you will need. Then, you'll set up an account to use (usually a checking account). You can't do anything in Quicken until you've got at least one account to work in. When you set up the account, you'll give it a name and enter the start date and the account balance.

So now, click the Next button so you can continue to set up Quicken. You'll then see the first in a series of windows that Quicken displays to help you set up Quicken so that you can get started.

How should I organize my transactions?

The first window you see, shown in Figure 1.3, lists some questions you need to answer so that Quicken can help you determine the categories that you want to use. Tell Quicken whether you're married, have children, own a home, and if you will be using Quicken for a business that you own.

Fig. 1.3
Answer these questions and Quicken will determine which of its two predefined category lists you should use in your Quicken file. There's a predefined list for home use and one for home and business use.

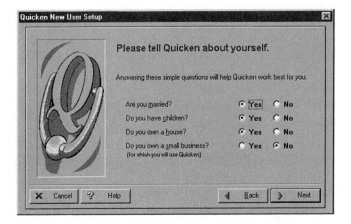

66 *Plain English, please!*

You're probably wondering how you use categories in Quicken. A **category** describes and summarizes your income and expenses and tells you where your money comes from and how you're spending it—an important part of organizing finances. In Quicken, when you enter a transaction, you assign a category to it. 99

Categories are simple to use. You can, for example, group your electric and water bills in a category called Utilities. Then at any time you can review all your utility bills by reviewing the Utility category.

There's a list of categories for home use and a list for business use. If you're using Quicken strictly for your personal finances, then Quicken will choose its Home category list. If you want to use Quicken to keep the books for your small business, Quicken will set you up with its Business category list. Or, if you want to combine your personal and business finances into one Quicken file, you'll get both the Home and Business category lists.

Now click Next, to move to the next window so that you can set up your first account in Quicken.

Setting up your first account

You can't use Quicken until you've set up your first account. The first account that you set up is usually a bank or checking account. Because you're new to Quicken, you get a lot of help in setting up this account. Quicken displays a series of windows that prompt you for the information it needs to set up your account.

You now see the first in a series of windows that Quicken displays to help you set up your account.

As you go through these windows, you

- Enter a name for your new account.

- Tell Quicken the start date for the account. This usually coincides with the ending statement date from your last bank statement.

- Finally, enter the account balance from your last bank statement.

This is all of the information that Quicken needs to set up an account.

TIP **After you've set up your first account, you'll be able to set up** others as you might need. In Chapter 3, I explain more about what accounts are, how they're used in Quicken, and how to set up more accounts.

Naming your new account

When you see the window with the <u>A</u>ccount Name box (see Figure 1.4), type a name for your account. You can call it "Checking" or use the bank name, like "First National." Just remember that you can use only as many as 30 characters and you can't use :][/ | ^ in the name.

Fig. 1.4
Name your new account anything that you want, but you can use only up to 30 characters.

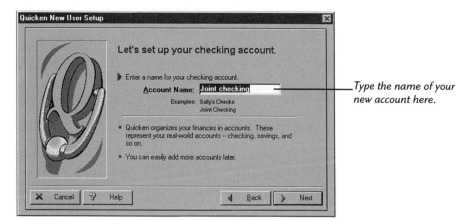

Type the name of your new account here.

Now, click the Next button and then decide whether you're going to use the information from your last bank statement to set up your new account.

Do I use my bank statement information?

The date on your bank statement probably won't be January 1, or the first day of any month, for that matter. In this case, you won't use the account balance from your statement as the starting balance in the account. Instead, you'll use the balance shown in your manual checkbook register as of January 1 or the first day of the month that you're starting.

If you haven't kept your manual checkbook up-to-date, well, you're like most people (at least those who aren't CPAs). No big deal. Use your last bank statement date and balance as the starting point for your new account, then bring Quicken up-to-date. Just enter in Quicken all uncleared transactions from your last bank statement.

 TIP   **Entering uncleared transactions is not difficult and not much** different than entering other transactions in Quicken. After you read Chapter 5, "Introducing the Quicken Register," you'll know exactly how to enter any type of transaction, whether current or past.

So, if you're going to use the information from your last bank statement, select Yes and then click the Next button and you're ready to enter the bank statement date and account balance.

If you're going to use some other date, select No and then Next to continue.

Entering your account statement date and balance

The window in Figure 1.5 is where you enter your account statement date and balance if you decided to use the information from your last bank statement. Enter the ending statement date in the Statement Ending Date box. Dates are entered in the MM/DD/YY format. So, August 16, 1996 is entered as **081696** (you don't have to enter the slashes).

Fig. 1.5
Use the information from your last bank statement to enter the starting date and account balance for your new account.

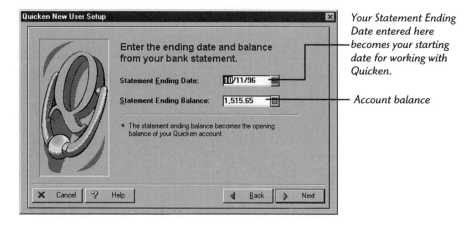

Your Statement Ending Date entered here becomes your starting date for working with Quicken.

Account balance

Now move to the Statement Ending Balance box and type the account balance shown on your last bank statement. Type the amount using the decimal point to separate dollars and cents, but no commas; for example, **1515.65**.

If you're not using the information from your last bank statement to start your account, Quicken automatically uses today's date and a $0.00 balance for your account. But don't panic, before you finish setting up your account, you'll get a chance to enter the date and account balance you want.

Make sure everything is correct

Click Next to see a summary of the information that you entered for your account (see Figure 1.6). If all your account information is correct, click the Next button. If not, move to the box with the wrong information and correct it.

If you didn't use the information from your last bank statement, this is the time for you to enter a new date and account balance. Just move to the Statement Date box and type in a new date and then go to the Ending Balance box to enter a different amount.

Click the Next button and Quicken introduces you to What's next? If you want to run through a ten minute overview of the program right now, click the Overview button. But, if you'd rather jump in and get started, click Done and you're there.

Fig. 1.6
Review your new account information carefully. Now is the time to make changes to your new account information.

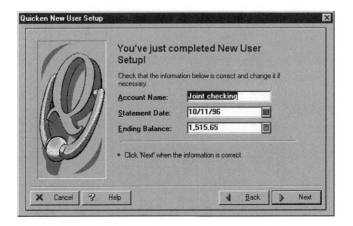

Time to quit

I know you're just getting into working with Quicken, but eventually you have to quit and fix dinner, play ball with the kids, or just go to bed. When you're ready to quit, just select File, Exit and Quicken automatically saves your work in the current file.

2

Learning the Quicken Ropes

● In this chapter:

- How do I get things done?

- What's in the Quicken window?

- Use the mouse or keyboard to travel

- Help is always close by

Get comfortable with Quicken. Take a few minutes to explore
Quicken and feel your way around . . . . ▶

I f you're a new computer user, there may be a lot of components to the Quicken screen you need to familiarize yourself with. You're in the right place. This chapter describes everything you see on your screen and shows you how to get where you want to go.

Even if you've used computers before but have never used Quicken, a quick review of this chapter will make you a more confident user.

How do I do things in Quicken?

So, you've got the Quicken application window on your screen, what do you do now? There's a lot of activities that you can perform in Quicken, like writing checks, entering transactions in registers (like your checkbook register), balancing your checking account, setting up a budget, and so on. But before you can do any of these things, you need to tell Quicken what you want to do. Quicken is kind of like a chauffeur—it'll take you anywhere you want to go once you decide where that is.

The elements you saw in the Quicken application window (like the menu bar and the iconbar) will help you perform activities. But you can use special key combinations on your keyboard, too.

A look at menus

The main menu bar you see at the top of your application window is simply a list of choices you have while working in Quicken. When you choose something from the Quicken main menu bar, a pull-down menu appears (see Figure 2.1).

Think of the main menu bar as a long curtain rod with each individual menu hanging from it in a neat line. Each menu unrolls like an old-fashioned window shade to reveal the list of choices underneath. Getting to a pull-down menu is easy—just point to one of the menu items on the Quicken main menu bar and click the left mouse button to unfurl it.

❝ *Plain English, please!*

A **file** is where Quicken stores your data. Quicken assigns a file name to each file. The file added to Quicken when you start it for the first time is named QDATA. Each of your Quicken files is stored in the directory (or folder) where you installed Quicken (such as C:\QUICKENW). ❞

What's in the Quicken application window?

Like all other Windows programs, Quicken has a lot of different windows you can work in and have open at the same time. These windows are displayed within a bigger application window that shows the same things all the time. All the elements in the Quicken application window are there to help you perform tasks and work faster.

As with all windows programs, the Title bar contains minimize, maximize (or restore), and close buttons. Note that if you're working in Windows 3.1, these buttons will look different.

The Title bar tells you the name of the application (or program), the file that you're currently in, and the name of the active window. Here, Quicken 6 for Windows is the active program, QDATA is the current file, and the Account List is the active window.

The Quicken main menu bar includes six different menus that you can choose from to do your work.

The iconbar includes (you guessed it) icons, or little pictures, that you use to select tasks or activities that you would normally select from a menu.

Windows that you open in Quicken are shown beneath the iconbar.

The How Do I? button is included in each key Quicken window to give you assistance with common tasks.

If this button is flashing, then you've got some things to do in Quicken, like checks to print, bills to pay, or notes to review in your calendar.

Fig. 2.1

Everything you could possibly want to do in Quicken, you can do from a pull-down menu. Use the File menu, for example, to open a file, start a new file, or even to back up a file.

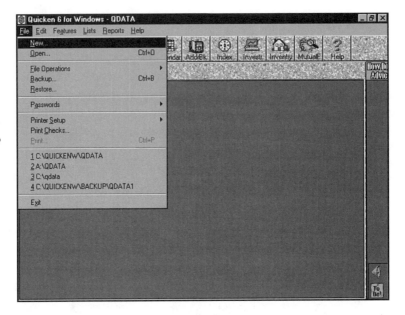

Main menu items or choices are fixed; that is, the available choices remain the same, no matter what you're doing in Quicken. Every time you start Quicken you see the same menu items—File, Edit, Features, Lists, Reports, and Help. Sometimes, however, the choices on a pull-down menu vary, depending on what you have selected or the activity you're performing.

Q&A **My mouse works, but I prefer the keyboard. How can I make menu choices without a mouse?**

Press the Alt key and the underlined letter of a menu name to open a menu or highlight a command. (To choose a menu that doesn't have an underlined letter, press the Alt key, press an arrow key to highlight the menu, and then press Enter.) Press the down arrow to move the highlight down the list of commands in a menu. Press Enter to choose the command, or Esc to close a menu.

TIP **Anything you can do in Quicken, you can do with the help of a** menu. It might not always be the fastest way, but it's guaranteed to work. If you're ever stumped at how to get a particular job done in Quicken, your best bet is to look on every menu you can find—sooner or later, you'll find the command you're looking for.

Sometimes, choosing a menu item does something right away. If you choose Edit, Transaction, Void, for example, the current transaction is immediately voided. But sometimes a menu choice does nothing at all. You can point and click until your finger falls off and nothing happens. What's going on? You've stumbled on a menu choice that's temporarily unavailable. (Unavailable menu items appear dimmed.) Maybe you selected Edit, Transaction, Go To Matching Transfer and nothing happens. That's because this menu choice is available only if the current transaction is a transaction that affects another Quicken account. If not, you can't, or don't need to, use this menu item.

When you select a menu item followed by ... (an ellipsis), a dialog box pops up with more choices for you to make. For example, when you choose File, Backup, the Select Backup Drive dialog box opens. Obviously, from here you can make choices about the disk drive you want to back up to. When you select a menu item followed by an arrow, a submenu appears with additional options.

Hey, I don't want these menus on my screen anymore! Well, get rid of them by clicking the menu item in the main menu bar or press Esc twice.

Icons make Quicken easier to use

The row of icons, or pictures, that you see under the main menu bar is called the **iconbar**. This row of icons represents some of the more common windows and activities you'll be using in Quicken. Clicking an icon to select a window or activity is quicker and easier than going through the menu. Although quicker, the end result is still the same.

Want to access the Account List? You can just click the Accts icon in the iconbar and Quicken instantly displays the Account List on your screen. Selecting Lists, Account does the same thing. If you really like using your keyboard, you won't be able to use the iconbar; it's mouse-operated only.

66 *Plain English, please!*

An **icon** is a graphic image or picture that represents a Quicken window, list, or activity. Clicking an icon instantly opens a window or list, or performs an activity. 99

Here are the icons that Quicken puts in your iconbar by default:

The icon	What it means in plain English
Registr	Display the register for the current account
Accts	Access the Account List
Recon	Start reconciling the current account
Reports	Put together a report
Online	Go online to do your banking or pay bills
Calendar	Show the Financial Calendar
AddrBk	Look up something in the Address Book
Index	Show the index of Help topics
Investr	Track your stocks with Investor Insight
Inventry	Inventory your household belongings
MutualF	Use the Mutual Fund Finder
Help	Give me some HELP!

TIP **When you're using Quicken, you may find that you'd like other** activities and windows represented as icons so that you can choose them quicker. No problem. You can take out some of the existing icons and put in your own. And if you don't like the iconbar at all, you can delete it from your screen altogether. Take a look at Chapter 24 to find out how to change the iconbar.

I can use Quick keys, too

If you want to use your keyboard to select a menu item or perform an activity, you can use **Quick keys**. Quick keys are a combination of two keys; usually the Ctrl, Alt, or Shift key with a letter key. To use a Quick key, press and hold the first key while you press the second key. If I tell you to use a Quick key to get something done, I'll show you the two keys separated by a "+", like Ctrl+A. Here are the Quick keys you can use:

Quick key	What it does
Ctrl+A	Displays the Account List
Ctrl+B	Backs up the current file
Ctrl+C	Shows the Category & Transfer List
Ctrl+D	Deletes a transaction or account
Ctrl+E	Edits a transaction or account
Ctrl+H	Starts to set up a loan
Ctrl+I	Inserts a transaction
Ctrl+J	Displays the Scheduled Transaction List
Ctrl+K	Brings up the Financial Calendar
Ctrl+L	Displays the Class List
Ctrl+M	Memorizes a transaction
Ctrl+N	Starts a new transaction or account
Ctrl+O	Opens a file
Ctrl+P	Prints
Ctrl+R	Goes to the register
Ctrl+T	Recalls a memorized transaction
Ctrl+U	Switches to the Portfolio View
Ctrl+V	Voids a transaction
Ctrl+W	Goes to the Write Checks window

continues

Continued

Quick key	What it does
Ctrl+X	Goes to a transfer transaction
Ctrl+Y	Displays the Security List
Shift+Del	Deletes a transaction and puts it in the Clipboard
Ctrl+Ins	Copies a transaction to the Clipboard
Shift+Ins	Pastes a transaction to the Clipboard
F1	Gives you help on the current window or menu item

Getting around in Quicken

Getting around in Quicken is fast and easy. You can go from field to field, activity to activity, or window to window using several different "modes of transportation." It's like getting around in New York City. You may walk to get from place to place, but if you're going very far, you'll take a taxi or the subway. (Certainly, getting around in Quicken is a lot easier than getting around in New York!)

Quicken provides several different "modes of transportation" through the program. Take a ride through Quicken using your mouse, the keyboard, QuickTabs, and the new Activity Bar.

Mouse and keyboard travel

As with any Windows-based program, using your mouse to move around and select menu items or activities is usually more efficient than using the keyboard. (Sometimes, however, using a combination of the mouse and keyboard makes sense.) The most important thing to remember when you use your mouse is to move the mouse pointer to the item that you want to choose first. In other words, make sure that the mouse pointer (that little arrow on your screen) is pointing to the menu item, icon, or transaction you want to choose. Once the pointer is where you want it, here's what you do next:

- **Click**. Selects an item or moves to where the mouse pointer (cursor) is pointing.

- **Double-click**. Also selects an item or enlarges a window or icon back to its original size.

- **Drag**. (Hold down the left button and move the mouse on your desk or mousepad.) Picks up an item, like an icon, and moves it. Dragging your mouse also highlights text so that you can move it.

You also can navigate your way around in Quicken using the keyboard. If you like using your keyboard, use these keys to move:

Which key to press	Where you go
←	One space left in a field
→	One space right in a field
↑	Previous transaction
↓	Next transaction
Page Up	Transaction at the top of the register window
Page Down	Blank transaction at the bottom of the register
Home	Beginning of current field
End	End of current field
Home (three times)	First transaction in the register window
Ctrl+End	Blank transaction at the bottom of the register
Tab	Next field
Enter	Records the current transaction; moves to the next transaction

Move easily through open windows with QuickTabs

Want to move to the Write Checks window or the register or any other open window? Just click one of the QuickTabs to get there. Each time you open a window, Quicken puts a QuickTab on the right side of your screen to represent that window. Figure 2.2 shows that you have several open windows you can quickly access by clicking a QuickTab.

Fig. 2.2
Use a QuickTab to go
to any open window in
Quicken.

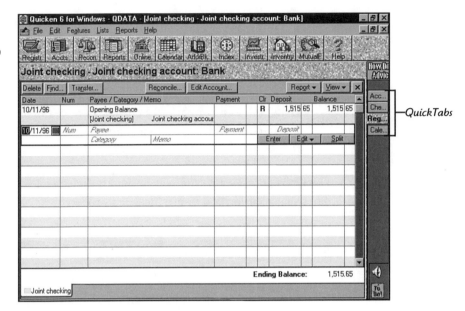

Q&A *What if I don't want or need QuickTabs on my screen?*

If you'd rather not take up space on your screen with QuickTabs, you can
get rid of the them by selecting the Quicken Program option that turns
QuickTabs off. Or, you can choose to display QuickTabs on the left side of
your screen instead, which is another Quicken Program option. You learn
how to set Quicken Program options in Chapter 24.

TIP **You can rearrange the order your QuickTabs are in by dragging a**
tab to where you want it and then releasing the mouse button. Quicken
then rearranges the other tabs accordingly.

TIP **If you're a creature of habit and would like to have the same**
windows open in a particular order each time that you start Quicken, you
can save your desktop (the arrangement of open windows). To learn how to
do this, see Chapter 24.

I want quick and easy access to Quicken tasks

Worried about getting lost once you're in Quicken territory? Don't be. If
you're feeling a little uncertain, use Quicken's new Activity Bar at the bottom

of every window that gives you quick and easy access to most commonly used tasks and features.

Just click on one of the icons in the Activity Bar and a quick menu pops up to let you choose which activity you want to perform. Figure 2.3 shows the activities you can perform when you choose the My Accounts icon. Select an activity from the menu by pointing to it with your mouse and clicking.

Fig. 2.3
Want easy access to Quicken's most commonly used tasks and features? Use the new Activity Bar.

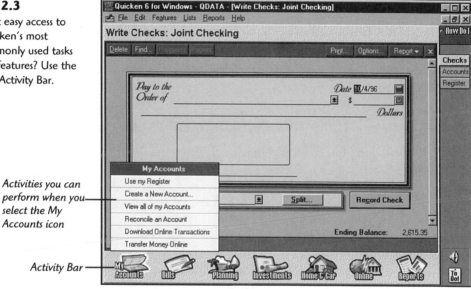

Activities you can perform when you select the My Accounts icon

Activity Bar

Time to get a little help

Quicken's an easy program to use, but there are going to be times when you have some trouble figuring out how to use a feature or what to do next. You can get all the help you need from this book, of course, but if you want online help from Quicken, there's lots available.

Here's a list of the types of help that you can get from Quicken:

Help available	What you get
Quicken Overview	Gives you a summary of Quicken's most popular features

continues

Continued

Help available	What you get
Qcards	Audio and video assistance the first time that you enter a key area of Quicken
Quicken Tips	Hints on useful features in Quicken
Troubleshooting	Lists the possible problems you may be having in the current window and then gives you solutions
Quicken Help	Library of helpful reference material on Quicken

And just to help you with Help, here's a brief look at what you'll find when you go to use it.

Give me a quick summary of Quicken

Don't worry about getting up early to catch the tour bus. You can take a quick tour with Quicken Overview anytime you want a brief, online tutorial of Quicken. If you're a new user, this overview is helpful because it gives a summary of Quicken, what it can do, and how it works.

To start Quicken Overview, choose Help, Quicken Overview. When the Quicken Overview window appears (see Figure 2.4), just click Next and your tour through Quicken begins. While you're "touring" through Quicken you'll see a Next button at the bottom of each window that you can click to move to the next window. If at any time you want to leave Quicken Overview, click the Cancel button at the bottom of the window.

Qcards give you a lot of help

Get audio and video assistance from Quicken with Qcards. If you used Quicken 5, you saw the old cue cards that popped up on your screen as you moved around in Quicken windows. But now, with Quicken 6, you get a more technologically advanced kind of help, complete with sound and visuals. You'll hear and see how to perform a task the first time that you enter an area in Quicken.

By default, Quicken assumes that you want to use these Qcards and turns them on when you install the program; therefore, they show up automatically. Don't worry though—if they start to bug you they can be turned off.

Fig. 2.4
Take a tour with Quicken Overview anytime you feel like it to get the rundown on Quicken.

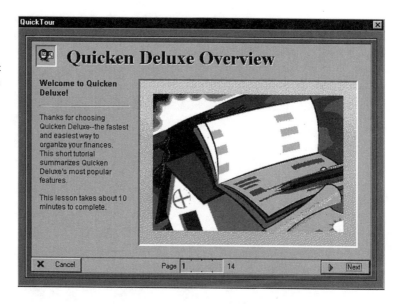

Figure 2.5 shows you the audio Qcard that appears when you start to enter a transaction in the register. Qcards are either audio or text messages. The first time you see a Qcard, you'll see the audio box where Quicken tells you how long the audio portion of the Qcard is and automatically plays it for you. To see the text message, click the T button in the upper-right corner of the audio box.

After you perform the action that you've just been given instruction for, a new Qcard (either audio or text box) appears with instructions for the next action that you need to take.

If you don't ever want to see another Qcard again, turn them completely off by selecting Help, Show QCards. (Notice that now, there's no checkmark beside this Help menu item to show that Qcards are turned off.)

Quicken tips are helpful

You get a "tip of the day" each time that you start Quicken. Tips cover features of the program and hints for how to do things faster and easier. You might get a tip, for example, on how to find items in lists by pressing the first letter of the item that you want to find or how to enter dates in the register quickly by using the + and – keys.

Figure 2.6 shows a typical tip. Your tip, however, will probably be different. After you've read your tip, choose Done to remove it from your screen.

Fig. 2.5
This audio Qcard tells you how to enter the date for a transaction in the register. Another Qcard appears after you've entered the date correctly and moved to the next field in the register.

Qcard prompts you to enter the date.

Click this button to see the text of this Qcard.

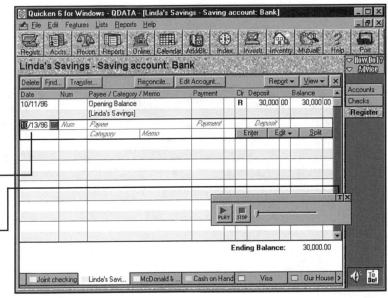

Fig. 2.6
Read Quicken tips for some great advice (straight from the source) on how to save time while you're working.

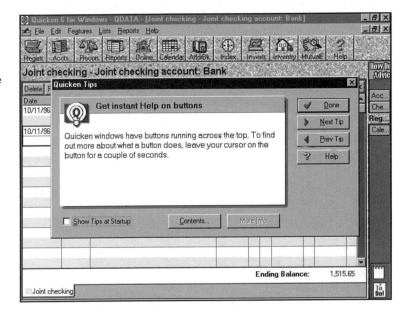

Anytime you want to see another Quicken tip while you're working, select Help, Quicken Tips. The Quicken Tips window opens with a new tip for you to read. If you want to read some more tips, click Next Tip. If you want to read an earlier tip, click Prev Tip.

Q&A *I like these Quicken Tips, but I'd like to turn them off so I don't see them every time I start Quicken. Can I do this?*

You sure can. See the Show Tips at Startup checkbox at the bottom of the Quicken Tips window in Figure 2.6? Just click the checkbox to remove the checkmark and Quicken Tips no longer appear when you start Quicken.

How does Quicken Help work?

As long as Quicken has been running under Windows, it's had a Help system that you're used to seeing in other Windows-based programs. Quicken Help assists with menu commands and options, provides definitions of terms that may not be familiar to you, explains how Quicken does things (like writing checks, printing, balancing your checkbook, and so forth), and gives you tips for using the program more efficiently.

 TIP **Click the Help icon or press F1 to access the Quicken Help** window.

There's an extensive library of helpful reference material in Quicken, mostly stored in the Quicken Help window. To access the Quicken Help window, select Help, Help on this Window. The information included in the Quicken Help window relates to the active window or menu item when help was selected. Figure 2.7 shows the Quicken Help window that's displayed when you ask for help from the Category & Transfer List.

Fig. 2.7
You can find out a lot about Quicken and how to perform tasks in the Quicken Help window.

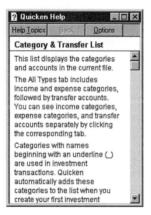

The information included in the Quicken Help window often includes additional topics you can select to see even more information. These topics appear in green and when you point to them with your mouse, the pointer changes to a pointed finger. To see additional information, just click.

If you're unable to find the topic that you need help with, click the Help Topics button and then enter the topic in the Index window (see Figure 2.8), or search through the list of topics.

Fig. 2.8
Every topic you would ever need to know about in Quicken is listed in the Index window.

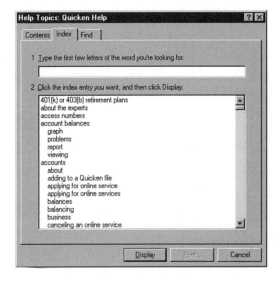

Once you're feeling Quicken-smart, close the Quicken Help window by clicking the Close button.

 TIP   **If there's too much help information to read on-screen, you can** print it by clicking Options (from the menu in the Quicken Help window) and then selecting Print Topic.

 TIP   **Want to see some tips that Intuit has put together to solve** common problems that Quicken users have while working in the current window? Select Help, Troubleshooting this Window to see the Quicken Help window with a list of troubleshooting questions that relate to the current window that you're working in. Just click the double-arrow button next to the problem that you'd like to see a solution for.

Using Accounts to Store Your Transactions

● **In this chapter:**

- How many accounts will I need?

- Add a new account

- Make some changes to an account

- Delete those accounts that you don't use anymore

- Hide an account in your account list

- Put your accounts in order

- Work with multiple accounts

Everybody's talking about the "Quicken" thing, so you just can't wait. Learn a few things about accounts first and you're on your way. . . . . ●▶

Accounts, accounts, accounts! Why do I keep talking about accounts? We're not setting up a bank here, are we? No, but from real life you already know about accounts, like checking accounts, savings accounts, credit card accounts (you know, VISA, MasterCard, American Express), brokerage accounts, and so on. You use these kinds of accounts in Quicken to keep track of your transactions. And don't forget about mortgages and car loans that also are accounts that represent your liabilities. You have to keep track of transactions in those accounts, too.

66 *Plain English, please!*

A **transaction** is any "action" you take that changes how much money you have or changes the value of things you own (like your house or any other investment). When you go to the bank machine to take out $20 for a movie and popcorn, that's a transaction because it changes how much money you have in your bank account. Or, when you spend $3,000 to add that new patio, that's a transaction because you changed the value of your house. 99

What are accounts and how do I use them?

You set up your first bank account in Chapter 1. But you probably need many more accounts if you want to stay completely on top of your finances.

Here are the types of accounts that you can use in Quicken:

- **Checking account**. You're going to use this account to write checks. You should have set up this account in Chapter 1.

- **Credit Card account**. Even though your grandparents never use credit cards, you do. So Quicken lets you set up accounts to keep track of your purchases (no matter how frivolous), payments, and those dreaded finance charges. Flip to Chapter 13 for more on credit card accounts.

- **Money Market account**. If you keep cash in a money market account, keep track of it in—what else—a Quicken Money Market account. You can even write checks from this account. Money Market accounts are set up the same way as other bank accounts, so stick with this chapter to learn more.

- **Asset account**. We all own something, right? So use this account to keep track of it—a house, a car, a boat, whatever. Chapter 12 tells you everything you need to know about asset accounts.

- **Savings account**. Whether you save your money under the mattress or at a bank, the Savings account tells you how much you've socked away. Keep reading this chapter for more.

- **Cash account**. Reach into your pocket. There's probably some cash there right now. Well, don't forget about keeping track of it. Read Chapter 12 to see how.

- **Investment account**. These accounts are not for those who have weak stomachs. Venture into these accounts at your own risk; they're deep and a little confusing. For you risk-takers, use them to track your stocks, bonds, and mutual funds. Proceed cautiously to Chapter 16.

- **Liability account**. Admit it. You aren't without debt. We all have some. And Quicken's not going to let you forget it. Liability accounts help you keep track of your debts so that you know how much money you owe. Proceed to Chapter 14 to learn about amortized loans and liability accounts for unamortized loans.

66 *Plain English, please!*

Liabilities are debts, or the money that you're "liable" for. If you buy a house and don't have enough money to pay for the whole thing (and who does!), you pay what you can (that's called a down payment) and borrow the rest (take out a mortgage). The mortgage is a liability because as long as you have the house in your possession, you are liable to the mortgage holder for the amount that you borrowed. 99

Q&A *But I don't want to use all of these accounts you keep talking about. All I want to do is use Quicken to print checks and balance my checking account.*

You can use Quicken any way you want. You don't have to set up any other account if you don't want to. Quicken works with one account or as many as you want. And to be honest, when I first started using Quicken, I used it just for my checking account. Heck, I used it for two years without even printing checks.

I'm merely suggesting that you get acquainted with these other accounts so that you can expand your use of Quicken to gain a complete picture of your financial situation.

Should I set up more accounts?

You already have a checking account set up in Quicken, right? You'll use this account to enter all of your checking account transactions, like checks, deposits, and withdrawals. And if you have more than one checking account, you guessed it, you can set up a Quicken account for each. You also can set up a Quicken account for each of your savings accounts, credit union accounts, money market accounts, and maybe even accounts for certificates of deposit (CDs).

Don't go crazy setting up accounts, though. If you don't have much activity in an account, don't bother to set it up. It really depends on how much detail you want Quicken to have.

I need to add an account

Accounts are easy to add. You can add them at any time on any day. Here, you'll learn how to add bank accounts that include checking, savings, and money market accounts.

Quicken's EasyStep feature makes adding accounts a breeze. With EasyStep, you just answer a series of questions to get your account going. It's like talking to an online interviewer who asks you questions about your account in a logical manner. When you're ready to set up an account, EasyStep is ready to help. This feature is always active, so you don't have to worry about turning it on or off. It's there to make your work in Quicken easier.

So now let's add a savings account. (You already set up a checking account in Chapter 1, so for variety, we'll add a savings account now.) The first thing that you need to do to add an account is click the Accts icon from the iconbar and then click the New button, or, click the My Accounts icon from the Activity Bar and then choose Create a New Account. When you do this, Quicken displays the Create New Account dialog box (see Figure 3.1).

Next, select the type of account you want to add. Because we're adding a savings account, click Savings and then click the Next button. You should see the Savings Account Setup dialog box (see Figure 3.2). Notice the tabs at the top of the window: EasyStep and Summary. If you want Quicken to give you step-by-step help as you set up your new account, stay where you are and Quicken will display a series of windows that ask for the information to set up your account. If you'd like to be on your own and enter all of your new account information at once, click the Summary tab.

Fig. 3.1
You can add eight different types of accounts in your Quicken file and as many accounts as you want.

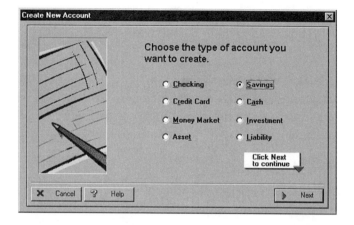

Fig. 3.2
Adding a new account in Quicken is simple. You can use EasyStep and get lots of help along the way.

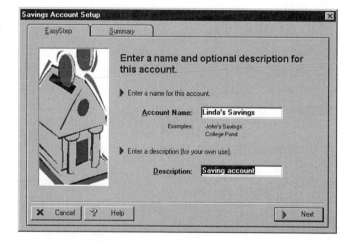

How much am I worth?

Ever heard of "net worth" and wondered what it was or thought that it applied only to the Donald Trumps of the world? Well, not true. Everyone has a net worth (it just may not always be a positive number). Your net worth is the difference between the total assets that you own and your total debts. So if your only asset is a house, car, and some cash worth $100,000

and your total debts are $50,000, then second grade math says your net worth is $50,000.

Quicken can Figure out your net worth. Just set up an account for each of your assets and each of your debts, print out a Net Worth report, and there you have it.

Since you're new to setting up accounts, let's choose the <u>E</u>asyStep tab so you can see how Quicken walks you through it.

Name that account

Now you're ready to name your new account and perhaps add a brief description (optional) about the account. As you see in Figure 3.2, EasyStep shows you what you need to do here. So type the name you want for this account, such as **My Savings**, **Joint Savings**, or just **Savings**—whatever you want. The only restrictions are that the name can only have up to 30 characters (including spaces) and *cannot* include any of these characters:

] [/ | ^ :

If you want to add a brief description about your account, you can enter that now.

Enter your balance

Now click the Next button and tell Quicken whether you have your last bank statement. If you're going to use the balance from your last statement, select <u>Y</u>es and then click the Next button so you can enter the ending statement date and the ending balance as shown on your statement. If you're not using the balance from your last statement, select <u>N</u>o and then Next.

What's in a name?

If you use the name of your bank as the account name, you also can add the last four digits of the account number. This helps if you have more than one account at the same bank so that you can distinguish your accounts more easily. For example, you might name three accounts at the same bank as follows:

1stNat'l-Savings

1stNat'l-Checking

1stNat'l-Money Market

Remember, though, you can use up to only 30 characters.

The next window is where you enter the date of your last bank statement and the ending account balance. In the Statement Date box, enter the ending date as shown on your last bank statement. Then, press Tab to move to the Ending Balance box to enter the amount shown on your statement as the account balance as of the ending date.

Note that if you selected not to use the information from your last bank statement, Quicken will use today's date as the starting date for your new account with a zero balance, but don't worry if this is not right. You can change the date and balance later.

CAUTION **Don't use commas or dollar signs when you enter your bank** account balance. If the balance for an account is zero, be sure to type 0. You can't leave the text box blank or Quicken will give you an error message.

TIP 🖩 **When you're entering your bank statement date, you see a** little icon at the end of the text box. If you're wondering what this is, it's a mini-calendar that you can click to see an on-screen calendar. When the calendar is on-screen, you can click the date that you want to enter as the Statement Date. In Chapter 8, I'll tell you more about the mini-calendar and some other neat Quicken shortcuts.

Interested in banking online?

After you've entered the date and account balance for this new account, select Next and tell Quicken whether you want to set up the account for online services, like banking or bill paying. If you're not going to use these services, you can skip this. If you are, you'll need to specify which service, or services, you want to use and then provide the name of the financial institution, the routing number, the account number and type, and your Social Security number.

Q&A *What if I don't select these online options now? Can I do it later?*

Yes. You may not even know that you're going to use online services right now. That's OK. You can set up a bank account as a traditional account now, and then later change it to an online account by editing the account.

Need to change anything?

Now Quicken shows you a Summary window that recaps the information you just entered. Notice you're now at the Summary tab at the top of the Savings Account Setup window. This Summary window shows the account name, description, date, and account balance (see Figure 3.3). Review this Summary window carefully and make changes if you need to.

Fig. 3.3
Make sure all of the information about your account in the Summary window is correct. If it's not, change it here.

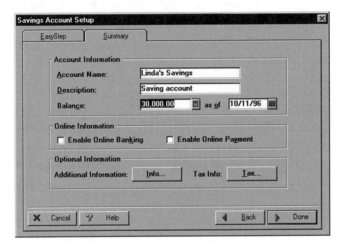

I want to keep track of some other bank information

To enter optional information about your account, you can click the Info button in the Summary window. Figure 3.4 shows you the type of information you can add about your account.

This information is completely optional; enter only information that may be helpful to you later. When you're finished, click OK to return to the Summary window.

Now, let's add the new account

So you're still reviewing the information in the Summary window, where you're probably noticing that there's a Tax button but you didn't enter any tax information while you were setting up this account. This information is optional, but necessary, if you want to designate the earnings from the account as tax-deferred or if you want to designate a tax schedule to assign to transactions you enter in this new account. You learn about assigning tax schedules to accounts in Chapter 17.

Fig. 3.4
Here's all of the additional information you can enter about your new account.

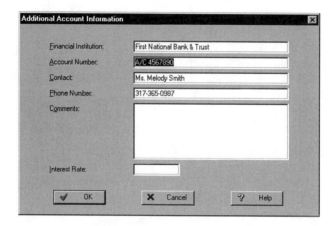

After reviewing the Summary window, click Done and you've just added a new account in Quicken.

Note that if you set up your new account for online services, you'll see a second Summary window that shows all of the online account information that you entered. Review this window carefully and click Done to add your new account.

Where can I see a list of all my accounts?

If you just added one new account or several new accounts, you may be wondering where you can go to see a list of all your accounts. Your accounts are all listed—in alphabetical order by account type—in the Account List. And you can see the Account List at any time by clicking the Accts icon in the iconbar or clicking the My Accounts icon from the Activity Bar and then selecting View all of my Accounts. Figure 3.5 shows you what the Account List looks like.

The button bar at the top of the Account List includes buttons you can use to work with accounts. You can use these buttons in place of the main menu to speed up your work. Instead of choosing Edit, Account, New, you can click the New button in the button bar.

Fig. 3.5

All of your accounts are listed in the Account List.

The button bar performs tasks in the Account List.

Use these tabs to sort your Account List by account type.

Here's the total of all your accounts in the Account List.

Do you want to see the accounts that you've hidden? If so, check here.

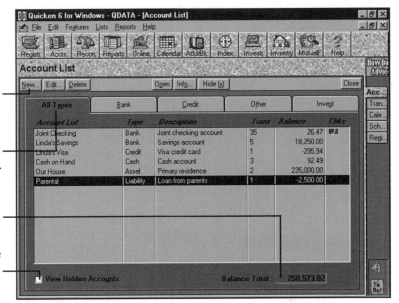

You can do all sorts of things to accounts from the Accounts List, like add a new account, edit an existing account, delete an account, sort the list, and even hide accounts that you don't want to show up in the list.

TIP **If you need information fast, look at the Balance Total at the** bottom of the Account List. This is a quick way to view your net worth because this figure includes all your assets and liabilities and comes up with your current net worth. Looking at this figure eliminates the hassle of printing tons of reports.

Can I change an account?

You can change an account at any time. You can change the account name, description, any of the additional information you may have entered, tax schedule assignments, and activate or deactivate online services for an account. About the only thing that you really can't change about an account is its account type. For example, if you set up an account as a bank account, you can't change it to a credit card account or an investment account.

CAUTION **If you discover that you set up an account as the wrong account** type, you'll need to delete the account and set it up again as the correct type. If you've already entered transactions in the account, however, you should first set up the new account and then copy the transactions to the new account register before you delete the incorrect account.

If you need to edit an account, find the account in the Account List and click the Ed<u>i</u>t button in the button bar. Quicken displays the Edit Account window (similar to the Summary window that you saw in Figure 3.3) with all the information that you can change for the account.

TIP **If you want to change only some of the additional information you** entered for an account, just select the account and then click the Inf<u>o</u> button in the Account List button bar.

To make a change, move to the text box you want to edit and type over the existing characters. If you want to edit additional information, click the Info button; if you want to edit tax information, click the <u>T</u>ax button from the Edit Account window.

After you've made all your changes, click the Done button.

So, you don't want this account anymore

If you decide you don't want to track the transactions in an account anymore (or you've closed the account), you can delete accounts from your Account List.

CAUTION **Be careful when deleting accounts. When you delete an account,** you delete all the transactions in that account. Obviously, if you've never used an account, it won't matter if you delete it.

So if you really want to delete an account, here's how:

1 Go to the Account List by clicking the Accts icon in the iconbar or clicking the My Accounts icon in the Activity Bar and selecting View all of my Accounts.

2 Find the account that you want to delete and click or highlight it.

3 Now click the <u>D</u>elete button from the Account List button bar.

4 Since deleting things is a serious matter in Quicken, you have to confirm that you really want to delete the account. Quicken displays a little warning box for you to confirm by typing **yes**. (If you change your mind, just click Cancel and then OK and Quicken will forget that you ever even thought about deleting this account.) Then click OK.

The account is instantly removed from your Account List. There will be no trace of this account left in your Quicken file—no account, no account register, and no transactions.

This account is inactive, but I don't want to get rid of it

You can hide accounts that you don't want to see in your Account List but you just can't part with. You're probably thinking that you're not so attached to any one account that you can't imagine when you'd need to use this feature. Well, how about when you've got some accounts that don't have any current activity but you don't want to delete them because they've got some past transactions that you want to keep? Or, maybe you want to hide some accounts to see how your Balance Total at the bottom of the Account List is affected without these accounts.

Whatever your reason, you can easily hide accounts from the Account List but still keep them in your Quicken file. To hide an account:

1 Select the account by clicking or highlighting it.

2 Then click the Hide button in the Account List button bar.

A message appears telling you this account will no longer be displayed unless you select the View Hidden Accounts checkbox at the bottom of the Account List. Click OK to hide the account. If the View Hidden Accounts checkbox is not checked, you won't see the account you just hid. If it is checked, you'll see the hidden account but there will be a little hand next to the account name in the Account list to show that it's a hidden account.

If you don't want to hide an account anymore, just select the hidden account in the Account List and click the Hide button again to "unhide" it.

Putting your accounts in order

Quicken sorts your Account List alphabetically, by account type. Unless you specify otherwise, all of the account types are shown in your Account List. Bank accounts are listed first, followed by credit card accounts, then other account types like cash, asset, and liability accounts, and last, investment accounts.

If you'd rather have your Account List include only one account type, you can change the accounts shown in the list.

The tabs that you see below the Account List button bar let you decide which types of accounts are shown in the Account List. In Figure 3.5, for example, all types of accounts are listed. So you see bank accounts, credit card accounts, a cash account, an asset account, and other liability accounts. But if you only want bank accounts to be listed, you can select the Bank tab and Quicken will hide all of the other accounts of other types and only list bank accounts. Sorting your Account List by type is helpful if you want to do a quick review of your accounts within each type. Or, if your list is too long, you may want to limit it to make it easier to find an account.

How do I work with all these accounts at once?

If you only have one account that you're using in Quicken, you never have to select which account you want to use. There's only one, so Quicken knows that it's the account you'll be using.

But what if you have lots of accounts? How does Quicken know which one you want to work in? Simple. You select the account in one of several ways.

If you're in the Account List, you just select the account from the list and click the Open button from the button bar. Quicken then opens the register for the account that you selected.

Another way to choose to work in an account is to select the account from the Account selection bar in any register or the Write Checks window. Figure 3.6 shows the register for the Joint Checking account with the Account selection bar just below the transaction lines.

To select another account to work in, just click the button for that account from this bar. If you have a lot of accounts and all of them are not visible in the Account selection bar, click the scroll buttons at the ends of the bar to view the accounts that don't fit.

TIP **You can rearrange the accounts in the Account selection bar so** that you always see the accounts you want to see. By default, Quicken arranges accounts by account type (just like they're arranged in the Account List). To switch account buttons, just drag (with the mouse, of course) the account you want to move to the spot where you want it. Then release the mouse button. If there are accounts that you use most often, you may want to rearrange the Account selection bar to group those accounts together so they show up on your screen all of the time.

Fig. 3.6
Each register in Quicken has an Account selection bar so you can switch from account to account with just a click.

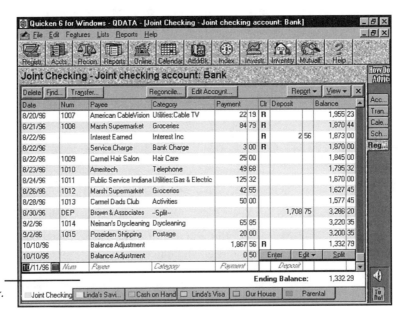

All of your accounts are arranged in this Account selection bar.

Tracking Income and Expenses with Categories

● **In this chapter:**

- **Find out what categories are and why they're important**

- **Figure out which categories you need**

- **Add a new category**

- **Add groups of categories at a time**

- **Get rid of categories you don't need**

- **See how subcategories work**

- **Shuffle the category list around**

- **Switch the category for transactions**

Categories are like electronic filing cabinets—use them to track everything you ever wanted to know about your money. . . . . ⊙

Do you stuff your receipts in envelopes or folders to differentiate all of the kinds of expenses you have? One envelope for utilities, one for groceries, one for entertainment, and so on. Well, get rid of that system and start using Quicken categories to track your income and expenses. Imagine having all of your expenses tracked in one place so that you can find out instantly how much you spent on clothes or dining out last month!

Sounds like a perplexing task, doesn't it? If I don't separate my receipts or fill out a multicolumn ledger sheet, how can I possibly know how much I'm spending on utilities every year? Or, if I don't keep all of my dividend vouchers, how will I know how much dividend income I had last year?

Categories are just what you need. Using categories in Quicken makes it easy to track all your income and expenses. If you assign each transaction to a category, you know, at any given time, how much you're spending on everything. You know how much money you've made from that second job, how much interest income you've received, how much you're spending each month on clothing (or how much your spouse is spending), how much on dinner out, and so forth. These are the things we need to know if we're to gain control of our finances!

Here's why categories are important

If there's one thing that I would advise you to use more than anything else in Quicken, it's categories. You can enter transactions in Quicken and not assign them to categories. But by doing this, you're really not using one of the real powers of Quicken. Categories group your income and expenses so that you always know exactly how much money you've made and from what source and how much money you've spent and on what.

By categorizing, Quicken can do the following difficult tasks:

- Break down checking account deposits and payments into groups of similar transactions so that you can summarize your income and expenses in reports and graphs

- Get your income and expenses and then compare budgeted amounts with actual amounts

- Track and calculate your taxable income and tax-deductible expenses

- Project your future income and expenses

Categories you should have

When you installed Quicken, you established your Quicken file with a set of categories. Quicken has a standard set of categories for home, or personal use. This set of categories can include those categories needed for married households, those with children, and homeowners. You'll find categories that you commonly use for your household finances, like Salary, Interest Inc (for interest income), Clothing, Entertainment, Groceries, Telephone, etc. Keep in mind that this is a general list of home categories and probably won't include every category you need. Don't worry; you can always add, delete, or change categories from the category list.

Quicken also includes a set of categories for use with a small business. If you run a small business and want to use Quicken to keep the books for your company, there's a whole set of predetermined categories that you will find useful in business accounting. Some of the categories included in the business category set are Gr Sales (Gross Sales), Ads, Meals & Entertn, Office, Returns, and so forth.

If you're planning to keep your home finances and your business finances together in the same file, you can combine both sets of categories in your category list.

About the cash flowing in and out

Don't confuse all cash inflows as income. If you sell a stock, for example, the money that you receive is not income to you. Income from the sale is the difference between what you paid for the stock and what you sold it for (if the result is negative, you have a loss). Medical insurance reimbursements also aren't income; they just offset your medical expenses.

Sometimes, you might mistake the cash that you pay out as expenses. Money spent for the purchase of major assets, like cars, boats, or an addition to your home are not really expenses. These types of cash outflows are just transfers from one account (the account that you use to pay for the asset) to another (the account that you set up for the new asset).

CAUTION **I don't really recommend that you combine your home finances** with your business finances in the same Quicken file. It's better to set up a separate Quicken file for your home use and one for your business. That way, you can keep all of your transactions separate without danger of misclassifying income and expenses. There is one drawback to using two different files, however—you cannot enter transactions that affect both a business and a personal account. For example, if you transfer funds from your business account to your personal account, you'll have to enter a separate transaction in your business file and another in your personal file. If you were using just one file, you could easily enter one transaction that transfers funds from one account to the other.

So how do you know if the categories that are already in your Quicken file are the ones you need? The category list that's already there will probably be sufficient for most of your transactions, but we're all different and have different kinds of income and expenses. Personalize your category list by adding some new categories, changing some that are already there, or getting rid of some that you know you'll never use. It's that simple. If you have some farm income, you'll want to add a category like Farm Income; if your kids take music lessons, you may want a category like Music or Piano Lessons; if you have expenses related to your pet cat, Felix, you may want a category called Pet or Pet Care, or even Felix Expenses.

Find your categories in the Category & Transfer List

Your categories are stored in a list called the Category & Transfer List (just like you found with accounts that are stored in the Account List). You can access the Category & Transfer List anytime you want. Just select Lists, Category/Transfer and you see the Category & Transfer List like the one in Figure 4.1.

This list is called the Category & Transfer List because it includes all of your categories (and subcategories) and all of your accounts (so that you can enter transfer transactions). (I tell you all about subcategories later in this chapter.) Quicken keeps the Category & Transfer List in alphabetical order by category and account type. All income categories are listed first, then expense categories, followed by accounts (in order by account type). Subcategories are listed in alphabetical order under the category in which they relate.

Fig. 4.1
All of your categories, subcategories, and accounts are listed in the Category & Transfer List.

The button bar performs tasks in the Category & Transfer List.

Use these tabs to sort categories by income or expense or to just list accounts in the Category & Transfer List.

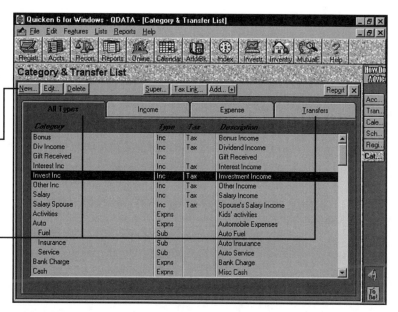

Q&A *I opened my Category & Transfer List but found I didn't open any categories in the list. What happened and what do I do now?*

Don't panic. When you installed Quicken, you must not have selected one of the predefined category lists included in the program, so Quicken thought that you wanted to enter all of your own categories. If this is not the case, you can still add categories from the predefined lists. You learn how to do this in the section, "I want to add a whole group of categories," later in this chapter.

TIP   **If you've already opened the Category & Transfer List during this** session, you'll find a Categories QuickTab in the right margin of the screen. Just click the Categories QuickTab anytime you want to access the Category & Transfer List again.

The button bar at the top of the Category & Transfer List includes buttons you can use to work with categories. You can use these buttons in place of the main menu to speed up your work. Instead of choosing Edit, Category/ Transfer, New, you can simply click the New button in the button bar.

You can do all sorts of things to categories from the Category & Transfer List, like add a new category, edit an existing category, delete a category, add a supercategory (you learn about these when you start budgeting in Chapter 15), assign tax schedules to categories, add or delete more than one category at a time, and even create a report on a category that includes all transactions assigned to that category.

TIP **It might be easier for you to review a printed copy of the Category** & Transfer List rather than scroll through the list on your screen. You can easily print the list by selecting File, Print List and then clicking OK. For more on printing lists, go to Chapter 18.

I want to add a new category

Okay, so you've decided there's a category you need that just isn't in Quicken's standard set of categories. It's easy to add any category that you want.

First, access the Category & Transfer List if it isn't already shown on your screen like in Figure 4.1 (choose Lists, Category/Transfer). Then click the New button in the button bar to see the Set Up Category dialog box shown in Figure 4.2.

Fig. 4.2
Just give your new category a name, an optional description, and tell Quicken whether it's an income or expense category or a subcategory.

As you can see from the Set Up Category dialog box, you need to name your category, give it a brief description (if you want), tell Quicken what type of category it's going to be, and, optionally, assign a tax form to the category.

Naming a new category

You can use whatever name you want for a new category. Just make sure there's not already a category with that name and that it's a name that is easy to recognize. You might not want to use many abbreviations in category names because you may not remember what they stand for six months from now. For example, if you want a category for Lawn Care, don't call it LC or LCare. Go ahead and use the full names for categories when you can. Quicken won't let you use more than 15 characters (you can include spaces) and you can't use any of these characters in the name:

:] [/ | ^

Now move to the <u>N</u>ame text box and type the new category name. Then press Tab to add a description of the category. In Figure 4.2, I set up a category called Music and then described it as Kid's music lessons so I know that this category is for my kids' music lessons expenses.

Next, you need to tell Quicken what type of category you're adding.

Selecting the category type

In the Type section of the Set Up Category dialog box (refer to Figure 4.2), you need to select which type of category you're setting up. As you can see, there are income categories, expense categories, and subcategories. If you're setting up a category that relates to income transactions (like wages or salary, interest income, dividend income, and so forth), then click the <u>I</u>ncome option. For categories that relate to your expenses (like rent, clothing, childcare, groceries, etc.), click the <u>E</u>xpense option.

The other type of category you can select is subcategories. Subcategories are a "subset" of categories. They simply break out your categories into more detail. Later in this chapter, there's a whole section devoted to subcategories and how to set them up. If you are adding a subcategory at this point, click the S<u>u</u>bcategory Of option, and then tell Quicken which category your new subcategory relates to by clicking the down arrow and selecting a category from the list that drops down.

If you want, you can assign a tax form to the new category. Assigning tax forms to categories is optional. But if you want to accumulate your taxable income and tax-deductible expenses so that you can use this information for income tax return purposes, you need to assign tax-related categories to tax forms and schedules. Chapter 17 covers income taxes and assigning categories to tax forms and schedules.

Adding your new category

After you've named your category and selected the type for your new category, you've entered everything Quicken needs to add the category to your

Category & Transfer List. You can stop now and add the category by clicking OK. Quicken inserts your new category in the Category & Transfer List in its proper alphabetical order by category type. In Figure 4.3, you see the new Music category is now added to the list.

Fig. 4.3
When you add a new category to the Category & Transfer List, Quicken puts it in its proper order in the list.

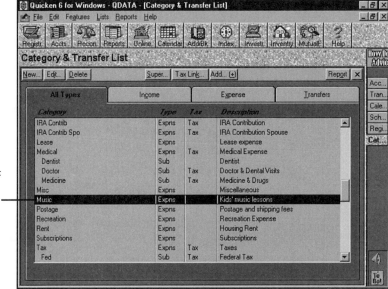

Here's the new Music category, placed alphabetically within all other expense categories.

I want to add a whole group of categories

Maybe you've decided that you don't really like some of the categories that are in the Category & Transfer List and you want to change the list. Maybe you want just some of the predefined home categories or a few of the business categories, too. It would take some time to individually add these categories one at a time, wouldn't it?

Quicken's Add button in the Category & Transfer List button bar lets you add groups of categories at one time. Click the Add button to see the Add Categories window in Figure 4.4.

Selecting categories to add

To select categories from the standard list, click the down arrow in the Available Categories drop-down list and select Standard. Quicken lists all of the standard categories in the Category list below. Select Business from the Available Categories drop-down list to select categories from Quicken's standard list of business categories.

Fig. 4.4
You can quickly add groups of categories from Quicken's standard category sets.

Here's the list of categories that you can add at one time.

If you want to add all of the available categories, click this button.

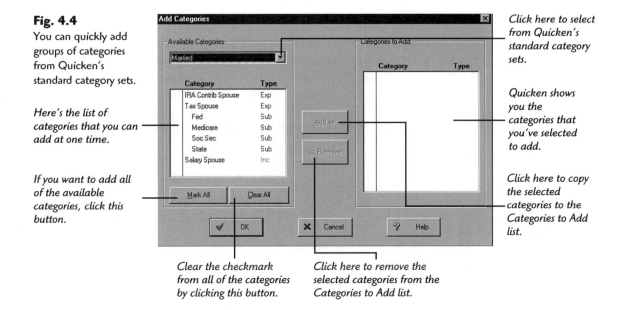

Click here to select from Quicken's standard category sets.

Quicken shows you the categories that you've selected to add.

Click here to copy the selected categories to the Categories to Add list.

Clear the checkmark from all of the categories by clicking this button.

Click here to remove the selected categories from the Categories to Add list.

Scroll through the category names in the Category list to see which ones you want to add. Before you can add categories, you have to mark each one in this list. Mark categories by clicking the category name.

TIP **Select all categories in the Category list by clicking the Mark All** button. Use the Clear All button to remove the checkmark from all of the categories. You may want to clear categories if you've reconsidered which categories you want to mark and want to start over.

Adding the categories

After you've marked the categories that you want to add, click the Add button to copy the marked categories to the Categories to Add list. In Figure 4.5, you see that I'm going to add two categories to my Category & Transfer List. If you're satisfied with these categories, just click the OK button and Quicken automatically adds the new categories to your Category & Transfer List and places them in their proper order.

I don't need this category in my list

What if there are some categories in your list that you know you'll never use? There's no need to have them there cluttering up your Category & Transfer

List if you don't need them, so just get rid of them. If a category has subcategories, though, you can't delete it until you first change its subcategories into categories or move the subcategories to another category. I'll explain more about this when I get to the section on subcategories. For now, just remember not to delete a category that has any subcategories.

Fig. 4.5
You'll see the categories that you've decided to add in the Categories to Add list. When you're ready to add them, just click OK.

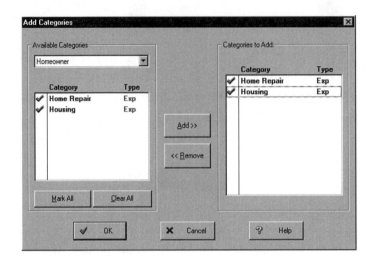

CAUTION   You can delete most categories from the Category & Transfer List except categories preceded by an underscore (_). These categories are automatically added to your list when you set up investment accounts in Quicken. You cannot delete these categories because they are needed to record transactions in your investment accounts.

When you're ready to delete a category, here's what you do. First, access the Category & Transfer List, then find the category that you want to delete and click or highlight it.

TIP   You can move really fast through the Category & Transfer List to find a category by using the Home key to move to the very beginning or the End key to move to the very end. Another speedy way to find a category is to type the first letter in the category name. Typing the first letter moves you to the first category in the list that starts with that letter. For example, when I type S, Quicken moves to the category called Salary because it's the first category that starts with S.

Now, click the Delete button in the Category & Transfer List button bar. So that you don't make a rash decision here, Quicken gives you an opportunity to keep the category and not delete it. When Quicken displays its warning message, click OK to go ahead and delete the category. If you decide to keep it, click Cancel.

CAUTION Be careful that you don't delete categories that you've previously assigned to transactions. If you do, Quicken removes the category from all of those transactions; your transactions are NOT removed. So, you'll have transactions without an assigned category and you'll need to go back and assign a new category to them. If there is a category that you've assigned to transactions that you want to delete, recategorize the transactions first and then delete it. You learn how to recategorize transactions a little later in this chapter.

TIP I just cautioned you not to delete categories that are assigned to transactions. Right? Well, here's an easy way to see if you've assigned the category that you want to delete to any previous transactions. Just select the category from the Category & Transfer List and then click the Report button. If Quicken finds any transactions with the category that you selected, you'll see them in a QuickReport on your screen. If you want to know a little more about QuickReports, read Chapter 18.

This category needs a change

Like most things in Quicken, you can change them if you need to. So, if you need to change a category name or description, change the type of category it is, or change the tax form or schedule assigned to the category, you can do so at any time.

There's only one group of categories that you won't be able to change and they're the ones preceded by an underscore (_). These are categories that Quicken automatically sets up when you add your first investment account. They are used for investment transactions and cannot be changed.

First, go to the Category & Transfer List and find the category you want to edit. Click or highlight the category name. Then, click the Edit button from the button bar. What you see next is the Edit Category dialog box. All of the information that you can change about a category is included in this dialog box.

Now, just move to the text box or option that you want to change and type over the existing information. When you're finished making changes to the category, click OK.

Subcategories work much like categories

Earlier in this chapter, you saw something called a "subcategory," and I know I explained only very briefly what it was. But now, we're ready to talk about subcategories, what they are, and how they work in Quicken.

A subcategory is similar to a category, but represents more detail than a category does. Subcategories are "subsets" of categories; they break down a category into smaller pieces. You might say that a category is a parent and subcategories are the children.

Take, for example, the category Utilities. The category Utilities is a general grouping for all of your utility expenses. And it's certainly okay to just group all of your utility expenses into this one category. But what if you want to know how much you spent on electricity last year or on water and sewer charges? If you have subcategories for each of these expenses under the general category of Utilities, then you can easily answer these questions. You could have the following subcategories for the category Utilities:

Electric

Water

Sewer

Gas

In this case, the subcategories of Electric, Water, Sewer, and Gas are subcategories of the parent category, Utilities.

Each time you pay an electric bill, you assign the subcategory Electric to the transaction. Then, you can easily determine how much your electric bills were for any given time.

TIP **Guess what? You can even have subcategories of subcategories.** These would even further break out the detail of a subcategory. There probably aren't many instances where you'll need these subcategories of subcategories. Here's one example. Say you have a subcategory called Condo Maint (for condominium maintenance) under the category Condo Exp (condominium expense). You could break out condo maintenance even further by creating subcategories called Cleaning and Lawncare. These would be subcategories of Condo Maint, which is a subcategory of Condo Exp.

Subcategories also are found in the Category & Transfer List

Subcategories are found in the same place you find categories—in the Category & Transfer List. You can tell which item in the list is a subcategory because it appears indented, right under its parent category, or the category to which it relates. In the Category & Transfer List shown in Figure 4.6, notice that there are three subcategories for the category Auto: Fuel, Insurance, Service. Then look in the Type column of the Category & Transfer List; Quicken shows Sub (for subcategory) as the type of category these are.

Fig. 4.6
When a category has subcategories, Quicken lists them in the Category & Transfer List right under the parent category.

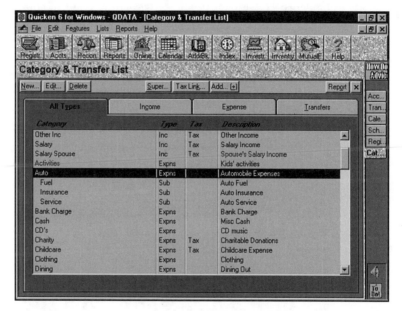

Adding, deleting, and editing subcategories

As I said earlier, subcategories are very similar to categories. And because they're similar, you add, delete, and edit a subcategory the same way that you do a category.

When you add a subcategory, follow the same instructions that I gave you for adding a category, but just be sure to click the Subcategory option. Then click the down arrow and select the category that you're setting up the subcategory for, or the parent category, from the list that drops down.

Deleting a subcategory works just the same way as deleting a category. When you delete a subcategory that you've assigned to transactions, Quicken automatically merges the subcategory into its parent category. So, if you have a subcategory called Movies under the parent category called Entertainment and you delete Movies, any transactions with Movies assigned to it will automatically be merged into the category Entertainment and therefore be assigned to this category.

You can edit a subcategory the same way that you edit a category. You can change the name, description, and even the parent category of a subcategory. So, if you decide you'd rather have the subcategory Art Fees under the category Activities instead of Recreation, you can change the parent category in the Edit Subcategory dialog box. I explain how to change a subcategory's parent a little later in this chapter.

Let's rearrange the category list

When I say you can "rearrange" your Category & Transfer List, I don't mean that you can put the categories in a different order. Quicken will always put your categories in alphabetical order by category type. All income categories are first, followed by expense categories, and then transfer accounts.

What you can do to your Category & Transfer List is change categories to subcategories (and subcategories to categories), change a subcategory's parent, and merge categories and subcategories together. The next few sections explain how to do this kind of rearranging of your list.

Changing a category to a subcategory and vice versa

Just like employees in corporate America, a category can lose its status and get demoted to a subcategory and a subcategory can climb the corporate ladder by getting a promotion to a category.

Let's say that you decide you've got a category called Tuition and you decide you want to group all of your school expenses into a category called Education. You'll have to demote the Tuition category to a subcategory of the category Education.

To demote a category to a subcategory, first select it from the Category & Transfer List. Then choose the Edit button in the button bar so that Quicken displays the Edit Category dialog box. Next, change the category type to a subcategory by selecting the Subcategory of option. So now that the category is a subcategory, tell Quicken which category is the parent by selecting the category from the Subcategory of drop-down list. Click the OK button and the category gets the bad news and becomes a subcategory.

If you want to grant a promotion to a subcategory, first select the subcategory from the Category & Transfer List and then click the Edit button. When Quicken displays the Edit Category dialog box for the subcategory, change its type from a subcategory to either an income or expense category and click OK.

Whether you've been heartless and demoted a category or benevolent and promoted a subcategory, Quicken will automatically change all previous transactions that were assigned to the category or subcategory.

Changing a subcategory's parent category

There are probably a lot of teens out there that would like to change their parent from time to time, but they're out of luck. But in Quicken, you can easily change a subcategory's parent without any legal hassles. You may want to do this if a subcategory seems better suited for another category rather than its own parent category. For example, if you've got a subcategory called Auto Lease, you may want to move it from the Auto category to the Lease Expense category.

When you're ready to make the switch, choose the subcategory from the Category & Transfer List and then click the Edit button from the button bar. When you see the Edit Category dialog box, open the Subcategory of drop-down list by clicking the down arrow. Then just scroll through the list to pick another category. Click OK and Quicken changes the parent category. You see in the Category & Transfer List that the subcategory is now listed under the new parent category.

Merging categories and subcategories

Sometimes you may want to condense your category list by combining categories and subcategories. When you merge two categories or subcategories, Quicken assigns the category or subcategory that you retain to transactions. For example, if you have a category to record interest income called Interest Inc and you really don't want to break out your investment income out into this type of income category, then you could merge this category into your investment income category, maybe Invest Inc. After you merge the two categories, Quicken changes the category assignment of any transactions that were assigned to Interest Inc to Invest Inc.

The first thing that you have to do when merging categories is to change the category that you want to merge into a subcategory (demote it). If you're merging a subcategory into another, make it a subcategory of the subcategory that you're merging with. You just learned how to promote and demote categories and subcategories, so you should be able to do this now.

Next, delete the subcategory that you want merged into its parent (either category or subcategory). Remember that when you delete a subcategory, Quicken merges it into its parent. So by deleting the subcategory, you're actually merging it into its parent category or subcategory. Any transactions that were assigned to the subcategory that was just merged will now be assigned to the parent category or subcategory.

I want to switch a transaction from one category to another

Oh no! You just realized that you've been assigning the wrong category to your rent payments. Instead of assigning the category Rent, you assigned the category Lease (which applies to your car lease payments). What do you do now? It will take forever to go back and find each rent payment transaction and assign the proper category.

Well, you really don't have to go through this ordeal. Quicken makes it quick and easy by finding groups of transactions and replacing the category in all transactions that you select with the category that you want.

Finding transactions

The first thing that you need to do when you want to switch (or recategorize) a group of transactions from one category to another is to have Quicken search through the register for the transactions assigned to the wrong category. Do this by selecting Edit, Find & Replace, Recategorize. Quicken displays the Recategorize window.

In the Search Category box, click the down arrow to display the list of categories and then select the category that you mistakenly assigned to transactions. In my example, I'd select the category Lease.

Then click the Find All button. Quicken searches the register for any transactions assigned to the category that you selected and displays them in the Recategorize window, like in Figure 4.7.

Fig. 4.7
When Quicken finds transactions assigned to the wrong category, it displays them all in the Recategorize window.

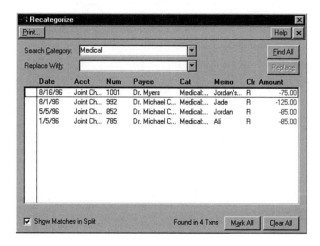

Sometimes, a transaction has more than one category assigned to it. This is called a split transaction. Split transactions break out the transaction into different categories. I give you lots more detail on split transactions in the next chapter. If you have any transactions that you assigned more than one category to, you can show each category in the transactions by clicking the Show Matches in Split checkbox at the bottom of the Recategorize window.

CAUTION **Quicken will not switch the category of the top level of a split** transaction in the Recategorize window. A split transaction has two or more levels (or two or more categories assigned to the transaction). The top level is the first line of the split transaction. If you need to recategorize the top level, go to the transaction in the register and change the category. I tell you all about editing split transactions in the register in the next chapter.

Marking transactions to switch

Now that you've found all of the transactions that you assigned the wrong category to, you can switch the category in all of the transactions, or select transactions that you want to switch.

To select a transaction so that Quicken recategorizes it, mark it by clicking the transaction in the Recategorize window. Quicken places a checkmark next to each transaction that you select. Figure 4.8 shows three marked transactions.

Fig. 4.8
Quicken changes only the category for the transactions that you mark in the Recategorize window. Quicken places a checkmark next to a transaction to show that you've selected it to be recategorized.

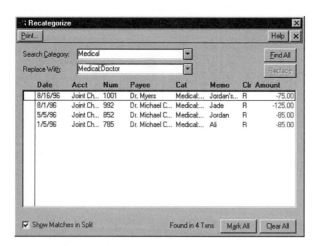

If you want to mark all of the transactions in the Recategorize window, click the Mark All button; to clear all marked transactions, click the Clear All button.

Recategorizing transactions

Once you've marked the transactions that you want to recategorize, just tell Quicken which new category you want assigned to the transactions. In the Replace With box, click the down-arrow key to display the category list and select the replacement category. Then click the Replace button. Quicken displays a confirmation message telling you how many transactions will be recategorized. Click OK to recategorize the transactions.

Q&A   *When I look through the Lists menu, I see something called Class. Is a class like a category, and how do I use it?*

Classes are similar to categories in that they help to break out transactions into income and expense groups. But classes add a second dimension to your transaction data by breaking it out in different ways. For example, if you want to track an expense by job or project, by salesperson or product line, or by geographic location or functional company area, you can use classes to record the expense.

Classes are very useful to business users of Quicken; however, they probably serve no real purpose for the Quicken home user.

Introducing the Quicken Register

● **In this chapter:**

- **See what the register looks like**

- **Move around the register**

- **Enter a transaction in the register**

- **Split a transaction**

- **Learn about transfer transactions**

- **Sort the register**

Quicken's register takes the hassle out of tracking all your facts and figures. . . . . ➤

Quicken's registers look like the register you're used to seeing in your checkbook. You know, you write a check and then flip back to the register to record the date, check number, payee, and the amount of the check. We all are very diligent about recording each and every check that we write and we even subtract the check amount from the account balance so that we always know exactly how much money we have. Not! Most of us try to keep on top of our finances but with today's time constraints we don't always get the job done.

But now that you've decided to automate your finances, you can rely on Quicken to keep track of your transactions and do all the arithmetic for you. Never again will a simple math error cause you to bounce a check!

Tell me about the register

Quicken registers do just what the name implies: they "register" (or record) your financial activity in a ledger-like format. Quicken's register is the program's major component. Every other feature in Quicken depends on the register to function. Look at how the register interacts with other features in Quicken:

- The check-writing feature records your checks in the register

- The bank account reconciliation feature uses the transactions in the register to balance your account

- The reporting and graph features use the data from your register to create summaries of your transactions

- Quicken's budgeting features use the information in the register to show you how actual data measures up to budgeted data

- The tax features in Quicken rely on the information in your register

Here's what you do with a register

Any financial activity you have can be recorded directly into a Quicken register. Sometimes you'll enter transactions directly into a register and other times Quicken enters the transaction in the register for you.

Here's when you're going to need to use a register:

- To enter checks you write manually

- To enter bank deposits and ATM (automatic teller machine) transactions

- To enter other types of transactions, such as interest you earn on a bank account or bank service charges

- When you want to review your transactions

- If you want to edit or delete a transaction

- To void a check or other transaction

- To find a transaction

- If you want to print transactions

Getting to the register

Open an account and Quicken automatically displays its register on your screen.

Let's review the different ways to open an account (and therefore its register):

- Click the Accts button from the iconbar to open the Account List. Then select the account from the list and click the Open button from the button bar (see Figure 5.1). Quicken opens the register for the specified account.

- If you've already got any account register open, select another account from the Account selection bar (see Figure 5.2) at the bottom of the register (you learned about the Account selection bar in Chapter 3). Open an account register by clicking the account name in the Account selection bar.

- If you're working in the Write Checks window for an account, you can open the account's register by clicking the Register button from the iconbar.

Fig. 5.1
Click the Open button
in the Account List to
open the selected
account's register.

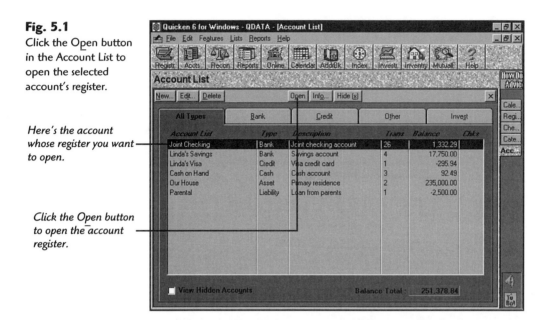

*Here's the account
whose register you want
to open.*

*Click the Open button
to open the account
register.*

Fig. 5.2
Click an account from
the Account selection
bar in any register.

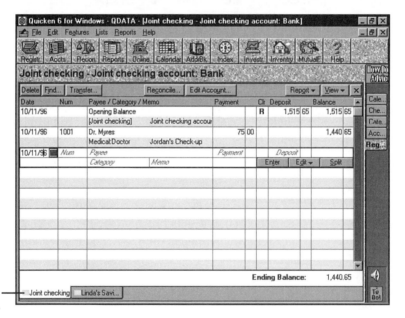

*The Account selection
bar includes a button
for all of your accounts.*

What you'll find in the register

Registers in Quicken look much like the register in your checkbook. Format aside, the information that you're used to entering in your checkbook is the same for a Quicken register.

Button bar
Use these buttons to perform tasks in the register, like deleting a transaction, finding a transaction, entering a transfer between two accounts, reconciling the account, editing the account, creating a QuickReport of transactions with the same payee, and sorting the transactions in the register.

Transaction toolbar
Use this toolbar to enter (record) a transaction, change a transaction, or split a transaction (assign more than one category to it).

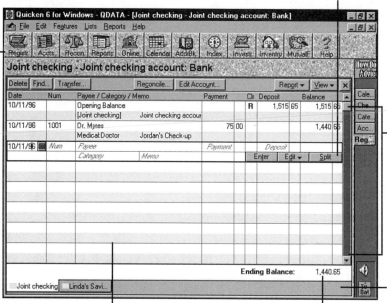

Scroll bar
Use the scroll bar to move through the register. To move up one transaction at a time, click the up arrow; to move down one transaction, click the down arrow. Drag the scroll box up or down to move quickly through lots of transactions. As you drag the scroll box, Quicken shows you the date and check number of the current transaction.

Account selection bar
Quickly switch account registers by clicking another account button on the Account selection bar.

Transaction lines
Here's the guts of the register, where you enter the date, identifying transaction information (like the check number), the payee for a check or the source of a deposit, the amount of the transaction, assign the category, and enter an optional memo.

Balance
Quicken always shows you the balance in your account.

Seeing more transactions in the register

Quicken shows you two lines of information for each transaction in the register. This is called two-line display. With this format, you can't see very many transactions at a time. Click the View button in the register button bar and then select One-Line Display from the View menu so that more transactions fit in the register (see Figure 5.3). Don't worry, you haven't lost any of your transaction data; it's just hidden from view.

Fig. 5.3

If you want to see more transactions in the register at one time, select the One-Line Display option from the View menu.

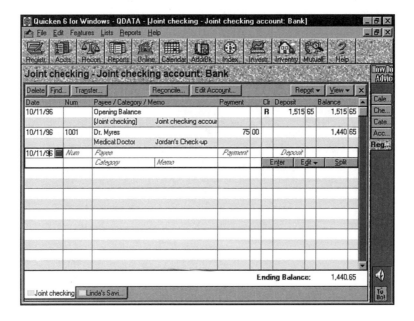

Of course, you can change the register back to displaying two lines per transaction by selecting the One-Line Display option again.

TIP

Need to make a change to the account whose register you're working in? It's easy with Quicken 6. Just click the Edit Account button in the register button bar to get to the Edit Account window where you can change the account name, description, and other information. Chapter 3 is where you learned all about editing accounts.

Entering a transaction is easy

Before entering a transaction in the register, make sure you're working in the appropriate account. If you're entering transactions for checks you've written from your 1st National checking account, make sure that the 1st National checking account register is the one that's open on your screen.

Moving to a blank transaction line

It's probably obvious that you want to move to a blank transaction line first before you start to enter a transaction. Just make sure you do. If you start entering a transaction where one already exists, Quicken will write over the old transaction and you'll lose it.

The first blank transaction line is always at the end of the register, so move to a blank transaction line by pressing Ctrl+End.

TIP **You also can get to a new transaction line by choosing <u>E</u>dit,** T<u>r</u>ansaction, <u>N</u>ew or pressing Ctrl+N. You also can insert a blank transaction line between two existing transactions. Figure out where you want to insert the transaction and highlight the transaction below the one that you want to insert. (Quicken inserts transactions above the highlighted transaction.) Then choose <u>E</u>dit, T<u>r</u>ansaction, <u>I</u>nsert or press Ctrl+I.

If the current field (the one with the flashing cursor) is not the Date field, press Home twice to get there. The date is the first piece of information you'll need to enter.

Plain English, please!

A **field** in a register is a blank area where you enter information. The current field is the one with the blinking cursor. Usually, pressing the Tab key moves the cursor from field to field. **"**

Entering the transaction date

After arriving at the Date field in the blank transaction line, you'll notice that Quicken already has today's date entered. Quicken automatically enters the system date in the Date field. You can enter any date you want by typing over the date that's already there. The date you'll want to enter is the date of the check or other transaction. If your check's written on 10/15/96, you'll enter this date in the MM/DD/YY format. You don't have to type the slashes though, so just type 1015 (entering the year isn't necessary either because if it's the current year, it's already entered for you).

Here's two other quick ways to enter dates in the Date field in the register:

- Press the + or – keys on the numeric keypad to change the existing date one day at a time. So, if the date that's already entered is 11/14/96, just press + once to change it to 11/15/96 or press – twice to change it to 11/12/96.

- Click the calendar icon in the Date field (see Figure 5.4) to see Quicken's mini-calendar. Then click on a date in the calendar to enter it in the register. I explain more about the mini-calendar in Chapter 8.

Fig. 5.4
Quicken's mini-calendar appears when you click the calendar icon in the Date field.

Click the calendar icon to see the mini-calendar.

You can select any date from Quicken's mini-calendar.

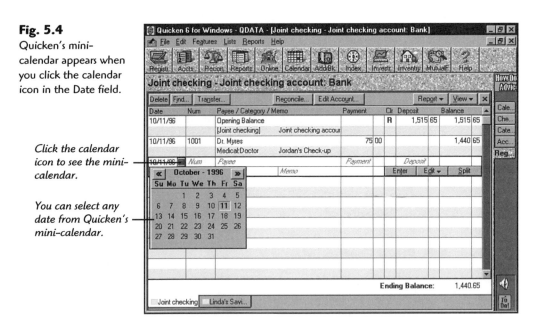

After you've entered the transaction date, press Tab to move to the next field to enter the check number or other identifying symbol.

Recording the transaction (check) number

If you're entering a transaction for a check that you've written, enter the check number in the Num field.

There are three ways to enter the check number:

- Type in the check number using the numeric keys on your keypad.

- Press the + and – keys on the numeric keypad to change the check number one at a time. So if the check number entered is 1345 and you press + twice, the check number changes to 1347. If it's 1345 and you press – twice, it changes to 1343.

- Select Next Check Num from the drop-down list that appears when you move to the Num field. Quicken automatically adds one to the last check number entered in the register.

There are several options in the Num field drop-down list. Here's when to use them:

- **Next Check Num.** To have Quicken automatically add one to the last check number entered in the Num field.

- **ATM.** To enter an Automatic Teller Machine transaction.

- **Deposit.** Used for deposit transactions.

- **Print Check.** To tell Quicken to print a check for the transaction you are entering.

- **Send Online Payment.** To send payment instructions for electronic bill paying.

- **Transfer Funds.** To enter a transfer of funds from one Quicken account to another.

- **EFT.** To enter electronic funds transfers.

- **Edit List button.** When you want to change one of the items in the Num fields drop-down list. Just click this button to make your change.

 TIP **Typically, you enter checks you want Quicken to print for you in** the Write Checks window (which I get to in the next chapter). Checks you write by hand (or manually) are entered directly into the register. You also can enter checks that you want Quicken to print into the register if you select Print Check in the Num field (so Quicken knows to print it).

After the Num field is filled, press Tab to move to the Payee field.

Tell Quicken who the payee is

Now you're ready to fill in the Payee field. Quicken uses the term payee generically to describe transactions in the register. Obviously, the payee in a check transaction is the person or business to whom you are writing the check. But there really is no payee for a deposit transaction or a withdrawal from the ATM. So just consider the Payee field as a description of the transaction that you're entering. For a deposit transaction, for instance, you could enter the source of the cash, like Weekly Payroll or Stock Dividend. For an ATM withdrawal, you could describe it as Cash Withdrawal or just Cash.

You can type the entry in the Payee field (using up to 40 characters) or you can select it from the drop-down list that appears when you move there. The list that you see is comprised of all of the payees that you've entered in Quicken registers. So if you write a check to Municipal Utilities every month, you're going to see Municipal Utilities in the drop-down list.

Q&A ***When I start typing a payee's name in the Payee field, Quicken finishes entering the name for me. What's happening here?***

You've just discovered QuickFill. QuickFill is a feature that saves you tons of time. When you type a few characters in a field, Quicken searches previous transactions in the register and in the Memorized Transaction List (you don't know about this list yet, but you can turn to Chapter 9 if you're dying to know) to find a match. When Quicken finds a match, the QuickFill feature fills in the rest of the field. I explain a lot more about QuickFill in Chapters 8 and 9.

The amount of the transaction gets entered next.

Now enter the amount of the transaction

So, is this a payment that you're making or a deposit? If it's a payment, Tab once from the Payee field to arrive at the Payment field. If the transaction is a deposit, Tab twice to get to the Deposit field.

Now, enter the amount of the transaction. You can enter amounts using up to 10 characters and as large as $9,999,999.99 (the decimal point counts as one character, but the dollar sign and commas do not). By the way, you don't have to type dollar signs or commas.

Q&A *I want to add several amounts together to figure out how much my deposit is. Is there a calculator I can use in the Deposit field?*

Yes. As a matter of fact, Quicken's mini-calculator is available from both the Payment field and the Deposit field. Just click the calculator icon (see Figure 5.5) to make it appear on-screen. Then, perform your calculations and press Enter to record the result in the Payment or Deposit field. The chapter on Quicken shortcuts, Chapter 8, tells you more about the mini-calculator.

Fig. 5.5

Need some help figuring out amounts to enter? Use Quicken's mini-calculator to help by clicking the calculator icon from the Payment field or the Deposit field.

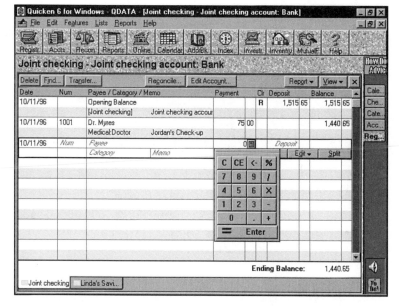

Q&A *What's the Clr field and what do I enter here?*

This is the Clear field and shows whether a transaction has been recorded by the bank (cleared). When you're entering current transactions, you don't enter anything in this field. When you balance your account (which we get to in Chapter 7), Quicken enters a **c** in this field to show that you've marked the transaction as cleared. Once you complete the reconciliation process, Quicken changes the **c** to an **R** to show that the transaction is cleared and reconciled with your bank statement.

If you are entering past transactions in Quicken that have already cleared, click the Clr field (Quicken enters a **c**). After you reconcile your account, Quicken changes the **c** to an **R**.

Assigning a category is important

Here's one of the most important fields that you need to complete in a transaction. The Category field is where you assign the category, subcategory, or other account (for transfers) to a transaction. If you don't assign something here, the transaction does not get classified into an income or expense category. It just ends up in an Other category and you won't know what it's made up of.

 Q&A ***How can I make sure that I assign all of my transactions to a category? Quicken doesn't make me do this, does it?***

Quicken will record a transaction in your register whether or not you've assigned a category. If you want to make sure that a category has been assigned to your transactions, there's a register option you can select in Quicken to help you remember. When you select this particular option, Quicken displays a warning message when you try to record a transaction that's uncategorized. Later in this chapter, I talk about how to set register options, and this option is one of them.

Press Tab to move to the Category field. When you get to the Category field, you see another one of those drop-down lists. Included in this list is all of your categories, subcategories, and accounts so that you can just select one to enter in the Category field. (If the drop-down list doesn't automatically appear, just click the down arrow.)

If you'd rather just type in your category, start typing the category name. Again, you'll notice that after you've typed a character, Quicken fills in the rest of a category name for you. This is QuickFill at work.

 By the way, if you're assigning a subcategory to a transaction, you also can just type in the subcategory name and Quicken automatically identifies the category that it goes with and enters it, along with the subcategory, for you. This makes assigning subcategories quick and easy. For example, to assign the category Medical and subcategory Doctor to a transaction, just type Doctor and Quicken enters Medical:Doctor for you.

You also can assign an account to a transaction by selecting or entering the account name in the Category field. This is called a transfer transaction, which transfers funds from one Quicken account to another. Later in this chapter, I talk more about transfer transactions and how to enter them.

TIP **If you're entering a transaction and decide that you need a** category that's not in the Category & Transfer List, you can add the new category on-the-fly by just typing the new category name in the Category field. When Quicken doesn't find it in the Category & Transfer List, the New Category window appears so that you can add it now. After you add it, it will then appear in your Category & Transfer List.

I'd like to enter a transaction memo

The Memo field follows the Category field and is completely optional. If you want to enter a transaction memo, press Tab to move to this field and type up to 54 characters. I use memos to provide as much information about a transaction as I can. If I write a check for something unusual or to someone I may not remember six months later, I usually enter a memo to describe what the check was for, like birthday gift for mom, or reupholster great room chair.

You're almost finished with your transaction. The only thing left to do is record it so that Quicken saves the data in the register.

Recording your transaction

After you've filled in all of the information for a transaction, you can save it in the register by clicking the Enter button from the Transaction toolbar or pressing Enter.

When you enter a transaction, Quicken places the transaction in the proper order (by date) in the register and updates your account balance accordingly. If the balance is too large (wouldn't we love that!), Quicken displays asterisks in the Balance field. If the balance is negative, a minus sign precedes the amount. On color monitors the balance appears in red.

I've got a transaction that affects two accounts

When you have a transaction that affects two accounts, in essence it's a transfer of funds from one account to another. This is called a transfer transaction. Suppose that you go to the ATM and transfer $500 from your savings account to your checking account. You would have to enter a transfer transaction to show the transfer of funds from your savings account to your checking account. It really wouldn't matter in which account you entered the transfer transaction. When you enter this type of transaction in one account, Quicken automatically enters a corresponding transaction in the other account (the account that you select or enter in the Category field).

There are two ways to enter a transfer transaction:

- In the register for either one of the accounts, enter the transaction like any other, except select Transfer Funds in the Num field (and Quicken enters TXFR) and select the other account in the Category field.

- In the register for either one of the accounts, click the Transfer button from the button bar. Quicken displays the Transfer dialog box that you see in Figure 5.6. Select the account to where you're transferring funds, and then fill in the date, description, and the amount of the transfer. Click OK to record the transfer transaction in the register.

Fig. 5.6
Here, I'm transferring
$500 from my joint
checking account to
my savings account.

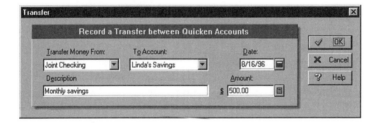

TIP **If you want to see the corresponding transfer transaction in** the other account that Quicken enters, highlight the transfer transaction and press Ctrl+X.

Go ahead, assign more than one category

When you see a transaction line in the register, you see only one field for assigning a category. But that doesn't mean you can only assign one category to a transaction. As a matter of fact, you can assign up to 30 different categories to a single transaction. Assigning more than one category to a transaction is called splitting a transaction because you're splitting the amount of the transaction between two or more categories.

Here's a good example of a split transaction. Let's say you go to Wal-Mart and write a check for $129.55 to cover your purchases. So what did you buy? Probably a lot of different things that fit into different categories, like toiletries, household items, a CD, hardware, and some grocery items. When you enter the transaction in your Quicken register, you'll need to break out the transaction to reflect the appropriate expense categories, maybe something like this:

Amount	Category
$24.67	Toiletries
$19.88	Household Items
$14.99	Music
$33.19	Hardware
$36.82	Groceries

So the single transaction for the check to Wal-Mart can be broken out into five different categories.

TIP **If you want to track your expenses closely, enter split transactions** for all of your expenditures. If you just dump some of your expenditures into a catch-all category, like Miscellaneous, you really won't know where all of your money is going. Keep your receipts from department stores and discount stores so that when you're ready to enter the transactions in Quicken, you can look at the receipts to figure out which categories to assign.

Splitting a transaction

You already know how to enter a transaction in the register and assign one category. Assigning two or more categories (splitting a transaction) only requires a few more steps.

Here's how you split a transaction:

1 In the register, fill in the Date, Num, Payee, and Amount fields as usual.

2 Click the Split button from the transaction toolbar to open the Split Transaction Window (see Figure 5.7), which contains 30 lines for you to assign categories.

Fig. 5.7

You can assign up to 30 different categories to a transaction in the Split Transaction Window.

3 Begin entering or selecting categories in the Category field, enter an optional memo, and then enter the amount for each category. Press the Tab key to move from field to field in the Split Transaction Window.

4 When you're finished assigning categories, click the Finished button to return to the transaction in the register.

5 (Optional) Press Tab to move to the Memo field and enter a memo for the transaction.

Then you'll need to record the split transaction in the register by clicking the Enter button.

After you record a split transaction in the register, Quicken inserts —Split— in the Category field to show the transaction is split between two or more categories (see Figure 5.8).

 TIP **Use the Adjust button in the Split Transaction Window to calculate** the amount of a transaction. Perhaps you have several invoices from the same payee and each represents a different type of expense. If you don't already know the total amount of all the invoices, let Quicken calculate it for you. Open the Split Transaction Window (select Split) before entering the transaction amount; then enter all your categories and amounts for all of the invoices. When you're finished, click the Adjust button in the Split Transaction Window to have Quicken calculate the total of all the amounts you just entered. When you click Finished in the Split Transaction Window, Quicken returns to the register and enters the total amount of the transaction for you.

Fig. 5.8
Here's what a split
transaction looks like
in the register after it's
entered.

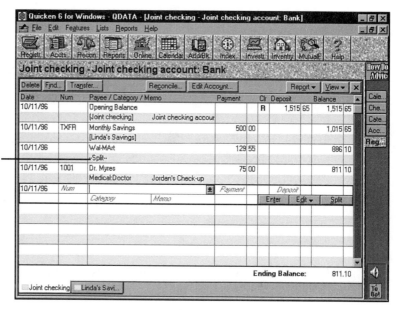

*Quicken inserts
— Split—to show this
is a split transaction.*

Changing a split transaction

If you need to change one of the categories or an amount in a split transaction, just click the check button to go back to the Split Transaction Window. Press Tab to move to the split line that you want to edit and then make your change. When you're finished editing the Split Transaction Window, click Finished to return to the register and then click Enter to record your changes.

CAUTION **If you change an amount in the Split Transaction window, your** transaction may no longer balance (the total in the Split Transaction window won't equal the transaction amount). If you need to change the transaction amount anyway, click the Adjust button to recalculate the transaction. If the original transaction amount is correct, change one of the other split line amounts so that the transaction balances.

Undoing a split transaction

If you enter a split transaction and later decide that you want just one category assigned to the transaction, you can undo the split by clicking the X button in the transaction line in the register. When you click the X button, Quicken asks whether you want to clear all split lines. Select Yes to delete all the split lines in the Split Transaction window and then select the single category from the drop-down list (displayed automatically by Quicken) that you want to assign.

Reviewing your transactions

It's a good idea to review the transactions you enter (especially if you're new to Quicken) to make sure that you've entered everything correctly. You also may want to review the transactions in your register to confirm whether a payment was made or if you've entered a deposit.

To review transactions, just use the scroll bar or the keyboard arrow keys to move through the register to see the transactions that don't fit on your screen.

Even though you've already entered a transaction, at any time you can edit the transaction, delete it, or void it. The next few sections explain how to perform these actions on transactions.

I see a mistake in the register and need to change it

Want to make changes to a transaction? Maybe you entered the wrong payee or the wrong check number. Or, maybe you entered the wrong amount or entered a payment transaction that should have been a deposit.

It's easy to edit a transaction. Just highlight the transaction that you want to change and then move to the field that's wrong. Either type over the existing information or select a new item from the drop-down list. Then, click the Enter button to record the changes to the transaction.

The Edit button in the transaction toolbar opens an Edit menu that can be used to make changes to transactions.

 Q&A ***What if I'm editing a transaction and then decide it shouldn't be changed?***

While you're editing the transaction, you can change it back to the way it was originally by selecting Edit from the toolbar in the transaction and then selecting Restore Transaction. Quicken restores the transaction to the way it was before you started editing it.

TIP **If you need to copy a transaction from one account to another,** highlight the transaction and choose E_dit, _Copy Transaction. Then, go to the account register where you want to enter the copied transaction, go to a blank transaction line, and select E_dit, _Paste Transaction.

I need to get rid of this transaction

If you enter the wrong transaction in an account register or a transaction in the wrong account, you can easily delete it. Be sure you want to delete it because once you do, it's removed permanently from the register.

CAUTION **Don't mistake deleting a transaction with voiding a transaction. If** you inadvertently enter a transaction that you never should have entered, you delete it. But, if you enter a transaction for a check that you've written and you later lose the check or stop payment on the check, you void the transaction. When you delete a transaction, you remove all record of the transaction. But when you void a transaction, Quicken retains the transaction information in your register, but not the amount. The next section explains how to void a transaction.

Once you've decided that you do indeed want to delete a transaction in the register, here's what you do. First, select the transaction that you want to delete. To show it's selected, it should be highlighted. Then, click the Delete button from the button bar. Quicken won't let you make hasty decisions so it displays a confirmation message to make sure that you really want to delete the transaction. If you do, click Yes. If you don't want to delete it, click No and the transaction remains untouched.

If you delete a transaction that is part of a transfer transaction (where you transferred funds from one Quicken account to another), the corresponding transaction in the other account is also deleted.

When deleting a transfer transaction that is part of a split transaction, you have to delete the transaction from the account where the transaction was originally entered. If the transfer transaction between your savings and checking accounts also was a split transaction and was entered in your savings account register, you have to delete the transaction from the savings account register.

And I need to void this transaction

You may need to void a transaction in the register for a check that you've already written. You now want to:

- Stop payment on the check

- Replace a lost check

- Print another check to replace a misprinted check

So what's the difference between voiding a transaction and deleting one? When you void a transaction, Quicken keeps your transaction information in the register but erases the amount and adjusts your account balance. In contrast, when you delete a transaction, Quicken wipes out the transaction completely. You have no record of the transaction in your register.

To void a transaction, highlight the transaction in the register and then choose Edit, Void Transaction. Quicken inserts **Void** in the Payee field (just before the payee name), erases the transaction amount, and places an R (for reconciled) in the Clr field. Then click the Enter button to record the voided transaction.

When Quicken erases the amount in a voided transaction, the account balance is adjusted accordingly. Voided transactions do not increase or decrease your account balance.

 TIP **You can change the way your register appears on-screen, how you** enter information in the register, and how the QuickFill feature works in the register. Click the View button in the Register button bar and then select Register Options. Quicken displays the Register Options window which includes three tabs (Display, Miscellaneous, and QuickFill) so that you can select the type of register options you want to change. Read Chapter 24 to learn more about customizing your register.

 TIP **6** **With Quicken 6, point to a transaction and click the right** mouse button to see a quick menu of editing activities you can perform, like cutting and copying to the Clipboard, voiding, memorizing, scheduling, or finding a transaction. You can also choose to print a report of all transactions to that particular payee.

Now you can sort your transactions

You'll notice that by default, your Quicken register is sorted by the date of the transaction. So, a transaction dated 8/16/96 comes after any transactions dated 8/15/96 or before.

If you want to sort your register in another way, say by amount (largest to smallest, or smallest to largest), you can easily do so with Quicken's new register sort feature. Sorting the register in no way affects the information in transactions in the register. Don't worry, you won't lose any transactions when you sort, you'll just change where they're placed in the register.

To sort the register, just click the View button from the button bar. Quicken opens the View menu, as shown in Figure 5.9, where you can select one of six different ways to sort the register. Just click to make a selection and Quicken re-sorts the register before your eyes.

Fig. 5.9
If you want to sort your register, select one of these options from the View menu.

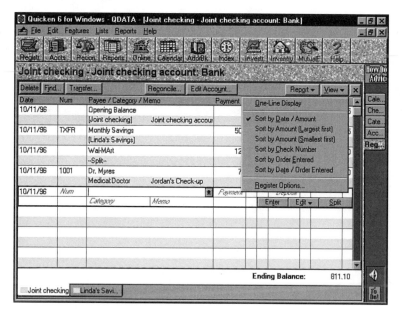

6

Writing Checks

● In this chapter:

- Order preprinted checks

- See what a check looks like on your screen

- Write a check

- Print checks

Forget those two hours you spent paying bills last month. With Quicken's printing feature, you can now pay your monthly bills in less than half the time . . . . **❯**

You're well aware of how long it takes to write checks each month, record the checks in your checking account register, and then update your account balance. What a tedious job. Right?

Well, now that you're using Quicken, you can speed up this process significantly. Using Quicken's check-writing feature, you can write a whole month's worth of checks in just a few minutes. Quicken not only prints your checks, but also records them in your checking account register and automatically updates your account balance. And your printed checks are ready to sign, stick in envelopes, and mail.

Deciding which checks to use

So you've decided that you want to use Quicken to print checks. Great! But first you need to order preprinted computer checks from Intuit that are compatible with your printer. You'll have to decide the check size, style, color, and whether you want multipart or voucher checks.

The best way to decide which checks work best for you is to review the Intuit Check Catalog that was included in your Quicken Deluxe package.

 TIP **When you order preprinted checks, you have to tell Quicken the** check number that you want to start with. If you're still using your manual checks, start your computer-printed checks with a number that won't overlap your manual checks. For example, if the next check number in your manual checkbook is 2890, then start your computer checks with the number 4000 or even 5000.

Ordering checks from Intuit

Order checks or any other Quicken supplies online through Intuit Marketplace or more traditionally by fax or mail.

You can order online

If you've got a modem, it's quick and easy to order your Quicken checks online through Intuit Marketplace. You can access Intuit Marketplace from Windows 95 by selecting the Marketplace program from the Quicken Deluxe program folder in Windows 95. If you're using Windows 3.1, just click the Intuit Marketplace icon in the Quicken program group to open the Intuit Marketplace window that you see in Figure 6.1.

Fig. 6.1
Use Intuit Marketplace and your modem to order checks and other supplies.

Click this button to order checks.

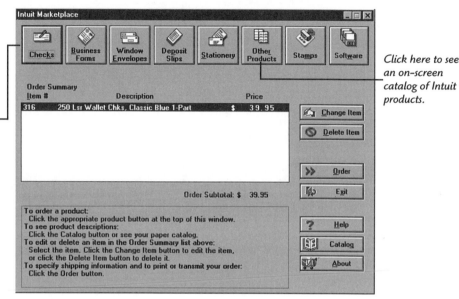

Click here to see an on-screen catalog of Intuit products.

Click the Checks button to order checks. Click the Continue button in each of the dialog boxes that follow, to enter information about your bank, printer, and the size and style of checks that you want to order.

After you've entered all the information Intuit needs to process your check order, review the Verify Check Order dialog box (see Figure 6.2) to make sure that all the information is correct and then click OK.

Computer checks are going to cost you more!

Preprinted computer checks are going to cost more than manual checks you order through your bank. You might expect to pay about $39.95 for 250 wallet-sized checks through Intuit and around $15 for manual checks. Of course, the time you'll save with computerized checks is worth something; however, you'll have to weigh the benefits.

Fig. 6.2
Review this dialog box carefully so that your checks get printed correctly. If you need to make a change, click the Ba<u>c</u>k button to get to the dialog box with the incorrect information and then correct it.

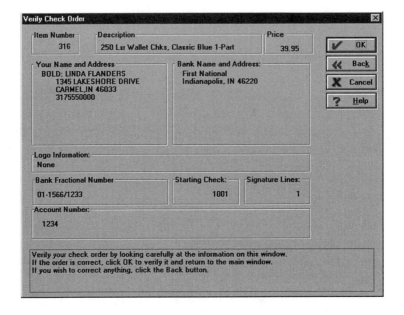

When you're ready to send your order, click the <u>O</u>rder button. Then enter your payment and delivery information. You have to pay by credit card when you order through Intuit Marketplace. So, be sure to provide a valid credit card number and expiration date. Because you're ordering online, be sure to select the <u>M</u>odem option in the Ordering by box. Now, click OK and select the <u>T</u>ransmit option from the Preview Order dialog box to send Intuit your check order.

TIP   **You also can use Intuit Marketplace to print an order form to mail or** fax to Intuit. Just enter check information as you would if you were sending your order by modem, but choose Mai<u>l</u> or FA<u>X</u> as the ordering option instead. Then select the <u>P</u>rint button to print the completed order form.

Order by mail or fax

If you don't have a modem, you can fill out the Intuit Supplies Order Form found inside the Supplies Catalog. Send your completed order form to Intuit:

- By mail to:

   Intuit, Inc.
   Supplies Department
   P.O. Box 34328
   Seattle, WA 98124-1328

- By fax to:

  1-206-925-9301

- Or phone in your order to Intuit's customer service staff from 6:00 A.M. to 5:00 P.M. PST:

  1-800-433-8810

Where do I write checks?

Remember back in Chapter 5, you entered manual checks in the check register? But now that you're using Quicken to print checks, you should use the Write Checks window to enter check information.

You can write checks only from bank accounts that you've set up in Quicken (like your checking account, savings account, or money market account). Obviously, you can't write checks from a credit card account or an asset account. If you have more than one bank account set up in Quicken, then you'll want to make sure you're using the appropriate account when you open the Write Checks window. After I show you how to open the Write Checks window, I'll tell you how to select the bank account you want to use with it.

You can get to the Write Checks window a few different ways:

- Click the Bills icon from the Activity Bar and then select Write a Check to Print.

- If you've already opened the Write Checks window during this Quicken session, click the Checks QuickTab on the right side of the screen.

- Press Ctrl+W.

 TIP **If you like using the register better than the Write Checks window,** you can still enter checks that you're going to print in the register. Just be sure to select Print Check in the Num field so that Quicken knows it needs to print a check for the register transaction. After you print checks, Quicken replaces the word "Print" with the appropriate check numbers.

What you find in the Write Checks window

Here's what the Write Checks window looks like when you open it. Notice the check in the middle of the window that looks just like one of your personal checks. And it's just as easy to fill out.

Button bar
Use this button bar to delete a check, find a check, view scheduled transactions and online payees, print checks, change check options, create a Report, and display an expense graph.

Current bank account
Here's the bank account that you're currently using to write checks.

On-screen check
Write a check by filling in this on-screen check.

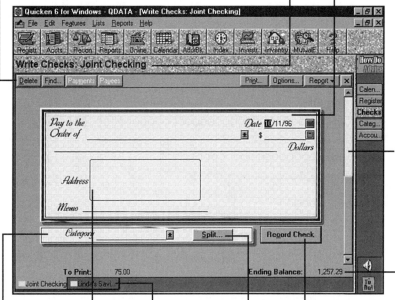

Scroll bar
The scroll bar helps you flip through the checks you've written (but not yet printed). To see the previous check, click the up arrow; to see the next check, click the down arrow. Drag the scroll box up or down to move quickly through lots of checks.

Quicken always shows you the balance in your account after checks have been written.

Category
Assign a category to your check transaction.

Account selection bar
The Account selection bar lets you quickly switch to another bank account to write checks from by clicking another account button.

Record Check button
This button is used to record a check when you're finished writing it.

Payee's address
If you want to use window envelopes to mail checks, type the payee's address here.

Split button
This button is used to open the Split Transaction window so that you can assign more than one category to your check.

Moving around the Write Checks window

In addition to the scroll bar and your mouse, you can use these keys to move around the Write Checks window quickly:

Press this key...	To move here...
Tab	Next field
Shift+Tab	Back one field
Home	Beginning of the current field
Home (two times)	First field in the check
End	End of current field
End End	Last field in the check
Ctrl+ →	To the next word in a field
Ctrl+ ←	To the previous word in a field
Page Up	Previous check written
Page Down	Next check written or blank check
Home (three times)	First check written (but not yet printed)
End (three times)	To a blank check

Now you're ready to write a check

You've opened the Write Checks window and there's a blank check staring you in the face. To write a check in Quicken, just fill in the on-screen check in the Write Checks window and then record it.

Before writing your first check, make sure that you're writing the check from the appropriate account. If you're writing a check from your joint checking account, make sure that the Write Checks window for Joint Checking is the one that's open on your screen. In Figure 6.3, you know that you're using the correct account because Quicken shows the name Joint Checking in the Write Checks window. If you need to change the account, just click one of the account buttons in the Account selection bar.

Fig. 6.3
When this Write Checks window is open, you'll be writing checks from the Joint checking account.

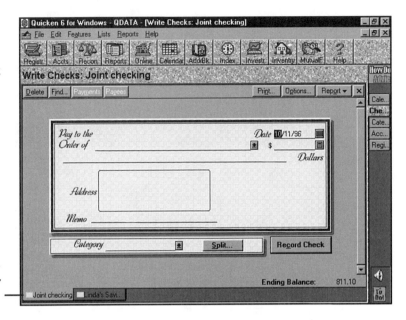

Select another account to write checks from by clicking an account button.

Entering the check date

Usually, when you open the Write Checks window, the cursor is already positioned in the Date field. If it's not there, press Tab to move forward one field at a time or Shift+Tab to move backward.

When you're in the Date field, type the date of the check. Enter dates in the MM/DD/YY format. So, to enter 9/4/96, type **94** (Quicken automatically enters the current year so you won't have to type 96 in this example if the current year is 1996).

Here are two other quick ways to enter check dates in the Date field:

- Press the + or – keys on the numeric keypad to change the existing date one day at a time. If the date that's already entered is 11/14/96, just press + once to change it to 11/15/96 or press – twice to change it to 11/12/96.

- Click on the calendar icon in the Date field (see Figure 6.4) to see Quicken's mini-calendar. Then click on a date in the calendar to enter it in the Date field. I explain more about the mini-calendar in Chapter 8.

After you've entered the check date, press Tab to move to the Pay to the Order of field.

Fig. 6.4
Quicken's mini-
calendar appears when
you click the calendar
icon in the Date field.

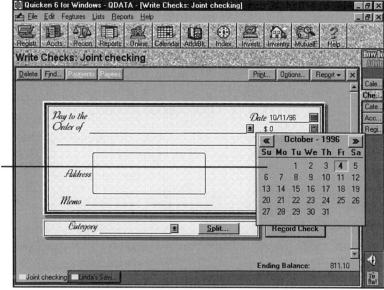

*You can select any
date from Quicken's ———
mini-calendar.*

Enter the payee

Obviously, the payee is the person or business to whom you are writing the
check.

You can type the entry in the Pay to the Order of field (using up to 40 characters) or you can select it from the drop-down list that appears when you
move there. The list that you see is comprised of every payee that you've
entered in the Write Checks window or in Quicken registers. So, if you write
a check to Public Service, Inc. every month, you're going to see Public
Service, Inc. in the drop-down list.

Q&A ***What's going on here? When I start typing a payee's
name in the Pay to the Order of field, Quicken finishes
entering the name for me.***

When you type a few characters in a field, Quicken searches previous
transactions in Quicken registers and in the Memorized Transaction List (you
don't know about this list yet, but you can turn to Chapter 9 to find out
about it) to find a match. When Quicken finds a match, the QuickFill
feature fills in the rest of the field. I explain a lot more about QuickFill in
Chapter 8.

The check amount is next

After you've entered the payee's name, press Tab to go to the $ (Amount) field so that you can enter the amount of the check. You can enter check amounts as large as $9,999,999.99 using up to 10 characters (the decimal point counts as one character, but the commas do not). And by the way, you don't have to type dollar signs or commas.

After you've entered the check amount and pressed Tab, Quicken writes out the amount on the next line of the check just as you would do if you were writing a manual check. Some of the words in the written amount may be abbreviated by Quicken to save space; like "Hundred" is Hndrd, "Thousand" is Thsnd, and "Million" is Mill.

 TIP **See the calculator icon in the $ (Amount) field in the Write** Checks window? You can click this to open Quicken's mini-calculator and use it to calculate the check amount. For example, if you have several invoices payable to the same payee, you can add the invoice amounts together with the mini-calculator and then press Enter to record the result in the $ (Amount) field. The chapter on Quicken shortcuts, Chapter 8, tells you more about the mini-calculator.

Filling in the payee address

You can enter the payee's address on checks if you want to use window envelopes to mail checks. When you enter an address for the payee in the Write Checks window, Quicken prints the address on the check so that it shows in the envelope window. You can type up to five lines in the address and use up to 30 characters in each line.

If you're going to enter the payee's address, press Tab to move to the Address field in the Write Checks window. Then begin typing the payee's name and address. Use the Tab key to move to the next line.

 TIP **Here's a little timesaver for you. If you want the payee name in** the address to be exactly as it is entered in the Pay to the Order of field, type an apostrophe (') in the first line of the Address field. Quicken copies the name from the Pay to the Order of field and puts it in the first address line. Because the Pay to the Order of field has space for 40 characters and the address line has space for only 30, the last 10 characters of the payee's name may get cut off.

Adding a memo

The Memo field in the Write Checks window is completely optional. If you want to enter a check memo, type up to 54 characters in the Memo field. I use memos to provide the payee of a check with information so that he can match my check to an invoice. I may enter the invoice number, my account number, or just **April Rent** to identify my check.

Q&A *Does the memo that I enter in the Write Checks window get printed on the check?*

Yes. So, if there's information that you don't necessarily want the payee to see, don't enter it as a memo in the Write Checks window. Instead, you can omit the memo, print the check, and then go to the register where Quicken records the check transaction and enter the memo there.

Assigning a category to a check

If you read Chapter 4, you know how important I think it is to use categories in Quicken to track your income and expenses. Assigning a category to a check tells Quicken the type of expense the check is being written for, such as utilities, interest expense, entertainment, clothing, etc. The Category field is where you assign the category, subcategory, or other account (for transfers) to a check. If you don't assign something here, the check does not get classified into an expense category. It just ends up in an Other category and you won't know where the money went.

When you get to the Category field, you see another one of those drop-down lists. Included in this list is all of your categories, subcategories, and accounts so that you can just select one to enter in the Category field. (If the drop-down list doesn't automatically appear, just click the down-arrow to see it).

If you'd rather just type in your category, start typing the category name. Again, you'll notice that after you've typed a character, Quicken fills in the rest of a category name for you. This is QuickFill at work.

By the way, if you're assigning a subcategory to a check, you also can just type in the subcategory name and Quicken automatically identifies the category that it goes with and enters it, along with the subcategory, for you. This makes assigning subcategories in checks quick and easy. For example, to assign the category Utilities and subcategory Water to a transaction, just type Water and Quicken enters Utilities:Water for you.

Q&A   ***What if the category that I need to assign to the check that I'm writing doesn't exist? How do I add it from here?***

If the category that you need to assign to a check isn't in the Category & Transfer List, you can add the new category on-the-fly by just typing the new category name in the Category field. When Quicken doesn't find it in the Category & Transfer List, the New Category window appears so that you can add it now.

You also can assign an account to a check by selecting or entering the account name in the Category field. This is called a **transfer transaction**, which transfers funds from one Quicken account to another. I talked about transfer transactions in more detail in Chapter 5.

Q&A   ***Do I use the <u>S</u>plit button to assign more than one category to a check?***

Yes. Remember in Chapter 5 when I talked about splitting transactions so that you can assign more than one category to a transaction? Splitting a check is done in just the same way. Just click the <u>S</u>plit button to open the Split Transaction window and assign categories to your heart's content (but only 30, please!). If you're not feeling quite sure how to split a transaction, go back to Chapter 5 and read the section, "Go ahead, assign more than one category."

Recording a check

When you've filled in the check in the Write Checks window, you're ready to record it. Review the check first to make sure the amount is correct and that you've written it to the appropriate payee, and then click the Re<u>c</u>ord Check button.

When you record a check in the Write Checks window, Quicken enters the check transaction in the register for the account from which you wrote the check. Figure 6.5 shows a check that I just wrote and Figure 6.6 shows the check transaction in the register after it's recorded.

Fig. 6.5
Here's a check I wrote in the Write Checks window from the Joint Checking account before it has been recorded.

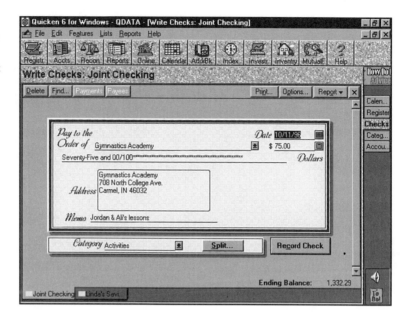

Q&A   ***Wait a minute! I didn't enter the check number anywhere. Don't I need to?***

No. You don't enter the check number when you're writing checks. When you're ready to print the checks that you've written, Quicken asks you to enter the next check number from your preprinted checks. It then assigns the appropriate check number to the checks that you print. So don't worry about check numbers until you get ready to print.

After you record a check, it scrolls off your screen and a blank check appears so that you can write another one. After you've written and recorded a check, it's ready to print. I'll tell you how to print your checks a little later in this chapter.

It's good to review the checks you've written

If you want to look over the checks you've just written, now is the time to do it. Don't wait until they're already printed because you may waste some of your preprinted computer checks.

Fig. 6.6

Here's the check transaction that Quicken enters in the Joint Checking account register after I recorded the check.

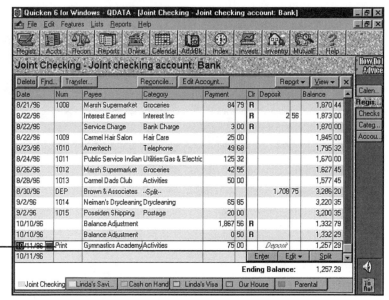

Quicken inserts the word "Print" here to show that this is a check that needs to be printed.

Quicken stores the checks that you write in the Write Checks window until you print them. Once you print the checks that you've written, they're no longer in the Write Checks window. Instead, Quicken records them in the register for the account from which you wrote them. If you wish, you can review them in the register.

Q&A

6 Can I change a check back to the way it was before I started editing it?

While you're editing a check, you can change it back to the way it was originally by clicking the right-mouse button to see a menu of procedures you can perform in the current check. Just click the Restore option and the check now looks the way it did before you started editing it. The Restore option works only if you select it before you record the changes to your check. Once you click the Record Check button to record changes to a check, you cannot restore the check.

I don't really want this check

What if I write a check for a bill that I've already paid? How do I get rid of it? I certainly don't want to print it. Well, because checks in the Write Checks window have not been printed yet (because if they had been, they wouldn't be there; they'd be in the register), you can delete the check at any time.

First, flip to the check that you want to delete so that it's the one shown in the Write Checks window. Then click the Delete button from the button bar. Quicken won't let you make hasty decisions so it displays a confirmation message to make sure that you really want to delete the check. If you do, click Yes. If you don't want to delete it, click No and the check will remain untouched.

Here's how you void a check

Even though we're talking about the Write Checks window in this chapter, you don't void checks from this window. And here's why. Checks in the Write Checks window have *not* been printed yet. They're the checks that you've just written but have not gotten around to printing. Because you never need to void a check that hasn't been printed, you don't void checks from the Write Checks window.

Make sense? Well, let's look at an example. Let's say that you write a check in the Write Checks window to M&M Plumbing for $165.00 to repair your leaky water faucet. You then discover that your husband already paid M&M by credit card. If you haven't printed the check yet, it's still in the Write Checks window and you can just delete it (like you learned in the previous section).

But, if you did print the check to M&M Plumbing, you will need to void it so that it can't get cashed. You void the check in the register for the account from which you wrote the check. You already learned how to do this in Chapter 5, so turn back if you need to review voiding transactions again.

 TIP   When you void a check, make sure that you write VOID in big letters on the printed check so that it can't mistakenly get cashed.

Let's print checks now

So, you've written a few checks in the Write Checks window that you're ready to print. Don't press the Print button yet.

Getting Quicken ready to print

You have to give Quicken some information about your printer and your checks before you can begin printing, like:

- Which printer you're using

- How checks are fed into your printer

- What kind of preprinted computer checks you'll be using (standard, voucher, or wallet)

- How you'll load partial pages of checks into your printer

Give Quicken the information about your printer by selecting File, Printer Setup, For Printing Checks. You'll see the Check Printer Setup dialog box, like the one in Figure 6.7, where you can begin setting up Quicken to print checks.

Select your installed printer from the drop-down list.

Click the Font button to change the font style and size for check printing.

Fig. 6.7
Tell Quicken every-thing it needs to know about your printer and checks in the Check Printer Setup dialog box.

Click the button for the type of paper feed your printer uses.

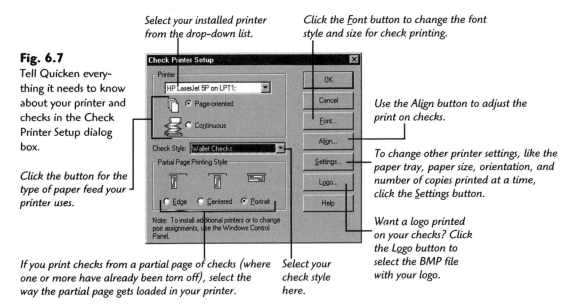

Use the Align button to adjust the print on checks.

To change other printer settings, like the paper tray, paper size, orientation, and number of copies printed at a time, click the Settings button.

Want a logo printed on your checks? Click the Logo button to select the BMP file with your logo.

If you print checks from a partial page of checks (where one or more have already been torn off), select the way the partial page gets loaded in your printer.

Select your check style here.

When you've entered the printer information that Quicken needs, click OK in the Check Printer Setup dialog box and you're one step closer to printing those checks.

Now, let's align my checks

These preprinted computer checks were more expensive than the checks you're used to carrying around with you, so you certainly don't want to waste any of them because the print isn't properly aligned.

So let's take a little time and align your checks so that you don't have to scrap any of them because they weren't printed correctly. The best way to make sure your checks are properly aligned is to print a sample check. You can use the sample checks that Quicken enclosed in the Quicken Deluxe software package so that you don't have to use one of your own preprinted checks.

Q&A ***Am I going to have to go through this alignment process every time I print checks?***

No, no, no. Quicken would never have you waste your time like that. You'll just have to align your checks once. Quicken saves the alignment settings so that they stay the same each time you print.

Now, go ahead and insert Quicken's sample checks into your printer. Then select File, Printer Setup, For Printing Checks to get back to the Check Printer Setup dialog box that you saw in Figure 6.7. What happens next depends on the type of printer that you have.

Aligning continuous-feed checks

You should be looking at the Check Printer Setup dialog box right now. So, click the Align button so that you can start getting your checks aligned. In the next dialog box, select the method that you want to use to align your continuous-feed checks. Select Coarse alignment to adjust the text on your printed checks by one line or more; select Fine to make small horizontal or vertical alignments.

If you selected Coarse alignment, select OK next to print a sample check. Don't do anything right now to the checks in your printer. Just let the sample check print and then remove it so that you can see how the text was printed on the check. You'll now see the Coarse Alignment dialog box (see Figure 6.8) on your screen where you can give Quicken some feedback on the sample check so it knows how it printed.

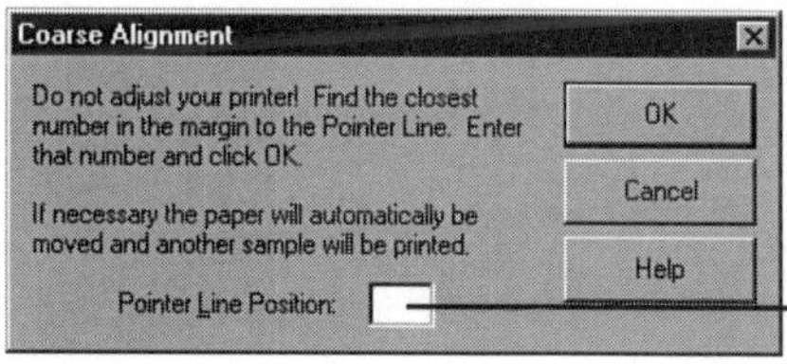

Fig. 6.8
Tell Quicken how well, or not so well, the text was aligned on the printed sample check.

> **Coarse Alignment**
>
> Do not adjust your printer! Find the closest number in the margin to the Pointer Line. Enter that number and click OK.
>
> If necessary the paper will automatically be moved and another sample will be printed.
>
> Pointer Line Position:
>
> OK
> Cancel
> Help

Find the Pointer Line on the sample check and its position number from the check form's pin-feed strips and enter it here.

If the text isn't properly aligned, Quicken automatically adjusts the checks in your printer and prints another sample check. If the text is aligned correctly, you're set. Just make note of the position of the checks in your printer and reload them the same way the next time you print checks.

If you selected Fine alignment, use the Fine Alignment dialog box to move the checks in your printer by increments of 1/100 of an inch (see Figure 6.9).

Fig. 6.9
Fine-tune the alignment of your continuous-feed checks by making very small adjustments.

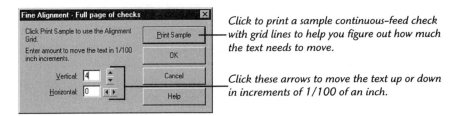

Click to print a sample continuous-feed check with grid lines to help you figure out how much the text needs to move.

Click these arrows to move the text up or down in increments of 1/100 of an inch.

When the text is properly positioned on the checks, make a note of the position of the checks in your printer and reload them the same way the next time you print checks. Click OK in the Check Printer Setup window to save your alignment settings.

Aligning single-sheet or laser checks

For those of you with single-sheet printers, like laser, inkjet, PostScript, or other page-oriented printers, your job in aligning checks is not so involved. You'll be performing only the fine alignment of your sample checks.

Start from the Check Printer Setup window and then click the Align button. You see the Align Checks dialog box next (see Figure 6.10). Even if your checks come three to a page, you won't always have a full sheet of checks in your printer to print checks on. You have to give Quicken the alignment settings for one, two, or three checks per page.

Fig. 6.10
Ready to align your single-sheet checks so they print correctly? Select the number of checks per page that you want to align.

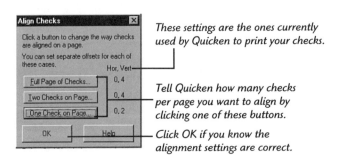

These settings are the ones currently used by Quicken to print your checks.

Tell Quicken how many checks per page you want to align by clicking one of these buttons.

Click OK if you know the alignment settings are correct.

If you need to adjust the alignment settings that were shown in the Align Checks dialog box, click the button for the number of checks that you want to align. For example, to align a full page of checks, click the Full Page of Checks button; to align a page with only one check, click the One Check on Page button.

Now, Quicken displays the Fine Alignment dialog box (shown earlier in Figure 6.9) where you can adjust the way text prints vertically and horizontally on checks. If the text on your single-sheet checks is not aligned properly, adjust the text vertically or horizontally in 1/100-of-an-inch increments.

To determine how the text will print on your preprinted computer checks, insert one of Quicken's sample checks or plain paper into your printer and click the Print Sample button. Quicken prints a grid on the sample check that you can use as a gauge for text alignment. After the sample check prints, check the alignment of the text. If you printed a sample check on plain paper, overlay it on top of one of your preprinted checks to check the alignment.

Each box in the alignment grid represents 10 units of height and 10 units of width. So, if the text is too high by one grid box, subtract 10 from the Vertical field value. If the text is too far left one-half grid box, increase the Horizontal field value by 5.

Print as many sample checks as you need to get the text aligned properly. After you've made the adjustments you need to get the text aligned, click OK twice to return to the Check Printer Setup window. Then click OK again to save your alignment settings.

Ready, set, print

Now you're ready to see how fast Quicken prints all those checks you just wrote. You're not going to believe how fast this whole process is. Because you're not going to have to align your checks anymore (you have to do it only once), writing and printing checks is a snap.

After you've written and reviewed your checks, just click the Print button in the Write Checks window when you're ready to print and Quicken shows you the Select Checks to Print window as in Figure 6.11. Then tell Quicken the check number of the next blank, preprinted check, which checks you want to print, and print away.

Selecting checks to print

Unless you specify otherwise, Quicken prints all of the checks that you've written in the Write Checks window. Notice in the Select Checks to Print window in Figure 6.11 that the All Checks option is already selected when you open the window. When this option is selected, Quicken prints all written checks when you click the OK button.

Fig. 6.11
When you're ready to print checks, tell Quicken the next check number to use and then select which checks you want to print.

Make sure the correct check style appears here. If it's not, select the right one.

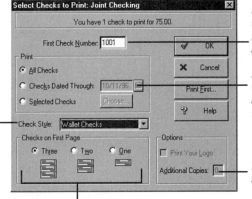

Here's where you tell Quicken what the next preprinted check number is. Press the + or the – key to change the check number by increments of one.

Select to print all the checks you've written, only those checks that are dated through a certain date, or just the ones that you specify.

If you want to print more than one copy of a check, select this option.

If your computer checks are on single sheets, tell Quicken how many checks are on the first page of checks it will be printing to.

But what if you don't want to print all checks right now? Maybe you wrote checks for the entire month and want to print only the checks due through the 15th. Or, you may just want to print one or two checks right now and print the rest later.

To print checks dated through a certain date, click the Checks Dated Through option and then enter the date. For example, entering 12/15/96 means that Quicken will print checks only with dates prior to 12/15/96.

If you want to hand-pick the checks that Quicken prints, click the Selected Checks option and then click the Choose button. Quicken displays another window that lists all the checks that you've written but not yet printed.

Click each check that you want to print or highlight the check and press the spacebar. When you select a check, Quicken puts a checkmark in the Print column to show that it will print. Click the Mark All button to select all checks, or click the Clear All button to remove all of the checkmarks from the Print column and start over selecting checks. When you've selected the checks that you want to print, click the D<u>o</u>ne button to return to the Select Checks to Print window.

Printing checks

After you've selected the checks that you want to print, you're ready to begin printing. From the Select Checks to Print window, click the OK button to print all of the selected checks. If you want to see how the first check looks before printing all of them, click the Print <u>F</u>irst button to print only the first check.

Quicken prints your check(s) and asks whether they printed correctly. If they did, click OK. If one or more of the checks didn't print properly, type the number of the first check that didn't print correctly and then click OK. Quicken goes back to the Select Checks to Print dialog box so that you can reprint the checks that didn't print correctly.

 TIP **If you lose a check that you've printed or a check gets misprinted** or destroyed somehow, you can just reprint. First, find the check transaction in the register for the account that the check was written from. Then, move to the Num field and type the word Print (or select Print Check from the drop-down list) over the check number. This tricks Quicken into thinking that it has not yet printed a check for this transaction. When you go to the Write Checks window and select the Pri<u>n</u>t button, Quicken will reprint the check. Now don't forget that you'll have to enter a voided transaction for the check that got lost or destroyed so that all of your checks are accounted for.

Let Quicken Help Balance Your Checkbook

● **In this chapter:**

- ● **Learn why balancing your checkbook is important**

- ● **Mark cleared transactions**

- ● **Balance your checkbook**

- ● **Print a reconciliation report**

- ● **Make adjustments so your check-book balances**

Save yourself bounced check fees and some stress by letting Quicken help you balance your checking account this month. . . . . ▶

know a lot of people who don't ever balance their checkbook.
They proclaim that it's a waste of time and that they don't need to
do it; and certainly, you won't get arrested if you don't. But it's my contention
that you can't really have a handle on how much money you have in your
checking account if you don't do the balancing act.

Balancing your checkbook is like going to the dentist. You know you have to
do it, but you put it off and dread every minute of it. Well, with Quicken,
balancing your checkbook really doesn't have to be so frightful. (And I'll
assure you it'll be more appealing than your dental checkup!)

Why do I need to balance my checkbook?

We all make mistakes. Right? Financial institutions, like your bank, aren't
always perfect either. So when you balance your checkbook, you're performing a "check" of *your* records against the *bank's*; you're comparing the
transactions and balance in your checkbook register against the transactions
and balance shown on your bank statement. If you or your bank has made a
mistake, you'll catch it when you balance your checking account.

One of the most common mistakes people make in their checking accounts,
including me, is forgetting to record withdrawals from the ATM. It's easy to
forget these transactions; there's no check involved so you usually don't have
your checkbook register handy when you step up to the machine. So, if
you've forgotten about $500 in withdrawals, how are you going to remember
to account for them down the road? You'll think you have more money in
your checking account than you really do. And what if that causes you to
bounce a check?

66 *Plain English, please!*

If you're not sure what I mean by **ATM**, it's the Automated Teller Machine
that enables you to transact electronically with your bank. 99

If you balance your checkbook on a regular basis (each time you receive your
bank statement), you'll catch forgotten withdrawals or other transactions
before they cause you headaches. And if your bank has made a mistake by
omitting a deposit to your account or debiting your account for an erroneous
amount, you won't know about these errors unless you balance your account.

It'll be easier for you to catch errors and omissions if you balance your account each time you receive your bank statement.

Let Quicken do the hard jobs

When you use Quicken to balance your checking account, it does all the hard jobs for you. All you have to do is enter the information from your bank statement and let Quicken do the rest.

Here's what you'll need to do so that Quicken can balance your account:

- Choose the account you want to balance

- Enter the opening and ending statement account balances

- Enter the amounts and dates of other transactions shown on your bank statement, like service charges and interest earned

- Mark the transactions that have cleared your bank (the ones that are shown on your bank statement)

The next few sections teach you how to perform your part in the balancing act. Hopefully, when you're done, your account will balance to the penny!

Tell Quicken which account you want to balance

You can balance, or reconcile, any bank account you have in Quicken. You can reconcile checking, savings, or money market accounts. When you reconcile an account, you're simply comparing the transactions and balance in your Quicken account register with the transactions and balance from your bank statement.

 Plain English, please!

When you **reconcile** a bank account, you're comparing the cleared balance that the bank says you have in your account with the cleared balance shown in your Quicken records. The cleared balance is the amount left in your account after all transactions have been presented to the bank. **"**

If you have more than one bank account in Quicken, you need to tell Quicken which one you want to balance. So, when you click the Recon icon, Quicken displays the Choose Reconcile Account dialog box. Click the down-arrow in the Account box to see your list of bank accounts and then select one. Click OK to open the Reconcile Bank Statement window and you're on your way.

If you're already in the register for the account that you want to balance, just click Reconcile from the iconbar. Because Quicken already knows the account you want to reconcile, the Reconcile Bank Statement window opens with the name of the account at the top.

The Reconcile Bank Statement window is your starting point for balancing your account. Here is where you enter the information from your bank statement that Quicken needs for its balancing computations.

Enter information from your bank statement now

Look over your bank statement carefully to familiarize yourself with the information that appears. Here's some of the important stuff you should see:

- Your bank account number

- The beginning and ending statement dates

- The beginning and ending account balances

- Interest earned during the period, if any

- Bank fees charged during the period, if any

Your statement may include other information like the annual percentage yield on interest-bearing accounts, interest paid to date, your taxpayer ID number, and so forth. This information is not important to the reconciliation process.

So now you're ready to tell Quicken what your bank statement balance is.

CAUTION
If you haven't balanced your account in a while, don't just pick up the last bank statement and start balancing. You need to go back to each bank statement you haven't reconciled and start from there. If you try to reconcile only your latest statement, you won't know which checks had cleared previously and you won't know if there were any balancing differences in previous periods. Balancing your account this time will be a nightmare!

Just click to mark cleared transactions

Moving from the Reconcile Bank Statement window where you enter bank statement information, Quicken displays another Reconcile Bank Statement window listing all of your transactions in your bank account register that have not yet cleared (see Figure 7.1).

 Plain English, please!

A **cleared transaction** is a transaction that has been debited or credited to your account by your bank.

Now you're ready to mark the transactions that have cleared your bank. All cleared transactions appear on your bank statement; if they're not there, they haven't cleared. To mark a transaction as cleared, highlight the transaction and press the spacebar. When you press the spacebar, Quicken puts a checkmark by the transaction in the Clr column and moves down to the next transaction. If that transaction has cleared, press the spacebar again, and so on. Continue marking transactions until all those shown on your bank statement are shown as cleared in the Reconcile Bank Statement transaction list.

TIP
You also can mark a transaction as cleared by clicking the transaction. When you mark a transaction this way, however, the highlight bar doesn't move to the next transaction after you click.

Notice that in the list of uncleared transactions, any transactions you entered from the bank statement (like interest earned or service charges) are already marked as cleared.

The Reconcile Bank Statement Window

Here's the Reconcile Bank Statement window for the account that you want to balance.

Quicken enters the ending balance from the last time it reconciled the account as the opening balance this time. If you've never balanced the account before, the opening balance is the balance that you entered when you set up the account in Quicken.

Any bank fees or service charges should be entered here.

If you're balancing an interest-bearing account, enter any interest earned for the period.

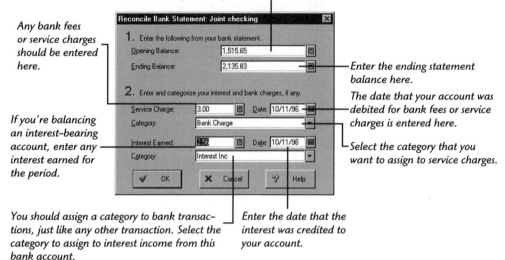

Enter the ending statement balance here.

The date that your account was debited for bank fees or service charges is entered here.

Select the category that you want to assign to service charges.

You should assign a category to bank transactions, just like any other transaction. Select the category to assign to interest income from this bank account.

Enter the date that the interest was credited to your account.

When the Reconcile Bank Statement window is complete, click OK and you're ready to start marking cleared transactions.

Delete transactions that shouldn't be in the list by clicking the Delete button.

Want to go back to the Reconcile Bank Statement window to see the statement information that you entered? Click the Statement button.

Fig. 7.1
Quicken lists all of the transactions that have not yet cleared the bank. From this list, mark the transactions that your statement shows as cleared.

If you need to add a new transaction while you're reconciling, click the New button.

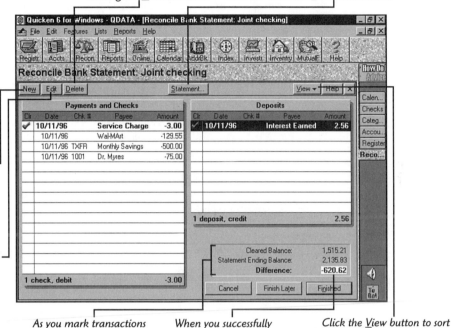

You can make changes to a transaction by highlighting it in the list and clicking the Edit button. Quicken goes to the transaction in the register so that you can edit it.

As you mark transactions as cleared, Quicken updates these balances.

When you successfully balance your bank account, the Difference amount will be $0.00 (zero).

Click the View button to sort transactions by date, instead of by check number.

TIP **Your bank statement usually lists the check number next to each** cleared transaction. If there are several checks in sequential order that have cleared, say 1234 to 1249, you can quickly mark a range of transactions as cleared, instead of marking them one by one. Just click the first transaction in the range that you want to mark, then move to the last transaction and press the Shift key as you click.

Q&A ***What if, by mistake, I mark an uncleared transaction as cleared?***

That's easy to fix. Just click the transaction to "unmark" it and remove the checkmark. Toggle between marking and unmarking transactions by clicking.

TIP **If you discover a transaction on your bank statement that you** haven't entered, just click the Ne<u>w</u> button to insert it in the register. You can also edit and delete transactions while you're reconciling by clicking the Ed<u>i</u>t and <u>D</u>elete buttons.

Q&A ***Something just came up and I don't have time to finish balancing my account. I'm in the Reconcile Bank Statement transaction list right now. What do I do?***

Quicken lets you quit balancing your account even if you're not finished. See the Finish La<u>t</u>er button at the bottom of the Reconcile Bank Statement transaction list in Figure 7.1? Just click this button and Quicken saves your work in the Reconcile Bank Statement transaction list. When you're ready to resume balancing your account, just click the Re<u>c</u>oncile button in that account's register button bar.

CAUTION **Don't leave the Reconcile Bank Statement transaction list by** clicking the Cancel button. When you select Cancel, Quicken does not save your work and you'll have to start over the next time.

Look! My checkbook balanced

Hopefully, now is your moment of triumph. You've entered all your bank statement information and marked all cleared transactions. You may have even added a transaction or two or edited a transaction while you were reconciling your account. So how do you know if your account balanced? Look at the Difference amount at the bottom of the Reconcile Bank Statement window. The Difference amount should be $0.00, which means that the cleared balance that you show in your account register is the same as the ending balance on your bank statement.

When the Difference amount is $0.00, you've successfully balanced your account and you're finished. So click the Fi<u>n</u>ished button. Quicken congratulates you (and so do I) in Figure 7.2 and asks if you want to print a reconciliation report.

TIP **After you balance your account, you won't be aware of this at the** time, but Quicken puts an R (for reconciled) in the Clr column of each cleared transaction in the register.

Fig. 7.2
Let me congratulate you, along with Quicken, on balancing your account. Good work! Now decide whether you want to print a Reconciliation Report.

Print a reconciliation report

After you finish balancing your account, you can print a report that shows the details of the reconciliation you just did. As shown in Figure 7.2, Quicken asks whether you want to print a reconciliation report. Click Yes if you want to print the report and Quicken displays the Reconciliation Report Setup dialog box (see Figure 7.3) for you to complete.

❝ Plain English, please!

A **Reconciliation Report** is a printed record of the reconciliation you just performed. It lists all the cleared transactions and also lists all checks and deposits still outstanding. **❞**

Enter a title for your report using up to 25 characters.

Fig. 7.3
Complete the Reconciliation Report Setup dialog box if you want a printed report of your account reconciliation.

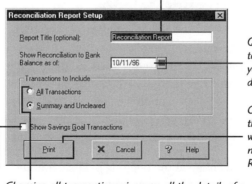

Quicken inserts today's date here or you can enter a different date.

Click this button to open the Print Report window where you tell Quicken more about printing the Reconciliation Report.

Click this option if you want your savings goal transactions to appear in the Reconciliation Report.

Choosing all transactions gives you all the details of every transaction, cleared or uncleared; if you want Quicken to summarize cleared transactions but give details of uncleared transactions, choose to include summary and uncleared transactions.

When you click <u>P</u>rint from the Reconciliation Report Setup dialog box in Figure 7.3, Quicken displays the Print Report dialog box. This is the generic print dialog box that Quicken always displays when printing reports. Complete the Print Report dialog box and then select OK to begin printing the Reconciliation Report.

Oh no! My checkbook didn't balance

If your account didn't balance (the Difference amount in the Reconcile Bank Statement transaction list window is any number other than $0.00), don't get uptight. Maybe you marked a transaction as cleared that really hadn't cleared the bank. Or vice versa. Or, maybe you recorded the wrong amount for a transaction in your register. Or, you may have inadvertently entered the wrong amount as the ending balance on your statement (with all the amounts shown on your bank statement, this is easy to do). So check the amounts you entered carefully, as well as the transactions that you marked as cleared. If you can't find the discrepancy after your review, you may have to enter an adjustment transaction so that your account balances.

There are two types of adjustment transactions—one for an opening balance difference and one for other differences.

 CAUTION   **If your account didn't balance the last time you performed a** reconciliation with Quicken, then you can't expect it to balance this time. Don't let balancing differences build up. The first time your account doesn't balance, look for the difference. If, after much deliberation, you don't find it, go ahead and make a balance adjustment. Then, the next time you balance your account, you should have no differences.

Adjust the opening balance

Remember when you started balancing your account? You saw the Reconcile Bank Statement window that asked for the bank statement ending balance and other transactions from your bank statement. And remember that Quicken automatically entered the opening balance for you. The amount that Quicken used here was the ending balance from the last time you balanced your account. But if you didn't balance your account, Quicken uses the starting balance from when you set up your account as the opening balance.

Well, what if you changed the opening balance amount when you started balancing your account to match the balance shown on your statement? If you did, Quicken shows an Opening Bal. Difference in the Reconcile Bank Statement window, like in Figure 7.4.

Fig. 7.4
When you change the opening balance, Quicken shows an Opening Balance Difference that's the difference between the balance you entered and the one that Quicken thinks you should have.

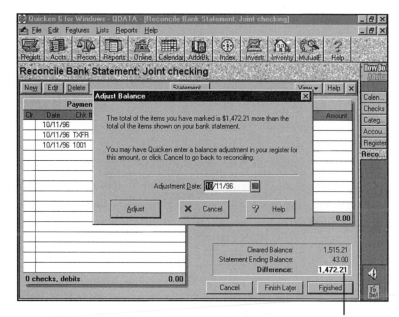

Here's the opening balance difference that may cause your account not to balance.

Here are some reasons why you may have an opening balance difference:

- This is the first time you've balanced your account with Quicken so Quicken is using the starting balance in your checking account as the bank statement opening balance. If you didn't use the ending balance from your last bank statement as your starting balance when you set up your checking account, this may be the difference.

- You're not reconciling your account with the right statement. Maybe you haven't balanced your account in a while. If you pick up your latest bank statement and start to reconcile it, your opening balance will be way off. Go back to the first bank statement you haven't reconciled (even if it's six months ago) and start with it. Then balance your account with each subsequent statement until you're up-to-date.

- When you started using Quicken, you may have entered some transactions in the register that had already cleared the bank but that you hadn't marked as cleared. This really messes up your opening balance. If you're entering old transactions in Quicken, be sure that you mark them as cleared if they have shown up on previous bank statements.

When you click the Finished button to complete the reconciliation and you have an opening balance difference, Quicken asks if you want to create an adjustment to make your account balance. If you do, enter the date for the adjustment transaction and click Adjust.

Or, adjust for other differences

If Quicken shows a Difference amount in the Reconcile Bank Statement window that isn't related to an opening balance difference, you may want to make a balance adjustment as a last resort.

 Plain English, please!

A **balance adjustment** means that Quicken creates a transaction in your account register that forces your account to balance with your bank statement. Let's say that when you balance your account there's a $1.28 difference. You've looked all over the place for this difference and can't find it. It's a pretty immaterial difference, so you can get your account to balance by making a $1.28 balance adjustment. **"**

So, you're finished balancing your account and you have a difference. When you click the Finished button, Quicken asks whether you want to enter a balance adjustment for the difference.

Enter the date for the balance adjustment transaction, click the Adjust button, and Quicken enters it in the register for you. Then tell Quicken if you want to print a Reconciliation Report; click Yes to print the report or No if you don't want a report.

After you print the Reconciliation Report, you'll see the balance adjustment transaction in the register, like the one in Figure 7.5.

Fig. 7.5

Quicken enters the balance adjustment transaction in the register for you. If you want, you can change the balance adjustment transaction, but your account will not balance if you change the amount.

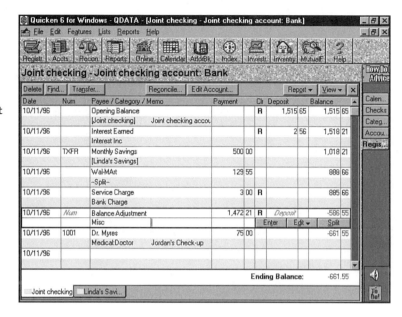

Part II: Saving Time with Quicken

Nifty Quicken Shortcuts that Can Save You Time

● **In this chapter:**

- Forget the wall calendar! You've got one on-screen!

- Forget the desk calculator! You've got one on-screen!

- Let QuickFill type for you

- I can recall a transaction with QuickFill and make changes in it

- Did you pay the electric company? Quicken's Find feature searches for transactions

I'll bet there are plenty of fun things you could do if only you had some spare time. Quicken's shortcuts can reduce your work time and add free time to your day. . . . . ❯

When you start taking advantage of the shortcuts Quicken provides, you'll feel like you have a personal assistant at your side, second-guessing your needs, handing you whatever tools you require and even ready to type transactions for you.

Quicken provides you with the next best thing to a personal assistant—shortcuts like a pop-up calculator and a calendar only a mouse-click away, and a filing system that never loses anything!

Write a check to your doctor, and the next time you pay the doctor all you have to do is type a couple of letters of the doctor's name and change the amount. Quicken fills in the rest of the information—the doctor's whole name and the expense category. You don't even have to worry about correct spelling!

Never type a date again

You know how irritating it is to type **10/18/96**—you search all over the keyboard for the number keys, you can never remember if you're supposed to type the slashes or if this is one of those programs that does the slashes for you (it is), then if you try to enter slashes your fingers trip over the slash and hit the period instead. And which slash key are you supposed to use, anyway?

Forget all that nonsense about typing dates. Quicken makes date-entering easy!

Today's date is a natural

When you open the check register, Quicken is ready for you to type a new transaction—and this program is one step ahead of you in the date department. Today's date is already waiting for your approval, as shown in Figure 8.1.

To accept today's date as the date you want to use, just advance to the next field (the Num field) like this:

- Click with your mouse in the Num field.

Or

- Press Tab to move to the Num field.

Fig. 8.1
Today's date magically
appears when you
open a register.

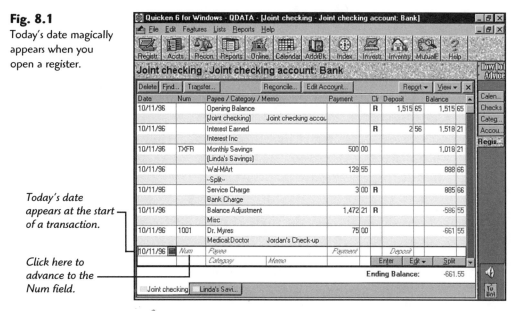

*Today's date
appears at the start
of a transaction.*

*Click here to
advance to the
Num field.*

TIP **To quickly enter today's date in a date field that has been** changed to a different date, simply press **T** (for Today).

Q&A *I'm entering several checks that are dated yesterday. Will I have to change the date from today's date for each check?*

No. When you enter a series of transactions, Quicken repeats the last date you used until you change the date yourself. So once you've entered yesterday's date in the first transaction, the same date will repeat for each transaction.

Change the date with a simple keystroke

Say you don't want to use today's date, but today's date is the date that's staring at you from the screen. How do you switch to a new date?

For starters, forget about typing a different date, that's the hard way. If you're not going very far with the date—just a few days in either direction—just use the plus and minus keys on your numeric keypad to make the date advance or retreat.

- Each time you press + the date advances one day.

- Each time you press – the date goes back one day.

Change the date with the pop-up calendar

You can press + or – until your fingers ache, but if you want to change the date in a big way (say you're entering last year's transactions) you need Quicken's pop-up calendar.

Look closely next to the date, and you'll see a button that resembles a calendar (see Figure 8.2). Click this button and a calendar pops up on your screen!

Now you've got all dates at your fingertips.

- Click any date in the calendar and Quicken types that date on-screen.

- Click the arrows to the right or left of the month in the calendar to move the calendar forward or backward a month (see Figure 8.2).

- Hold down your mouse button while pointing to one of the month arrows to move quickly into the future or through the past.

Let your fingers do the walking

There are keyboard shortcuts for changing your date. While in the date field, instead of typing a date, you can type one of these letters to place a date on the screen.

Key	Action
t	Today
m	First day of month
h	Last day of month
y	First day of year
r	Last day of year

Clicking an actual date puts the date on your screen and takes the calendar away.

Q&A ***What if I just want to use the calendar to check on what day of the week my birthday will fall, but I don't want to change the date on-screen?***

You can look up whatever date you want in the calendar and then press Esc. This takes the calendar away and leaves the date on-screen the way it was before you started looking around.

Fig. 8.2
An on-screen calendar
is only a click away.

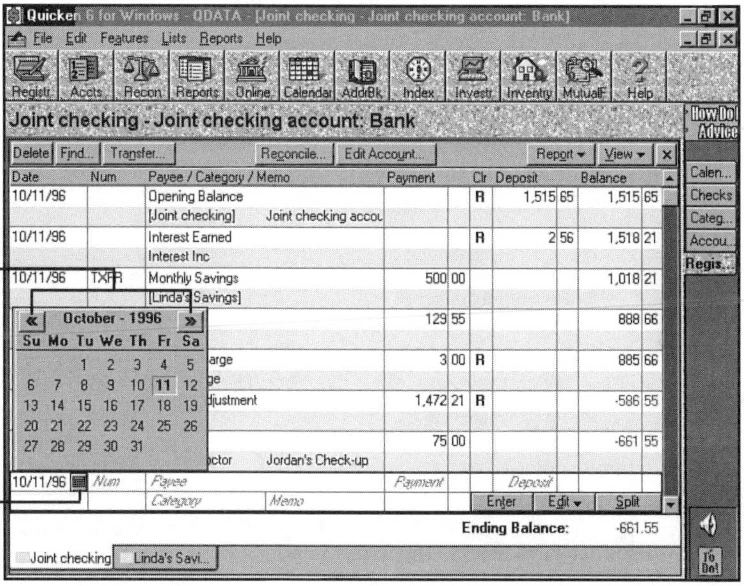

*Click one of these
buttons to change
the month.*

*Click this button and get
an on-screen calendar.*

On-screen calculators at your fingertips

You've entered the date, you've entered the name of the payee or payer—now you need to enter an amount.

First of all, there may already be an amount entered for you. If Quicken has entered the amount from the most recent transaction with this payee (or payer), that's what you'll see in the amount position. If that's the right amount and you don't need to make a change—you're finished here and ready to go to the next field.

TIP **Quicken's ability to automatically recall previous transactions is** part of a feature called QuickFill and is discussed later in this chapter.

But what if you need to perform a calculation to determine an amount? Perhaps you have two bills to pay to the same supplier and you need to add them up, or maybe you can take a two percent discount for an early payment and you need to figure out how much that is.

Quicken features an on-screen calculator that can come to your mathematical rescue.

To pull up the calculator directly from a number field:

- Click the calculator button in the Payment or Deposit fields (see Figure 8.3).

Or

- Press the + key.

Fig. 8.3
Use Quicken's pop-up calculator to compute amounts for Num fields.

Click the calculator button to display the pop-up calculator in a Num field.

Enter calculations in the calculator by using the number keys on your keyboard (or numeric keypad) or clicking on the numbers on the calculator with your mouse. Use the following mathematical symbols to perform operations:

+	addition
−	subtraction
*	multiplication
/	division

All of these math operators are represented by keys on the pop-up calculator so you can either click them on the calculator or type them from the keyboard. Finishing your calculation with the = sign (either type it or click it) or pressing Enter on the keyboard will put the answer on your screen and close the calculator.

There may come a time when you want to use the calculator from a field that doesn't have a calculator icon. Instead of using a pop-up calculator, you can bring Quicken's calculator to the screen anytime by selecting Edit, Use Calculator. The Quicken Calculator appears on-screen (see Figure 8.4).

*Drag here to move
the calculator.*

*Click here to close
the calculator.*

Fig. 8.4
Use Quicken's
calculator to perform
any standard math-
ematical operation.

*Copy the results of your
calculations into the
current field.*

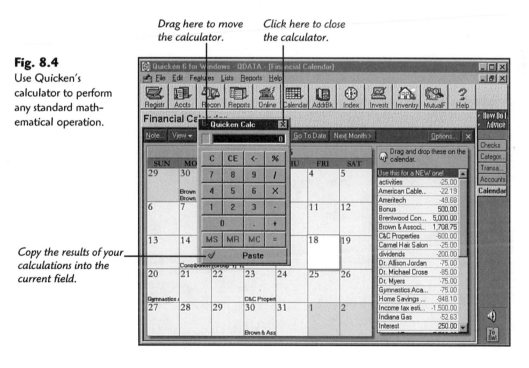

The Quicken Calculator (as opposed to the pop-up calculator) stays on-screen until you don't want it anymore. In fact, you may want to slide it off to the side (use your mouse and drag the title, "Quicken Calculator" off to the side of the screen) and keep it available for whenever you need it (refer to Figure 8.4). Remove the calculator from your screen by clicking the Close button (X) in the upper-right corner of the calculator.

 TIP **After performing a calculation in the Quicken Calculator you can** paste an amount from the calculator into your register so you don't have to type it. First, click in your register where you want the amount to appear. Then, click the Paste button on the calculator.

Let QuickFill do your typing

You don't have to perform any special tricks, nor do you have to click any little boxes to let Quicken do your typing for you. As long as Quicken is set up to memorize transactions (and, by default, it does this), you just have to start typing the payee or payer in a transaction in the Quicken register and Quicken will finish typing the name for you. This feature is called QuickFill and is always at work.

You can put your calculator on the iconbar!

If activating the Quicken Calculator by selecting Edit, Use Calculator is just too many steps for your taste, you can add a Calculator icon to the iconbar at the top of the screen. To add the Calculator icon, follow these steps:

1   Choose Edit, Options, Iconbar.

2   Click the New button.

3   In the Icon Action list, click Use Calculator. (Note that the items on this list are not presented in alphabetical order, so you may have to search a bit to find Use Calculator.)

4   Click OK and then click Done.

From now on, just click the Calculator icon on your iconbar whenever you want to use the calculator.

TIP **Quicken may be smart, but it's not a mind reader. If you're typing** in a payee's name you haven't used before, you'll have to type the full name. Once you've typed the name, Quicken will recall it as soon as you start typing the first letters of the name.

For example, as soon as you type a **P**, Quicken enters the first "P" company from your list of names you've typed previously, which may be "Poseiden Shipping Co." If the company you are really trying to type is "Pranitis Heating and Cooling," continue typing. By the time you have typed **Pr**, Quicken will have filled in the rest of the name for you. You don't have to type anything more. Click on the next field, or press Tab to continue to the next field.

Q&A *My transactions aren't filling in the way you described. I know I've typed this company's name before, but I still have to type the full name in each time I want to use it.*

Your transactions aren't getting memorized as you type them. Select Edit, Options, Register to display the Register Options dialog box. Then click the QuickFill tab to see the QuickFill options. Make sure the Complete Fields Using Previous Entries and Auto Memorize New Transactions options are checked, as illustrated in Figure 8.5. (For more on memorized transactions, see Chapter 9, "Speed Up Your Register Entries with Memorized Transactions.")

Fig. 8.5
Here's the options that need to be activated for QuickFill to work.

Make sure these two boxes are checked if you want QuickFill to automatically fill in your transaction for you.

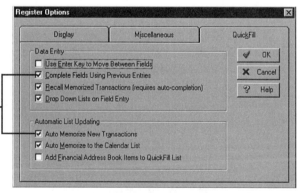

QuickFill repeats an earlier transaction

What a timesaver for entering payments! Enter the date and the check number (using the shortcuts you learned earlier in this chapter), then start typing the name of the payee. It's like a guessing game for Quicken. You tell the program to find the first payee starting with a particular letter. If the payee Quicken finds is not the one you want to use, give Quicken another clue by typing the second letter of the payee. Continue typing until Quicken has enough clues to fill in the entire name.

Here's what happens. As soon as you type the first letter, "P" for example, Quicken searches through the names you've previously typed and finds the first one, alphabetically, that begins with "P," and fills in the rest of the name. If that's the correct payee, you're finished! Click the amount field (or press Tab to move to that field) and enter the amount. But what if "Pancake House" isn't the payee you wanted? Type another letter, "R" for example, and Quicken continues the search until it gets to the first "Pr" payee, like Pranitis Heating & Cooling.

Of course, if this is the first time you have entered this payee, Quicken won't be able to guess the name you want. You'll have to type the entire name—but only this one time. The next time you enter a payment to this payee the name will be familiar to Quicken and will be on the list of names that can be recalled.

TIP **Capitalization isn't important when you expect Quicken to recall** a payee using the QuickFill feature. Type in lowercase and save the time it would take to type capital letters. However, if you are entering a payee for the first time, type carefully, watch your spelling, and use correct capitalization. This way Quicken is sure to recall the name later and present it just the way you want.

Notice that when Quicken uses QuickFill, not only the payee name is recalled, but the entire last transaction is recalled—the amount, category, and the memo. If everything stays the same, just click the Enter button and you're ready for your next transaction.

Quicken can help you find transactions

Use Quicken to search through your transactions and help you find something you entered in the past. Say you've got a statement in front of you from the electric company and you can't remember whether you paid it. Click the Find button in the register button bar or the Write Checks window button bar (or press Ctrl+F), and Quicken opens the Quicken Find dialog box. Here, you can enter pertinent information about the transaction for which you are searching.

In the Find box, type the text or an amount from the transaction you want to find. If you only want Quicken to search in a particular field, click the down arrow across from Search and choose the field you want to examine (see Figure 8.7). Or you can have Quicken look in all fields for your missing transaction information.

Click the Find button to find the first transaction in your register that matches what you typed. Clicking Find again and again will take you through your register, one item at a time, finding every item that matches your criteria. You can choose to search backward or forward through the register by selecting clicking the Search Backwards checkbox in the Quicken Find window.

Click the Find All button and Quicken gives you a list of all the transactions in your register that match the text or amount you typed. Double-clicking any item in the list takes you to the place in the register where you entered that item.

Fig. 8.7
Quicken can find transactions for you.

Click to add a checkmark and search backward through the register.

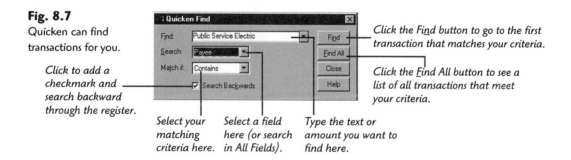

Click the Find button to go to the first transaction that matches your criteria.

Click the Find All button to see a list of all transactions that meet your criteria.

Select your matching criteria here.   *Select a field here (or search in All Fields).*   *Type the text or amount you want to find here.*

TIP **When using Quicken's Find feature, you don't have to type the** full name from a transaction. Say you're searching for a payment made to Dr. Vosicky. Typing **Dr. V**, then clicking the Fi<u>n</u>d button will take you to the first Dr. V transaction in your register. That may be Dr. Vosicky or it may be Dr. Voorhees, but it gets you close and saves you some typing. Keep clicking the Fi<u>n</u>d button until you reach the transaction you're searching for, or click <u>F</u>ind All to display a list of all the Dr. V transactions.

Speed Up Your Register Entries with Memorized Transactions

● **In this chapter:**

● **I can repeat an earlier transaction using the Memorized Transactions feature**

● **What if I need to change a memorized transaction?**

● **I'll never type this transaction again. Can I erase a memorized transaction?**

Tired of typing the same entry over and over? With Quicken, you never have to type the same entry twice! . . . . ▶

Once you enter a transaction in Quicken you never have to take the time to retype a similar transaction. This is an incredible timesaver. Pay the mortgage, enter it once, tell Quicken to memorize it, and Quicken will send it back to you, each month, whenever you ask for it.

Recall frequently repeated transactions

In Chapter 8, you learned how Quicken's QuickFill feature saves you typing time. Quicken has an even nicer feature for entering transactions that are the same every time, like monthly loan payments or your biweekly paycheck.

The Memorized Transactions feature is a powerful tool that lets you effortlessly repeat transactions. You can even teach it to enter transactions for you on specific dates.

I want to memorize this transaction

Here's how Quicken's Memorized Transactions work. You enter a transaction in the register. Say it's a monthly payment for a leased car. You type the name of the payee, the amount, and any memorandum information you may want to add, including a category. Then you press Ctrl+M or click the right-mouse button and select Memorize Transaction from the transaction menu. Quicken flashes a message on-screen that says, "This transaction is about to be memorized." Click OK to accept the memorization or Cancel if you don't want to accept it. A few little beeps signify that you've memorized a transaction!

You also can memorize a transaction you've previously entered. Maybe you entered your payment for cable television last month, it's time to pay cable again, and you realize that you're going to pay the same amount this month (and next month and so on). Here's how you memorize a transaction you entered at an earlier date:

1 Find the transaction you want to memorize in the register (you can use the Find feature you learned in Chapter 8).

2 Click the right mouse button to open the transaction menu and select Memorize Transaction.

3 Click OK.

Now I want to use the memorized transaction

Just as when you use QuickFill, you can begin typing a new transaction and, as soon as Quicken recognizes what you're typing, the rest of the transaction will fill in automatically.

Q&A *I don't get it. What's the difference between QuickFill and a Memorized Transaction?*

There are a lot of similarities between the QuickFill and Memorized Transaction features. But there are a couple of significant differences:

- You have the option of turning off the QuickFill feature and not using it, but even if you've done that, your memorized transactions are still available.

- With QuickFill, each time you change a transaction (for example, your electric bill changes each month), Quicken remembers the last entry you made when it recalls the transaction. With a memorized transaction, the entire transaction you memorize is the one that sticks. Even if you make changes in it (say you memorized your mortgage payment, but this month you paid an extra amount toward your principal so the amount changes), the next time you recall it, the fields you originally memorized are recalled.

Quicken stores all your memorized transactions in, what else, the Memorized Transaction List. Just press Ctrl+T to see the list. Double-click a transaction you want to recall and it is added to your register. Quicken automatically enters the transaction and uses the next available check number. You can use memorized transactions in credit card and investment registers, too.

CAUTION **Be sure you are ready to enter a new transaction when you begin** to recall a memorized transaction. If your cursor is placed on an existing transaction and you recall a memorized transaction, the existing transaction is replaced with the memorized one and you lose the transaction that was there in the first place.

The Memorized Transaction List includes all the transactions Quicken remembers, either because you specifically memorized them or because you've had the QuickFill feature memorizing them for you. Transactions you specifically memorized are marked with a little padlock (see Figure 9.1).

Fig. 9.1
Transactions with padlocks are transactions you told Quicken to memorize.

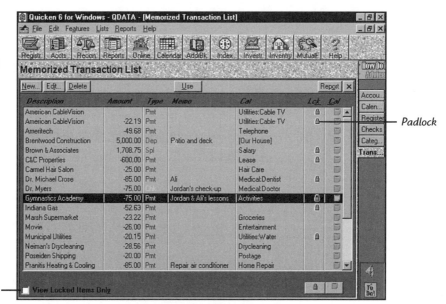

Click here to display only the transactions you told Quicken to memorize.

Padlock

What's a locked transaction?

Locked transactions, the ones you told Quicken to memorize, are the unchanging transactions. You can record all of the transaction and it always comes back the way you memorized it, even if you make changes when you enter it.

For example, say you frequently withdraw $50 cash from the ATM machine at your bank. When you enter an ATM withdrawal of $50, you memorize the transaction so you won't have to re-enter it each time. But this time you need extra cash and you withdraw $100. You recall the memorized transaction, it comes up with $50, and you change it to $100 before recording it.

The next time you want to enter an ATM withdrawal and you call up your memorized transaction, what amount do you think will appear? If you said $50, you're right. If you do the same thing using QuickFill, the $100 transaction would appear because it was the last transaction you used with your ATM account.

To see only the locked transactions when you display the list of memorized transactions, click the View Locked Items Only box at the bottom of the transactions list. From now on, the only transactions you see in the Memorized Transaction List are the ones you put there intentionally.

You can change a memorized transaction

Memorized transactions aren't written in stone. Maybe your monthly car payment has changed, or now you regularly take $70 from the ATM instead of $50. You can easily change a memorized transaction.

To change a memorized transaction, just enter the transaction the way you now want it to appear. Press Ctrl+M on the revised version of the transaction, and the "This transaction is about to be memorized" box appears. Click OK.

This time you see an additional box that reads: "Transaction Already Memorized." You can click Replace and your new transaction replaces the old one.

If you prefer, you can choose Add and your new revised transaction is added to the list, but the old one also remains on the list. You'll then have two memorized transactions with the same payee from which to choose. (Thereafter, when you begin to enter a transaction to that payee, the two memorized transactions come up in alphabetical order, by category. As soon as you see the first one in the Payee field, the down arrow on your keyboard will take you to the second memorized transaction to the same payee.)

Click Cancel if you want to change your mind and not memorize the new transaction.

You can edit an existing memorized transaction by following these steps:

1 Open the Memorized Transaction List by pressing Ctrl+T.

2 Select the memorized transaction you want to change.

3 Click the Edit button.

4 Make desired changes in the Edit Memorized Transaction dialog box that appears (see Figure 9.2).

5 Click OK to save the changes.

Fig. 9.2
You can edit any
memorized transaction
by making the
necessary changes in
the Edit Memorized
Transaction dialog box.

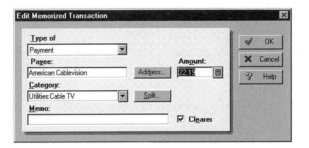

My car's paid off! I don't need this memorized transaction anymore!

When you don't need a memorized transaction anymore, you can remove it from your list.

To remove a memorized transaction, follow these steps:

1 Open your Memorized Transaction List (press Ctrl+T).

2 Select the transaction you no longer need.

3 Click the Delete button. A window appears with the statement: "You are about to delete a memorized transaction."

4 Choose OK.

The transaction is deleted from the Memorized Transaction List.

Other cool things you can do with memorized transactions

One of the nicest features you'll find in the Memorized Transactions List is the QuickReport feature. Select any item in the Memorized Transaction List, then click the Report button (see Figure 9.3), and voilà! You get a report on-screen showing all the transactions you've had with that particular payee.

Fig. 9.3
Quicken can print a
QuickReport of your
transactions with one
payee.

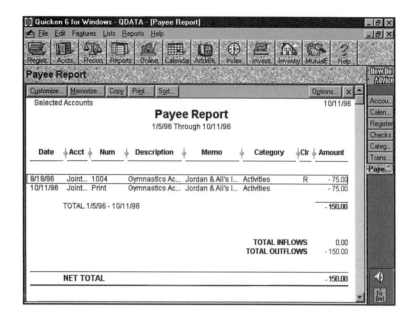

Say you want to see a total of how much you've paid your dentist. Just find
his name on the list, click it, click the Report button, and there before your
eyes is a list of every payment you've made to your dentist from your entire
register. Need a hard copy? No problem, just click the Print button at the top
of the report, then click OK from the Print Report window that appears on-
screen, and a copy of your report is sent to your printer.

TIP **Do you use a memorized transaction frequently? Consider placing**
an icon for that transaction in the iconbar—your memorized transaction will
be a click away! Go to Chapter 24 to learn how to add an icon to the
iconbar.

10

Scheduling Future Transactions

● **In this chapter:**

- ● **Create a scheduled transaction**

- ● **Pay the bills (and other neat tricks) with scheduled transactions**

- ● **Can I take a vacation and still pay the bills?**

- ● **Group scheduled transactions**

- ● **Quicken tells me when the rent is due**

- ● **Never miss a loan payment again**

Quicken's Financial Calendar takes care of scheduling financial events for you, giving you more time to relax. . .

E very month I pay the mortgage—same amount, same day of the month. I also make a monthly car payment. And then there are those pesky quarterly tax payments that creep up, not every month, but four times a year. When you stop and think about it, there are lots of things that repeat during the year. And it's not only expenses. Do you get a paycheck directly deposited in your checking account regularly?

Whether it's income or expenses, let Quicken save you the trouble of remembering to record and remembering to pay. It's just one fewer item that you have to remember in your busy life.

Never miss an important payment again

So, how is it that scheduling transactions in Quicken guarantees that I never miss an important payment again? Well, by scheduling your transactions in Quicken, you'll be prompted to make those payments at just the right time. So, put simply, scheduling transactions in Quicken is just what it sounds like. You set up transactions that happen at the same time every month, quarter, year, and so forth, for the same amount (perhaps, not always) and Quicken prompts you when they're due or need to be recorded.

With scheduled transactions, you tell Quicken when a payment or deposit is supposed to occur. Give Quicken all the details about that transaction, including the amount, the date, the payee, the category, and any memorandum information you may want to include. Then decide whether you want Quicken to take care of processing the transaction or just remind you to process it yourself.

You won't ever have to worry again about missing an important payment due date or forgetting to enter deposits in your checking account register (unless, of course, you forget to turn on the computer for a week or two—Quicken is good, but it's not that good).

Here's how you set up a scheduled transaction

Before you start telling Quicken what to do, decide for yourself what kinds of things you can schedule into your Quicken account system so that you won't have to think about them any more:

- Mortgage payments

- Loan payments

- Rent

- Recurring monthly utility bills (even if the amount changes each month!)

- Childcare payments

- Lease payments

- College tuition and housing

- Tax payments

- Salary income from a job

- Your mother-in-law's birthday (I'm not kidding!)

Basically, anything you can plan for in advance, you can schedule into Quicken and take advantage of the scheduled transactions.

When you're ready to set up a scheduled transaction, here's what you do. Select Lists, Scheduled Transaction (or press Ctrl+J) to open the Scheduled Transaction List (see Figure 10.1). Then click the New button to open the Create Scheduled Transaction dialog box that you see in Figure 10.2. Here's where you enter all the information about the transaction that you want to schedule.

Fig. 10.1
You can view, select, and edit scheduled transactions from the Scheduled Transaction List.

Click the <u>N</u>ew button to set up a scheduled transaction.

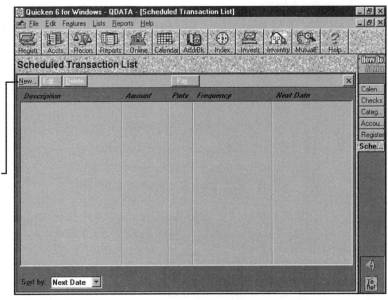

Choose the account to use.

Is this transaction a payment or deposit? Do you want Quicken to print a check, or will this be an online payment?

Fig. 10.2
Enter the information about the transaction you want to schedule in the Create Scheduled Transaction dialog box.

Enter a payee's address if you print checks with Quicken and want to use window envelopes to mail your checks.

Click here to see a list of the payees you've entered previously in Quicken.

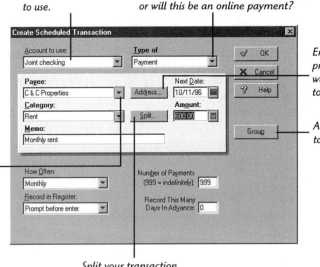

Add this transaction to a group.

Split your transaction among several categories.

There are several steps involved in setting up your scheduled transaction. Complete these steps once and you never have to repeat them again:

1 In the Account to use drop-down list, select the account (usually your checking account) in which this transaction occurs.

2 In the Type of Transaction drop-down list, select whether this transaction is a payment that you want to record in the register (but for which you will write a check yourself), a deposit, a payment for which Quicken will print a check, or an online payment you will perform electronically.

3 Choose the name of the payee in the Payee drop-down list (clicking the down arrow will create a drop-down list of all the payees in your register).

4 In the Next Date box, tell Quicken when the next payment is due or the next deposit will be made. Click the calendar icon to use the pop-up calendar to select the next date.

As soon as you select a payee, Quicken fills in the information from the last time you paid or received money from this payee. You can accept the rest of the information Quicken has filled in, or you can make changes. This additional information includes:

- **Category.** Enter the category you want assigned to this transaction.

- **Amount.** Enter the amount of the transaction—this amount becomes part of the scheduled transaction, but you can override this field (or any other field, for that matter) when you actually record the scheduled transaction.

- **Memo.** Enter a memo for your own use. Anything you enter here will not ultimately appear in the list of scheduled transactions, but if you come back to this screen to edit or view the details of this transaction, you will see the memo.

- **How Often.** Is this transaction monthly? Weekly? Quarterly? A once-only event? You decide how often you want this transaction to occur.

- **Record in Register.** Do you want Quicken to enter this transaction automatically? (For example, if your paycheck is direct-deposited, you would want that entered automatically so you'll always have the correct balance when you open Quicken.) Then you choose the Automatically enter option. Or, do you want to be prompted so that you can examine the transaction and be reminded to write a check? If so, choose the Prompt Before Enter option.

- **Number of Payments.** If the transaction is ongoing (like you hope your paycheck is, or like the monthly cable television bill), leave the number of payments at 999. This just means the transaction will continue to repeat itself, endlessly, with the frequency you requested. If there is a fixed number of payments (like your car loan that has only 18 months left), then change the number of payments to fit your needs.

- **Record This Many Days In Advance.** By default this is set to zero, but you can change it so that Quicken gives you a reminder that a transaction is forthcoming. To have a little advance warning that those nasty quarterly income tax payments are coming due, you might want to set this at 14 days to give you two weeks to prepare yourself. For a monthly transaction, you probably don't need much of a reminder.

Besides several boxes to fill in regarding your scheduled transaction, there are some other buttons in the Create Scheduled Transaction dialog box that allow you to customize this transaction further (see Figure 10.2).

- **Split.** Click this button to assign more than one category to the scheduled transaction. For example, you may split your paycheck so that the withholding amounts, such as taxes and medical insurance, get assigned to the proper categories.

- **Address.** If you use Quicken to print your checks, including this scheduled transaction, click the Address button to open the Printed Check Information dialog box so that you can enter the payee's address and an additional message. The address will print on the Quicken check (see Chapter 6, "Writing Checks," for information on writing checks with Quicken).

- **Group.** You can make this transaction part of a group of transactions that are all executed at the same time. See "Using Transaction Groups" later in this chapter for more information about groups.

After you've completed all the information for your scheduled transaction, click OK to add this transaction to your list of scheduled transactions (see Figure 10.3). Now on the designated date (or however many days in advance you asked to be prompted), Quicken gives you an on-screen prompt to remind you of your scheduled transaction.

Fig. 10.3
It's official! Your scheduled transaction gets added to the Scheduled Transaction List.

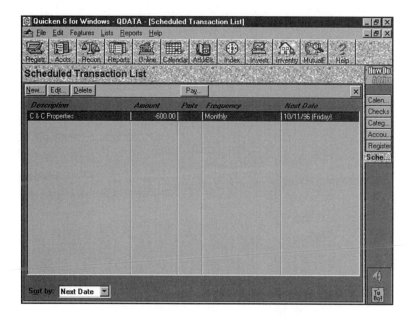

I want to pay a scheduled transaction

Now that you've entered some of your scheduled transactions, what happens when the due date for one of these transactions comes around?

As soon as you start Quicken, you see a reminder of your scheduled transaction (see Figure 10.4). You can rely on Quicken to keep you current with your payments. If you are in the habit of starting Quicken daily, you will receive your reminders in a timely fashion. To learn how Quicken can remind you of your transactions when you don't start the Quicken program, see the section "Let Quicken Give You Reminders," later in this chapter.

Fig. 10.4

Time to make a payment! The Scheduled Transactions Due reminder dialog box pops up on your screen as soon as you open Quicken.

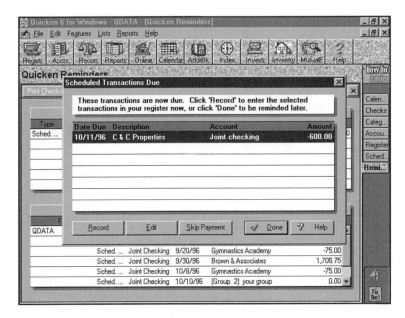

Paying your scheduled transactions on time (or choosing not to pay)

So you've got this reminder on the screen. Now what? Actually, you've got several choices:

- **Record.** Click this button if you are ready to add the transaction to your register. If you plan to write a manual check, now's the time to do it. It's dangerous to record transactions when you mean to write the check sometime in the future. If you're not ready to write the check, save the Record option for later.

- **Edit.** Choose Edit to go to the Edit Transaction dialog box and make some changes. For example, if your scheduled transaction is your mortgage payment and the bank charged you extra (because last month you hadn't set up your scheduled transaction yet and you made your payment late), you can edit the amount to include the penalty.

Q&A *If I choose to edit a transaction from the Scheduled Transactions Due dialog box, will that editing affect the scheduled transaction in the future?*

When you edit a scheduled transaction from the Scheduled Transactions Due dialog box your edit only affects the current payment of that transaction, not any of the future payments. To change a scheduled transaction for all future occurrences, open the Scheduled Transaction List (choose Lists, Scheduled Transaction). Any changes made here will affect all future occurrences of the transaction.

- **Skip Payment**. Choose this option to skip this month's scheduled transaction. Use this option only if you want to skip the transaction entirely. Skipping a scheduled transaction in the Scheduled Transactions Due dialog box will not delete the transaction permanently—you will still be reminded of this transaction next month.

- **Done.** Choose this option to take a pass on the transaction for now. Clicking Done closes the Scheduled Transactions Due dialog box without entering the transaction, but the next time you open Quicken you will receive the same reminder about this transaction.

How can I pay a scheduled transaction early (or in advance)?

You always have the option of paying your Scheduled Transactions early. Because you're paying before the due date you won't see those transactions in the Scheduled Transactions Due reminder dialog box. Instead, you have to go get the scheduled transaction in order to make the payment.

To pay a scheduled transaction early, open the Scheduled Transaction List (choose Lists, Scheduled Transaction), click the transaction you wish to pay, and click the Pay button at the top of the dialog box. The Record Scheduled Transaction dialog box opens. You can enter any changes you might want to make before paying (for example, maybe you want to write the check today but plan to postdate it, or maybe you get to reduce the amount by paying early). Click Record (see Figure 10.5) and the transaction is executed.

Fig. 10.5
You can make changes to your scheduled transaction in the Record Scheduled Transaction dialog box.

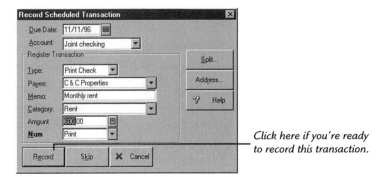

Click here if you're ready to record this transaction.

What if you change your mind and decide not to pay this transaction early? Just click Cancel and the dialog box disappears but your regularly scheduled transaction is not disrupted. If you decide you're not going to pay it at all and don't want to be reminded of the payment on the due date, click Skip. Quicken will come back next month (or whenever this transaction falls due again) to remind you to make a payment.

Using transaction groups

A transaction group is just that—a group of transactions, scheduled transactions, that is. Put several transactions that occur on the same day in a group and that group can be executed all at once. No matter how many transactions you put in one group, they all execute at the same time.

You don't need to set up your transactions as scheduled transactions before you put them in a group. In fact, if you do set up scheduled transactions and then add them to a scheduled group, you need to delete the individual transactions from your scheduled transaction list; otherwise, the transactions will be duplicated.

To set up a transaction group, open the Scheduled Transaction List dialog box (choose Lists, Scheduled Transaction), and then select New. Ignore the choices in this dialog box for setting up a scheduled transaction, and click the Group button. The Create Transaction Group dialog box opens (see Figure 10.6).

In the Create Transaction Group dialog box, select the date of payment, the account, and the Group Type. The Group Type choices are Regular and Investment. Choose Regular for now. You can read about investment groups in Chapter 16, "Staying on Top of Your Investments."

Fig. 10.6

Use this dialog box to designate a group of transactions that you will pay at one time.

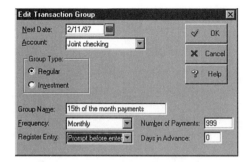

Select a name for your group. The name can be no longer than 28 characters (including spaces). Call your group something that will give you a clue about what goes in the group. The example in Figure 10.6 is "15th of the Month Payments." You can use a name like the one I've chosen, or maybe you want to create a group name that identifies payments that are of a similar type, such as "Utility Payments." It doesn't matter what name you choose as long as you pick a name that is meaningful to you.

After you name your group, select the frequency of payments, whether you want to be prompted for these payments, the number of payments (for something like a utilities group you would just leave the number of payments at 999 to indicate ongoing payments), and the number of days (if any) in advance of the due date that you want a reminder message. Fill in these items just as you did with a single Scheduled Transaction.

After you fill in all the information in the Create Transaction Group dialog box, click OK and a window opens listing all your memorized transactions (basically, all the payees in your register). From this list you can select the payees you want to add to your group. To select a payee for inclusion in the group, click the name of a payee, and then click the Mark button at the top of the Assign Transactions to Group window (see Figure 10.7).

Each group you create is given an identifying number by Quicken. This number appears in the Grp (Group) column at the right side of the Assign Transactions to Group window, alongside each payee's name that is included in the group.

Fig. 10.7

Assign transactions to your scheduled group in this window.

Click the Mark button to include the payee in your group.

Click the name of a payee you want to include in your group.

This is the group number in which this payee is included.

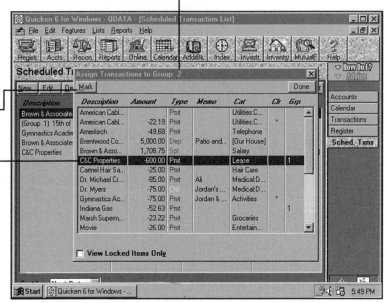

 CAUTION **Be sure you don't duplicate scheduled transactions. If you** originally set up a transaction to be scheduled by itself, then later added it to a group, go back and delete the original scheduled transaction from your Scheduled Transaction List. Otherwise, Quicken will try to execute both the original, single scheduled transaction, and the group that includes that transaction. You don't want to pay the mortgage twice!

You can change the contents of a group by opening the Scheduled Transaction List, selecting the group you want to change, and clicking Edit. To add to the items in the group or to remove an item from the group, click the OK button and the list of memorized transactions appears with the Group designations in the right column. Simply click an item you want to add to the group and then click the Mark button to add a transaction. To remove a transaction from the group, click the item you want to remove, and again click the Mark button. The Mark button turns on and off the group designation each time you click it.

When it is time for your scheduled group of transactions to be executed, Quicken pops up a reminder message, just as it did for a single scheduled transaction. Selecting Re<u>c</u>ord from the reminder window will have the effect of recording every item in the group at once.

You can schedule transactions quickly using the financial calendar

Now that you understand how scheduled transactions work, you can speed up the process a little and make it more visual. When you use Quicken's Financial Calendar, you see an actual calendar on-screen and you can enter your scheduled transactions right in this calendar.

To open the Financial Calendar, click the Calendar icon in the iconbar, or you can click the Bills icon in the Activity Bar and then select Schedule a Future Payment. On your screen you see the current month's calendar showing your transactions for the month. To the right of the calendar is a list of your payees (see Figure 10.8).

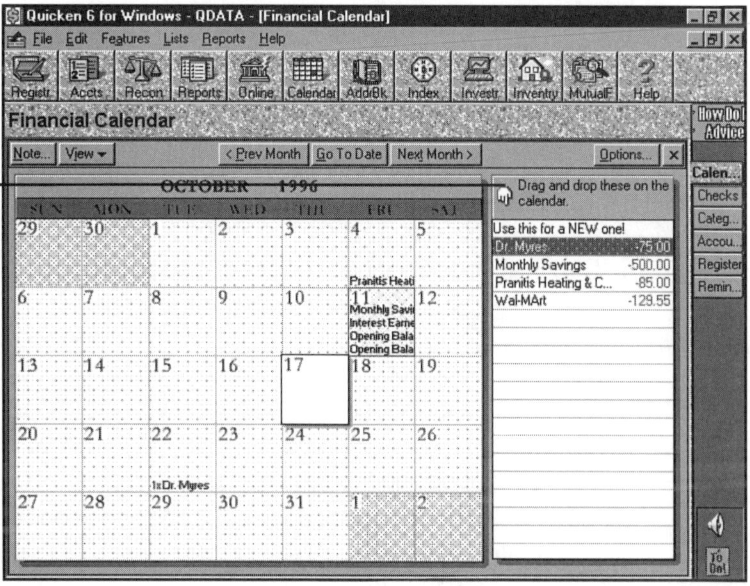

Fig. 10.8
Use your mouse with this cool calendar to drag your transactions right onto the dates on which they should occur!

Drag an item from this list right onto a specific date on the calendar.

To create a new scheduled transaction, select one of your payees from the list on the right side of the calendar and, using the mouse (which changes to a pointed finger), drag the payee onto the calendar on the date on which you want to schedule the transaction (you can change the pages of the calendar by clicking on the arrow buttons at the top of the calendar screen).

When you drag a transaction onto the calendar, the New Transaction dialog box opens (see Figure 10.9). To make this a scheduled transaction, click the Scheduled Transaction button in the middle of the New Transaction dialog box. Otherwise, you are entering a one-time-only payment right into your register (Register Transaction). The rest of the scheduled transaction options appear just as they did when you created a new scheduled transaction from the Scheduled Transaction List explained earlier in this chapter.

Fig. 10.9
This New Transaction dialog box opens in response to your dragging a transaction onto the calendar.

Select the Scheduled Transaction option to schedule a transaction for future execution.

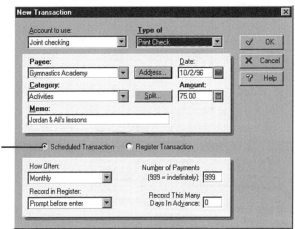

I can change a transaction in the calendar

You can change any transaction from the Financial Calendar, whether it is a transaction you entered in your register or a scheduled transaction. Just point with your mouse to the transaction in the calendar that you want to change and double-click on it. The Transactions On dialog box opens on-screen (see Figure 10.10) listing all the transactions for that day—register and scheduled. Click the transaction you want to change, then click the Edit button at the bottom of the dialog box to make changes.

Fig. 10.10

You can add, edit, remove, and pay transactions from the Transactions On dialog box.

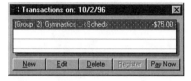

Notice you also can delete a transaction from the Transactions On dialog box, and request that a transaction be paid now. You also can enter a new transaction from this dialog box. In fact, another way to enter a new transaction in the Financial Calendar is to double-click on any day of the calendar. The Transactions due dialog box opens, even if there is nothing entered on that day, and then you can click on the New button to add a transaction.

If you double-click a date that contains scheduled transactions, you'll see the scheduled transactions listed in the Transactions due dialog box. You can request an early payment of that transaction by clicking the Pay Now button, and Quicken executes your scheduled transaction, even though you're paying it before the due date.

 TIP **Another easy way to enter a new scheduled transaction from the** Financial Calendar is to click on the top line of the list of payees (use this for a new one!) and drag that line to the date in the calendar when you want to schedule the transaction (see Figure 10.8). When you drag this line to a date in the calendar, the New Transaction dialog box appears so that you can enter the scheduled transaction information.

I'd like to see how my accounts are doing

You can see the balance in your checking account by clicking the View button at the top of the Financial Calendar and selecting Show Account Graph. What you get when you make this selection is a bar graph at the bottom of the screen that displays the daily balance in your checking account, based on the transactions entered in your register and the projected scheduled transactions in the Financial Calendar. Pause your mouse pointer on any one of the bars, hold down your mouse button, and you see the actual amount that was, or will be, in your checking account on that particular day.

Use this bar graph (shown in Figure 10.11) to see in an instant if you're going to need some additional cash to cover a particular transaction.

Fig. 10.11
View the account graph to see at a glance how your checking account balance is holding up.

*Select View, Show
Account Graph to
display the bar graph.*

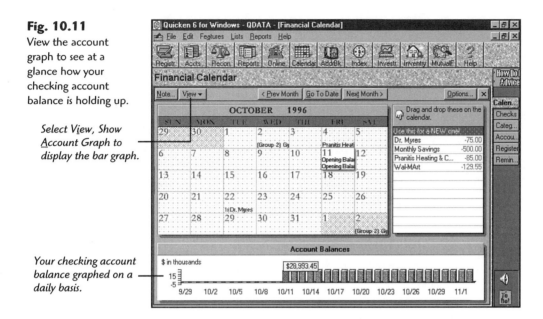

*Your checking account
balance graphed on a
daily basis.*

Neat! I can make notes in the calendar!

You can add any text you want to your Financial Calendar—after all, it's *your* calendar. To add a reminder note to yourself, click on the day on which you want to be reminded, then click the Note button at the top of the Financial Calendar. The Note dialog box appears in which you can write notes (see Figure 10.12). Click Save to keep the note, Delete Note to remove a note, and Cancel to change your mind and close the dialog box. These notes don't actually appear as text on the calendar; instead, they appear as a small, colored box in the corner of the calendar day (see Figure 10.13). Click the box to see the note inside.

 TIP **To distinguish notes from one another in the Financial Calendar,** you can color code them. You can make birthdays yellow, meetings green, special events blue, and so on. To change the color of a note, from the Note dialog box (see Figure 10.12), select the color you want from the Note Color drop-down list.

Fig. 10.12
Type your note in the
Note dialog box.

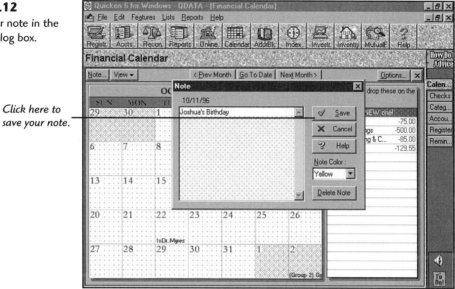

*Click here to
save your note.*

Fig. 10.13
Your notes appear on
the calendar as small,
colored boxes.

*Click here to
read your note.*

*Your note appears
on the date where
you created it.*

Let Quicken give you reminders

Now that you've entered all these scheduled transactions and notes into Quicken, take advantage of Quicken's ability to remind you of all these things. You've already seen how your scheduled transactions come up on-screen each time you start Quicken. You also can make Quicken present you with your notes each time you start the program. After all, what's the use of entering your mom and dad's anniversary into the calendar if you aren't reminded of it when the time comes?

What's more, you can have Quicken remind you of all these important transactions and events without your even starting the Quicken program.

Getting reminders from Quicken

To make sure that Quicken gives you reminders when transactions or notes are due, you need to activate the reminder settings in Quicken. To activate reminder settings, select Edit, Options, Reminders to open the Reminder Options dialog box. Check the Show Reminders on Startup box and the Show Calendar Notes box in this dialog box. Select the number of days in advance that you want to be reminded of transactions and notes and click OK. Now, each time you start Quicken, you'll see a window showing you the current reminder notes in your current file and any other Quicken files you have (see Figure 10.14).

Changing reminder options

You quickly can change the display of reminder notes. When the Quicken Reminders window is open, click the Options button to open the Reminder Options dialog box. From this window you can turn off any of the reminder features that are currently turned on.

See reminders anytime

You've probably noticed the To Do! button in the lower-right corner of your Quicken screen. When you have scheduled transactions that are due, notes, checks to print, or online payments that are due, you'll see the To Do! button flash. Just click this button at any time to see the same reminder notes that you see when you start Quicken (see Figure 10.14).

Fig. 10.14
Reminder notes are
presented on your
screen when you start
Quicken.

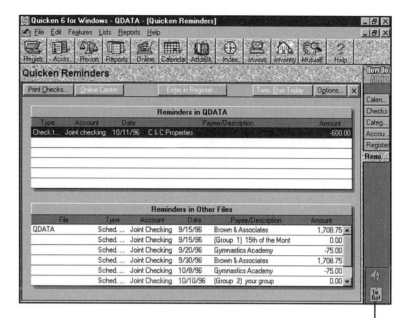

Click here to see a list of
your currently scheduled
transactions.

11

Storing Addresses in Quicken

● In this chapter:

- Open the Financial Address Book

- Where do these addresses come from?

- Add a new address

- Put addresses in groups

- Print addresses

Look! Quicken's got an Address Book that I can easily access and update to keep all the addresses and phone numbers I need in one place! . . . . ➤

Here's a feature in Quicken that makes your life easier by keeping all your work, family, friends, and Quicken addresses and phone numbers at your fingertips. The Financial Address Book is available to you while you're working in Quicken or any other program on your computer. Use it to look up addresses and phone numbers, or use it to print mailing labels. Updating address changes is easy in the Financial Address Book; no more messy-looking address books with pencil scratches marking out old information with the new.

The Financial Address Book organizes and stores the addresses you need to pay bills or perform other financial activities for each of your Quicken files. It holds addresses and phone numbers of your business associates, family members, or friends.

How do I open the address book?

You can open the Financial Address Book from Quicken or while you're working in another program. If you need to check an address or phone number, just open the Financial Address Book and look it up right on the spot.

If you're already in Quicken, open the Financial Address Book by clicking the Address Book (AddrBk) icon from the iconbar or selecting Lists, Track Important Addresses. Quicken opens the Financial Address Book for the Quicken file you are working in. There's a separate Financial Address Book for each of your Quicken files. Look at the title bar at the top of the Address Book to see in what book you're working.

Even if you're not working in Quicken, you can still open, and work in, the Financial Address Book. In Windows 95, just select the Financial Address Book program from the Quicken program folder, and the Address Book opens. From Windows 3.1, click the Financial Address Book icon in the Quicken program group to open the Address Book. So, if you're writing a letter in Microsoft Word and need to look up an address, just open Quicken's Financial Address Book and find it there.

A closer look at the Financial Address Book

Menu
The Financial Address Book has its own menu that you use to perform tasks.

Finding an address
Type a name here to quickly find an address.

Displaying a group
Select the group that you want to show at one time in the Address Book.

Button bar
Use the Address Book button bar to add, edit, delete, and find addresses. Also, print addresses, get help, and close the Address Book using the button bar.

Adding notes
Add more information for the highlighted name through *Notes*.

Scroll arrows
Click the arrows at each end to see more information in the List view of the Address Book.

List view
This part of the Financial Address Book is the List view where you see each name and address on one line.

Saving addresses
Save the new address or changes using this button.

Assigning a group
Assign a group to a name and address.

Detail view
The Detail view of the Address Book displays all of the information for the address highlighted in the List view above. Here's where you add new addresses or update existing ones.

QDATA - Financial Address Book

File   Edit   Sort   Options   Help

New   Edit   Delete   Search   Print   Help   Close

Find *Last Name:* [   ]   Group: <All Groups>

First Name	Organization	Street 1	City
<<New>>			
	Best Pest Control	3489 W. Michigan Aven	Carmel
	Castle Maid Services	P.O. Box 89	Carmel
	Municipal Utilities	1919 S. Washington Blv	Carmel
	Public Service Indiana	93456 W. Hwy 38	Indianapolis
	Cellular One	9700 N. College	Carmel
	Gymnastics Academy	708 North College Aven	Carmel

Last Name: _____   First Name: _____
Organization: **Cellular One**   Position: _____
Street 1: **9700 N. College**   Street 2: _____
City: **Carmel**   State: **IN**   Zip: **46032**
Phone: **555-8996**   Fax: _____
Notes: _____

[Record]   [Notes>>]   Assigned To Group: [Unassigned]

Here's where the addresses come from

So, you've opened the Financial Address Book for the first time and there are already some names and addresses there. How did they get there?

You know when you're working in Quicken and you enter an address for a payee? Quicken not only stores the address for you, but it also stores it in the Financial Address Book. Any payee names and addresses that you have set up in the Memorized Transaction List, the Scheduled Transaction List, or the Online Payee List also are copied into the Financial Address Book.

 TIP New Quicken users won't have anything in the Financial Address Book. As you begin your work in Quicken, the information that you enter for payees will automatically be imported into the Address Book.

 CAUTION When the Financial Address Book imports personal names from Quicken, the first and last name are placed in the Last Name field. That's because Quicken has no way of knowing whether the payee name is a personal name that should be divided into first and last name, or the name of an organization that shouldn't be divided.

If you want to sort the addresses in your Address Book, you must edit personal names to correctly divide the first and last names. I'll show you how to edit entries in the Address Book a little later in this chapter.

I'd like to update the Address Book

Some of the names, addresses, and phone numbers of the people and organizations that I deal with have changed. Can I change them in my Address Book? Sure. You can add new entries in the Address Book, too.

Before you make any changes, here are some things to remember:

- In the Financial Address Book, if you change Leo Smith to Smith in the Last Name field and Leo in the First Name field, Quicken changes the payee name in, say, your Memorized Transaction List.

- If you change Bob Jones's address in the Address Book, it also gets changed in the Memorized Transaction List.

- If you change the address for one of your online payees in the Address Book, you'll have to go to the Online Payee List in Quicken and make the change there, too.

If you make changes to payee names and addresses from within Quicken, here's what happens in the Address Book:

- When you enter a transaction in Quicken for a new payee, the payee name and address automatically gets sent to the Financial Address Book.

- If you delete a payee name and address from the Memorized Transaction List, the Scheduled Transaction List, or the Online Payee List in Quicken, it's not automatically deleted from the Address Book. You'll have to open the Address Book, find the name and address, and then delete it from there.

Let's add a new address

Open the Financial Address Book and then click the New button or double-click the New line in the List view of the Address Book. The cursor is moved to the first field in the Detail view of the Address Book so that you can begin entering a new name and address.

Entering information for a new address

Fill in the Detail view of the Address Book with as little or as much information as you want. For example, if you want only a name, street address, city, state, and ZIP, just fill in these fields and leave the others blank. Move forward from field to field by pressing the Tab key; to move back a field, press Shift+Tab.

Saving information in the Address Book

After you've entered the information for a new entry in the Address Book, save it by clicking the Record button. If you've selected to have the Address Book sorted by last name, the new entry is placed in the Address Book in alphabetical order by last name. If you've selected to sort by city, then the new entry is placed in the Address Book based on its city location.

TIP **Click the <u>N</u>otes button to display a notepad where you can enter** more data for a name in the Address Book. You can't sort the data that you enter in the notepad; it's for informational purposes only.

I want to change or delete an address

You easily can change or delete an entry in your Address Book. Just select the entry, and then choose whether you want to edit it or delete it by clicking the Edit or Delete button in the button bar.

TIP **Type a name in the F<u>i</u>nd box at the top of the List view to select** an address to edit or delete. The element that Quicken looks for in the F<u>i</u>nd box depends on what's displayed after Find (like Last Name, First Name, and so forth).

I want the Address Book sorted another way

Usually, you'll sort your Address Book by last name and that's how the Address Book is set up when you first use it. But if you need it sorted another way, like by organization or by city, you can do that too.

First, you'll need to open the <u>S</u>ort menu from the Address Book (see Figure 11.1).

Fig. 11.1
The Sort menu shows you the fields you can use to sort the Address Book.

Select one of the fields from the Sort menu to sort the list another way. If there's a field that you don't see in the Sort menu, perhaps you want to sort by ZIP code or phone number, select <u>B</u>y from the menu. Quicken shows you the other fields that you can sort by.

Using address groups

You can assign each of the entries in your Address Book to a group so that they're all together. For example, you may want all of your family member addresses together so that you can print mailing labels for birthday, graduation, or anniversary parties.

Your Address Book is already set up with five predefined groups: Quicken (assigned to all addresses that come from Quicken lists), Family, Friends, Work, and Unassigned. When you click the Group drop-down arrow in the Address Book, you'll see these predefined groups. You can add your own groups (as many as 100) or modify the ones already there.

If you want to assign a group to an address that's already in your list, just select the address, click the Assigned to Group drop-down arrow, and select the group that you want.

TIP   **You can add a new group by selecting Options, Set Up Groups to** open the Set Up Groups dialog box. From here, click New in the Available Groups list and then type the new group name in the box. Click the Record button to add the new group to the list of Available Groups.

Searching for an address

If you need to search through your Address Book for an item in more than one field or if you don't know which group an address is in, you can call an all-out search with the Search button. When you click Search, Quicken displays the Search dialog box that you see in Figure 11.2. Here, you can enter an item to search for, and tell Quicken which fields and groups to look in.

Q&A   *What's the difference between fields and columns?*

Absolutely nothing. You'll see the terms used synonymously in the Address Book. They both refer to the items of information you enter in the Address Book. For example, the Last Name field and the Last Name column are the same; the City field and the City column are also the same.

Type part of the address that you're looking for.

If you're not sure of the item that you're looking for, type something that sounds like it and click this option.

Fig. 11.2
Call an all-out search for an address in your Address Book using the Search window.

Click the field that you want Quicken to search in. For multiple fields, press Ctrl or Shift first and then click the field.

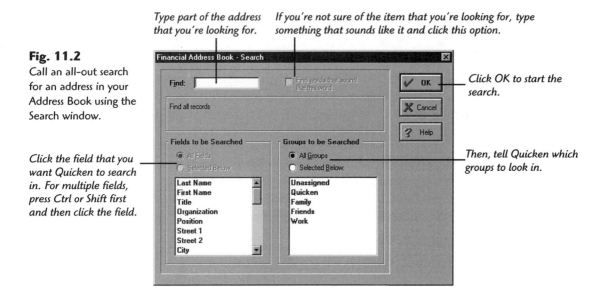

Click OK to start the search.

Then, tell Quicken which groups to look in.

I want to print addresses

Maybe you want to send invitations to a big birthday bash and need mailing labels for all your family members. Or, maybe you'd like to put together a call list of all your clients with their telephone numbers. Take advantage of having all of your names and addresses in one place that can be quickly printed for whatever reason.

The Financial Address Book lets you print addresses in several different formats:

- Names with complete addresses

- Names and telephone numbers

- Mailing labels with names, organizations, and primary addresses

- Rolodex cards (Avery #4168 for continuous feed printers; Avery #5385 for laser printers)

- #10 envelopes

If you're using mailing labels, here are the Avery label styles that are compatible with the Address Book:

Label #	Labels up	Label size	Description
4143	2	4" x 15/16"	Standard continuous
4144	3	2 1/2" x 15/16"	Standard continuous
4145	1	3 1/2" x 15/16"	Standard continuous
5160	3	2 5/8" x 1"	Standard laser
5161	2	4" x 1"	Standard laser

CAUTION **Before you start printing, you'll need to select the size and** orientation of the paper that you're printing on. To get Quicken ready to print from the Address Book, select File, Print Setup from the Address Book menu. Quicken opens the Print Setup dialog box where you enter printer settings.

Select the addresses you want to print

Before you begin printing, you'll need to select the addresses you want to print. If you don't select an address, Quicken will print all addresses within the current group.

Print just one address by clicking it in the List view of the Address Book. To select more than one address from the current group, press and hold the Ctrl key as you click each address.

To select a number of consecutive addresses, click the first address and then press and hold the Shift key while you click the last address you want to include. All addresses between the first address you clicked and the last address will print.

Printing addresses

Now that you've entered your printer settings and selected which addresses you want to print, click the Print button in the Address Book. Quicken opens the Print dialog box shown in Figure 11.3.

Complete the Print dialog box by specifying the print format, type of paper, the print range, and the font. Click OK to begin printing addresses.

Fig. 11.3
Complete the Print
dialog box to print the
selected addresses from
the Address Book.

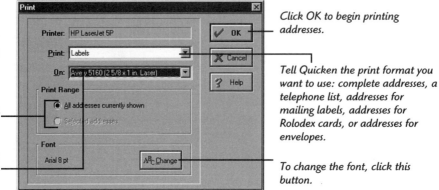

*Click OK to begin printing
addresses.*

*Tell Quicken the print format you
want to use: complete addresses, a
telephone list, addresses for
mailing labels, addresses for
Rolodex cards, or addresses for
envelopes.*

*If you're printing a
single address, click
Selected addresses.*

*Select what you'll
be printing on.*

*To change the font, click this
button.*

 TIP **If you want to see an on-screen preview of what will print before** you actually print on paper, labels, envelopes, or Rolodex forms, select File, Print Preview from the Address Book menu and then complete the Print Preview dialog box (which is identical to the Print dialog box in Figure 11.3).

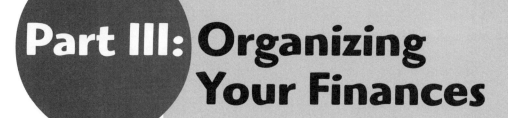

Part III: Organizing Your Finances

12

Tracking Cash and Other Assets

● **In this chapter:**

- Set up a cash account

- Track your cash expenditures

- Balance the cash in your pocket with your cash account

- Set up and use an asset account

If only I had a way to track how much cash I spend each month and how much I have. Wouldn't that make my life easier? . . . .

How did you pay for the things you bought today? Maybe you wrote a check to pay some bills, paid cash at the grocery store, and used a credit card at the shoe store. Quicken gives you a way to record all these expenditures so you can stay on top of your finances.

So, what do you do with cash expenditures? They can't go in the checking account register because the cash isn't in your checking account when you spend it. Quicken lets you set up a cash account to record your cash expenses. There's also a credit card account in Quicken (discussed in Chapter 13, "Managing Your Credit Cards").

Now, while we're talking about cash, did you know that cash is an asset? You may have noticed that in Quicken there are asset accounts, too. Well, even though I just told you that cash is an asset, you don't use an asset account to keep track of your cash. Quicken's provided a special cash account for that. You'll use the asset accounts in Quicken to track the value of the things that you own, like your house, cars, boats, furniture, and so forth.

66 *Plain English, please!*

An **asset** is any personal or business resource you own that has lasting value. The assets that you might own are your house, cars, furniture, and investments. Businesses' assets include money owed by customers (accounts receivable), inventory held for resale, and any fixtures or equipment used in the business. 99

Here's how you set up a cash account

Setting up any kind of account in Quicken is easy. If you remember from Chapter 3, Quicken guides you through the steps for setting up accounts with a series of windows that ask you for information. Cash accounts are no exception; they're easy to set up, too.

Here's what you'll need to do to set up a cash account:

- Assign a name to your cash account.

- Enter the amount of cash you have on hand to start your account and the date that you're starting the account.

- Tell Quicken some additional information about your account; however, this is probably not necessary with a cash account.

When you're ready to set up your cash account, click My Accounts from the Activity Bar and then select Create a New Account. Or, from the Account List, click the New button to display the Create New Account dialog box (see Figure 12.1). From here, you can select the type of account you want to set up. Obviously, for a cash account, you'll select Cash.

Fig. 12.1
Click the Cash option to set up a cash account.

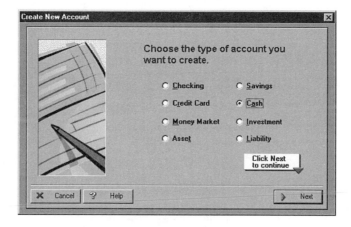

When you select Cash, Quicken opens the Cash Account Setup dialog box (see Figure 12.2) that starts you on your way to setting up a cash account.

Fig. 12.2
Quicken's EasyStep windows make it a snap to set up a cash account. Just follow the instructions in each window and you're there!

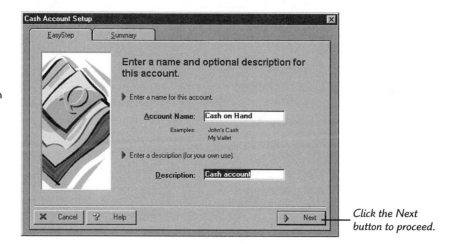

Click the Next button to proceed.

Earlier in this book, I explained how to set up bank accounts in Quicken. Setting up a cash account is very similar. Just follow the EasyStep Account Setup windows to name the cash account (remember, you can use only 30 characters, including spaces, but not :] [/ | ^), enter a start date and balance, and any other information you may want to add to your cash account.

When you're finished, Quicken displays the Summary window (see Figure 12.3) with the information you entered for your cash account. Look it over carefully to make sure it's all correct. If it's not, move to the box with the incorrect information and change it.

Fig. 12.3
Review your informa-
tion in the Summary
window for your new
cash account. If there's
anything that's wrong,
correct it here.

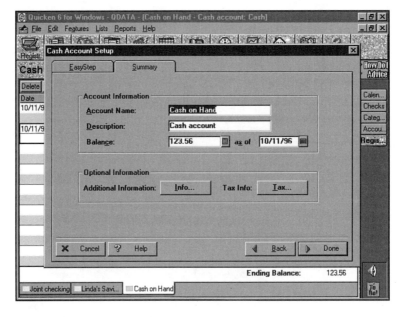

 In the Summary window, you see a Tax button. When you select this button, Quicken provides the Tax Schedule Information dialog box so that you can assign a tax schedule to the transfers that occur to and from your cash account. Because you'll have many different types of transfers in a cash account, you won't want to assign a tax schedule to it.

When you're sure that the information in the Summary window is correct, click Done and Quicken adds your new cash account to the Account List.

I'm ready to use my cash account

After you've set up your cash account, you can start using it to track those expenses that you pay cash for—like when you go to the movie theater and spend $14 for the movie and another $12 on popcorn and soft drinks. There's $26 that you've spent in cash that could go unaccounted for if you didn't enter it in your cash account.

When you're ready to enter a cash transaction, open your cash account register by selecting it from the Account List, or selecting it from the Account selection bar from any register.

When you open your cash account register, it looks like other registers you've already seen in Quicken (see Figure 12.4), except cash account registers have Spend and Receive columns instead of Payment and Deposit columns.

Fig. 12.4
Here's the register for my cash account. Notice that it looks just like other registers you've seen in Quicken.

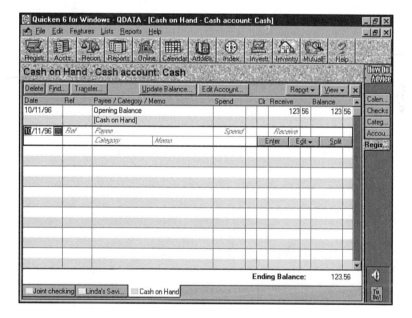

Once you've opened your cash account register, you're ready to enter some cash transactions.

Enter only cash expenditures in your cash account

Now that you're working with more than one account type (bank accounts and cash accounts), you'll want to make sure that you enter only cash transactions in your cash account. If you make a mistake and enter a cash transaction in, say, your checking account, you'll not only mess up your cash account balance, but your checking account balance will be off as well.

TIP **Did you know that each type of account's register is a different** color? Bank accounts are light green, cash accounts are yellow, credit card accounts are blue, and so forth. Quicken color codes your registers so that you'll quickly recognize the type of account that you're using. You won't likely enter a cash transaction in a register that's blue because you'll know it's a credit card account. Oh, and you can change the colors if you want a different color scheme. Just select the View button in any register and then select Register Options. You'll see a Colors button as one of the register display options. When you click this button, you'll see a color palette for each account type.

Enter a cash transaction in the cash account register just like you enter transactions in the checking account register. You'll enter the date of the cash expenditure, a description of the expense (this is optional) in the Payee field, the amount you spent in the Spend field, and then assign a category. Click Enter to record the transaction in your cash account register.

Figure 12.5 shows the cash transaction for a night out at the movies.

Keeping track of petty cash

If you're running a small business, I recommend setting up a cash account to track your petty cash fund. You'll benefit in two ways: one, you'll be accurately classifying each cash expenditure as to the type of expense, and two, you'll always know how much is in your petty cash fund. Petty cash is usually a tough one to track because more than one employee may have access to it. Tracking petty cash in a cash account will keep your employees honest because they'll have to account for any cash used from the fund.

Fig. 12.5
Entering a cash
transaction is just like
entering a transaction
in your checking
account register.
Quicken updates your
cash balance each time
you enter a cash
transaction.

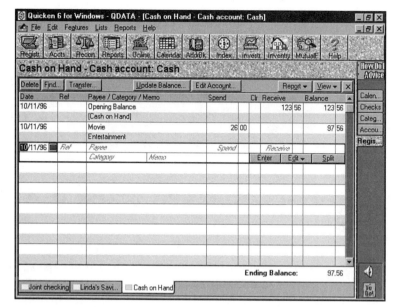

Adjust the balance in your cash account to match the cash you have

No matter how diligent you are in entering cash expenses in your cash
account, there are probably going to be some small ones that you miss. You
may forget to enter a transaction for your lunch or for the parking fees you
paid yesterday. These expenses may be small by themselves, but over an
extended period, they add up.

Periodically, you'll want to adjust the balance in your Quicken cash account
with the amount of cash you actually have on hand. If your cash account
register says you have $97.56 and you only have $92.49, then you'll want to
adjust your cash account for the difference.

Adjust your cash account balance by choosing Reconcile button from the
register button bar. Quicken displays the Update Account Balance dialog box
like you see in Figure 12.6. Complete this dialog box and click OK to update
your cash account balance.

Fig. 12.6
Update your cash
account balance in
Quicken to match the
cash that you actually
have on hand.

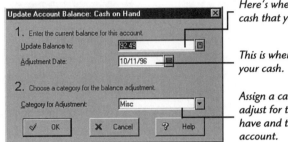

*Here's where you enter the amount of
cash that you actually have.*

*This is when you take an actual count of
your cash.*

*Assign a category that Quicken enters to
adjust for the difference in the cash you
have and the balance in your cash
account.*

Using asset accounts to track the things you own

If you want to use Quicken to track all of your assets, you have to set up an
asset account for each one. It's important to set up asset accounts if you
want to use Quicken to determine your net worth (remember back in Chapter
3, I explained that net worth is the difference between all your assets and all
your liabilities). Quicken won't know what your total assets are unless you
set up an account so that you can enter asset values for each. (Obviously,
you'll need to set up liability accounts for each, but you won't learn about
liability accounts until Chapter 15.)

Here are some of the assets you might want to set up asset accounts for:

- **Your home.** This is probably your most valuable asset, so you'll want to
  include its worth in a Quicken asset account.

- **Furniture and personal belongings.** In aggregate, these will be a
  significant part of your net worth.

- **Jewelry.** If the value of your jewelry is high, set up an asset account to
  track it.

- **IRA account.** IRA accounts can be set up as asset accounts if you don't
  want to track the price of securities held in your IRA. If you do want to track
  security prices in an IRA, it's better to set it up as an investment account.

- **A 401k or other retirement account.** Asset accounts can be used to
  track the value in retirement accounts and you can even designate the
  earnings from these accounts to be tax-free, if necessary.

- **Business property.** If you own a business, you'll want to set up an asset account for capital equipment and accounts receivable.

Q&A *What about my stock investments? They're certainly considered assets that I own.*

You're right. But you don't set up investments as asset accounts in Quicken. Quicken has special investment accounts that you use to track assets that you have invested in stocks and securities. The exception, here, is the IRA account. If you don't care to update prices for securities held in your IRA, you can set up your IRA as an asset account. See Chapter 16, however, to learn how to set up and use investment accounts.

Setting up an asset account

Setting up an asset account is pretty much like setting up a cash account as shown earlier in this chapter. If you refer to Figure 12.1, you see the types of accounts that you can add in Quicken. When you set up a cash account, you selected the Cash account type; to set up an asset account, you'll select the Asset account type.

When you select to set up an asset account, Quicken displays a series of EasyStep account setup windows (like you saw when setting up your cash account) that ask you for information . Here's what you'll need to enter:

- A name for your asset account and a brief description of the asset.

- The value of the asset and the date that you want to start using the asset account.

- Tell Quicken whether you're going to use the asset account to track an IRA or tax-free investment. Tax-free investment accounts are those whose earnings are not taxable. The earnings from an IRA, for example, are not taxable at the current time.

- Assign a tax schedule to transfer in and out of the asset account, if you want.

- Any additional information that you may want to attach to the asset account, like a bank name, contact person, account number, and so forth.

In Figure 12.7, I've set up an asset account to track the value of my house. After I click Next and then click Done at the last Summary window, my asset account is added. Quicken includes a register for the account that I can use to record any activity that affects the value of my house.

Fig. 12.7
Adding an asset account is similar to adding other types of accounts. Just name the account, enter the value and start date, and some tax informa-tion (if necessary), and you're done.

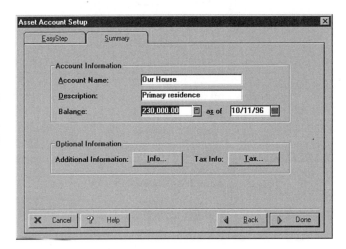

Recording activity in an asset account

After you've set up an asset account to track an asset's value, you can enter transactions in the account's register. Transactions are entered in asset account registers just like any other Quicken register that you may have already used. You'll see one difference in an asset account register from other registers. Instead of the Payment and Deposit columns that you see in your checking account register, or the Spend and Receive columns in your cash account register, you'll see the Decrease and Increase columns. The Decrease and Increase columns let you adjust the value of your asset.

So, if you spend $5,000 to add a new patio to your house, you can enter a transaction in the asset account register for your house to increase its value by $5,000. Figure 12.8 shows the asset account register for My House with a transaction for the $5,000 patio addition.

Fig. 12.8
Activities that increase or decrease the value of an asset can be entered as transactions in your asset account. Here, the value of this asset has increased by $5,000.

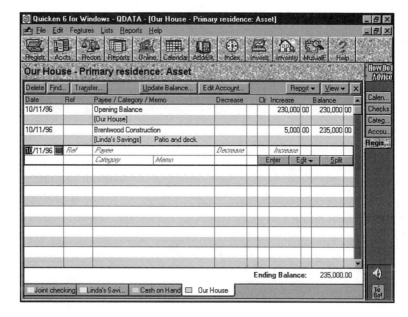

Working with transfer transactions

In Chapter 5, I told you a little about transactions between two accounts in Quicken, called **transfer transactions**. Now that we're working with asset accounts in Quicken, it might be a little easier to see how these kinds of transactions work.

66 *Plain English, please!*

> **Transfer transactions** are transactions in Quicken that affect two different accounts. In a transfer transaction, another account is assigned to the transaction in the Category field. 99

Look again at Figure 12.8 with the transaction for the addition of a $5,000 patio to the My House asset account. Notice that in the Category field, I assigned another account (the Linda's Savings account) instead of a category. What actually happened here is that the patio addition was paid for from the Linda's Savings account. So, this transaction affected two different accounts: the My House account and the Linda's Savings account. The value of the My House account increased while the value (or balance) in the Linda's Savings account decreased.

In Figure 12.9, you see what the other side of the transaction that you saw in Figure 12.8 looks like. This transaction was entered by Quicken when I assigned the Linda's Savings account to the transaction in the My House account.

Fig. 12.9

Quicken enters a transaction in the register for the account that you assign in the Category field of a transfer transaction.

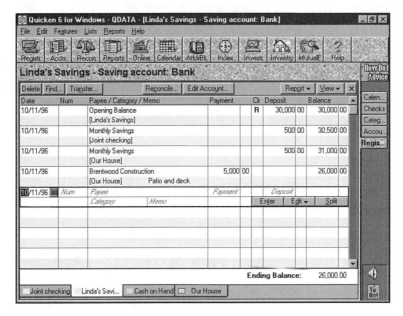

 TIP **A quick way to move between transactions in a transfer transac-**
tion is to highlight one side of the transaction and then press Ctrl+X.

13

Managing Your Credit Cards

● **In this chapter:**

- Set up a credit card account

- Enter credit card transactions

- Balance your credit card account

- Make a payment

Quicken can't pay those credit card bills, but record keeping will be a breeze. . . . . ●▸

Let Quicken help you get a handle on those credit card bills you have stacking up. You can set up a credit card account for each credit card you have and enter purchases and payments in registers that you're already accustomed to using. This way, you're sure to include credit card purchases as expenses and will have an easy way to track each of them by category.

Even if you're diligent and always pay your credit card balances each month, you can still benefit by using a Quicken credit card account. You'll still want to enter each credit card purchase as a transaction in your credit card account so that you can assign it to a category.

If you use credit cards, setting up a credit card account is essential if you want to accurately track *all* of your expenses.

Why you should set up a credit card account

So what kind of credit card user are you? Do you use your credit card instead of cash so that you have a record each month of what you spent? Do you use credit cards instead of writing checks because it's quicker when you're checking out? Or, do you use credit cards to finance your lifestyle (you know, buy something today and pay for it tomorrow)?

Whatever the reason, you can use Quicken's credit card accounts to stay on top of those credit card bills so they don't get ahead of you. When you use a Quicken credit card account, you've got a place to record your credit card purchases so that you can assign a category to them. If you use credit cards, you won't have an accurate picture of your finances if you don't include credit card transactions in Quicken.

 TIP You don't have to set up a credit card account in Quicken if you pay off your credit card bill each month. When you pay your bill each month, you can enter a split transaction in the register for the account that you pay bills from. Then, enter each credit card purchase as a separate line in the split transaction.

TIP **If you carry credit card balances, the amounts outstanding are** considered liabilities. If you want to use Quicken to determine your net worth, you must set up credit card accounts so that these liabilities enter the net worth equation. Remember, net worth equals your total assets minus your total liabilities.

Setting up a credit card account

By this time, you've probably set up several accounts in Quicken. In previous chapters, we've talked about bank, cash, and asset accounts. So I know you know how to set up an account by now. There's really not much difference when setting up a credit card account. You'll start from the Create New Account dialog box that you see in Figure 13.1. Select the Credit Card option to set up a credit card account and display the first Credit Card Account Setup dialog box. Here's what you'll need to enter to set up a credit card account:

- A name for the account and a brief account description.

- If you have your previous credit card statement, the balance and statement date. (If you don't have your previous statement, Quicken uses today's date and a $0.00 (zero) balance to start your credit card account.)

- If the credit card account you're setting up is for a Quicken credit card or another account that you want to use with online banking to download your statements, enter:

  The financial institution

  Credit card number

  Your Social Security number

  Your bank's routing number

- Your credit limit.

- Any additional information, like the name of the financial institution associated with the card, your account number, a contact person, and so forth.

Fig. 13.1
Open the Create New Account dialog box by clicking My Accounts in the Activity Bar and then Create a New Account.

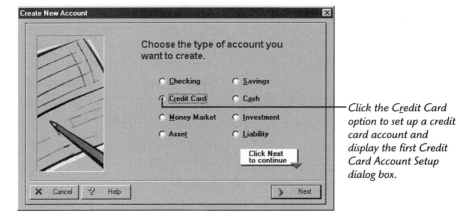

Click the Credit Card option to set up a credit card account and display the first Credit Card Account Setup dialog box.

Now, proceed through Quicken's EasyStep windows to enter a name for the credit card account and the balance shown on your last credit card statement with the statement date. Optionally, you can enter some additional information about your account.

You could always enter your credit card limit in previous versions of Quicken, but now with Quicken 6, it's important that you do this so Quicken can warn you when you approach your limit. If your limit is $5,000 and your balance is already at $4,950, then Quicken will give you an on-screen warning so that you're aware that you're approaching the limit.

If you're not setting up a Quicken Credit Card account or a credit card account that you'll use for online banking, then you'll see the first Summary window (see Figure 13.2) when you're finished entering credit card information.

Fig. 13.2
In the Summary window, you see all of the information that you've entered for your credit card account. Review it carefully and make changes here if you need to.

Click Next to see each Summary window. After you're finished reviewing the information in the Summary windows, click Done to add the credit card account to your Account List.

Q&A   ***I used to have an IntelliCharge credit card account and received my statements by disk or modem. What's different in this version of Quicken?***

The Quicken Credit Card replaces the IntelliCharge account; however, it's still used in the same way that you're used to. The Quicken Credit Card is now part of online banking and works like any other online bank account. Don't worry about what to do with your old IntelliCharge account. Quicken automatically updates your account to online banking during installation. In Chapter 26, I cover online banking and will show you how to handle Quicken Credit Card accounts.

Okay, now I can use my credit card account

Now that you have a credit card account set up in Quicken, you can start entering your credit purchases. Credit card accounts have registers just like bank accounts, cash accounts, and asset accounts. Figure 13.3 shows you the register for the Visa credit card account. Instead of the Payment and Deposit columns you see in bank accounts, though, credit card accounts have Charge and Payment columns.

Credit card transactions can be entered in your credit card register in one of two ways:

- Enter each credit card purchase as you make it. For example, when you come home from shopping, enter your credit card purchases. Even though you may have up to 30 days to pay for these purchases (depending on your statement cut-off date), they will be reflected in the outstanding balance in your credit card account.

- Wait until you get your credit card statement and then, at one time, enter all of the transactions that appear on your statement. This is not ideal, however. The problem that arises when you enter transactions from your statement is that not all of your purchases are reflected. For example, you may have made major credit purchases after your statement cut-off date that now won't be in your credit card account. The outstanding balance, therefore, is somewhat distorted. It will be more than Quicken says it is.

Fig. 13.3
Here's the register for a credit card account. Notice that it looks the same as other registers. You'll enter credit transactions just like you enter transactions in other registers.

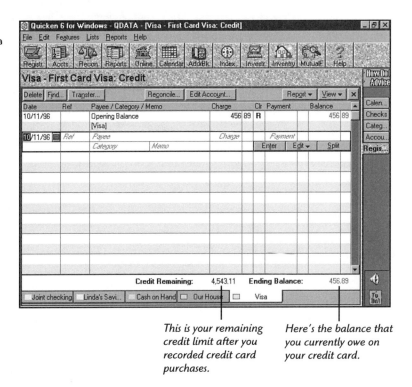

This is your remaining credit limit after you recorded credit card purchases.

Here's the balance that you currently owe on your credit card.

So what about credit card payments? Well, they're entered in the account that you use to pay your credit card bills. If you use your Joint Checking account to write the check to the credit card company, the payment is entered in that account.

Other credit card transactions, like finance charges or credits from returned items, are entered directly into the credit card account register. Or, if you choose to balance your credit card account, you can enter these transactions when you reconcile the account. (I tell you how to balance your credit card account a little later in this chapter.)

I'll enter each credit card purchase

Regardless of the method you choose to enter your credit card transactions, you'll enter them the same way. Here's what you'll need to enter for each transaction:

- The date that you made the credit purchase.

- In the Payee field, tell Quicken who you made the credit purchase with (if you made a credit card purchase at Sears, enter Sears in the Payee field).

- The amount of the credit purchase.

- The category that you want to assign to the purchase.

- A memo describing the purchase (optional).

Figure 13.4 shows a few credit card purchases entered in a credit card account register.

 TIP **You can edit and delete transactions in a credit card account** register the same way that you do in any other register. If you need some help working with transactions, go to Chapter 5 and read about editing and deleting transactions in the register.

Avoid high interest costs

Many credit cards allow you to get a cash advance and treat it as a credit purchase where you don't pay it back until you receive your statement. But don't make the mistake of assuming that the cash you receive is interest-free for up to 30 days (like purchases). Unfortunately, cash advances start accruing interest from the day the money is advanced to you. Sometimes, banks charge an additional fee of as much as 1.5 percent on cash advances. So, if you're in a bind for cash, take the advance but pay it back as soon as possible to avoid high interest costs.

Fig. 13.4
Credit card transactions are entered in the register just like transactions in other registers in Quicken. Be sure to assign a category to each of your credit card transactions.

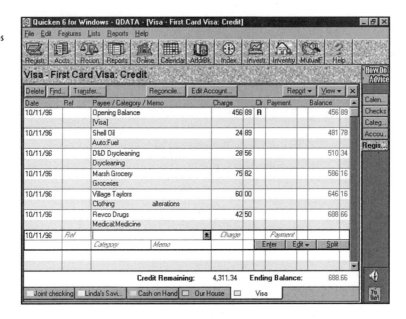

I can balance my credit card account to make sure it's accurate

In Chapter 7 I told you all about how important it is to balance your checkbook. Well, it's just as important to balance your credit card account against your statement to make sure that all of the transactions that appear are accurate. Balancing your credit card helps you uncover unauthorized uses of your credit card, errors recorded in your account by the credit card company, or any mistakes you may have made when you entered credit transactions. The time to balance your credit card account is before you make a payment. That way, you can first make sure that the balance is correct and then decide how much of the balance you want to pay.

Balancing your credit card account each month is not only smart, but easy. If you've already balanced your checking account with Quicken, then you know most everything you need to know to balance your credit card account. The steps are almost identical.

Entering information from your credit card statement

Enter information from your credit card statement first (see Figure 13.5).

Enter the total charges and cash advances as shown on your credit card statement.

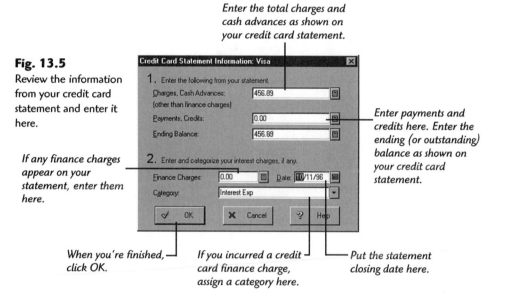

Fig. 13.5
Review the information from your credit card statement and enter it here.

If any finance charges appear on your statement, enter them here.

Enter payments and credits here. Enter the ending (or outstanding) balance as shown on your credit card statement.

When you're finished, click OK.

If you incurred a credit card finance charge, assign a category here.

Put the statement closing date here.

Marking transactions

Next, mark those transactions that appear on your statement (see Figure 13.6).

When your credit card account balances, you're ready to pay your bill.

 Q&A *What if my credit card account doesn't balance?*

First, go through all of your credit card transactions and make sure that you marked the right ones. Then, make sure that the transaction amounts are the same as those shown on your credit card statement. If it still doesn't balance, you may need to make an adjustment to your credit card account. When you click Finished, Quicken recommends the amount of the adjustment transaction to make your credit card account balance.

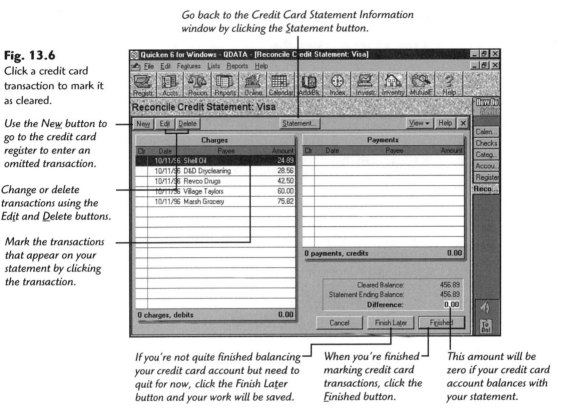

Go back to the Credit Card Statement Information
window by clicking the Statement button.

Fig. 13.6
Click a credit card
transaction to mark it
as cleared.

Use the New button to
go to the credit card
register to enter an
omitted transaction.

Change or delete
transactions using the
Edit and Delete buttons.

Mark the transactions
that appear on your
statement by clicking
the transaction.

If you're not quite finished balancing
your credit card account but need to
quit for now, click the Finish Later
button and your work will be saved.

When you're finished
marking credit card
transactions, click the
Finished button.

This amount will be
zero if your credit card
account balances with
your statement.

Time to make a payment

When you've successfully balanced your credit card account, Quicken
displays the Make Credit Card Payment dialog box shown in Figure 13.7.
Here's where you tell Quicken whether you want to make a payment now or
not. If you do want to make a payment, select the account to pay and how
you will make the payment.

Fig. 13.7

Are you ready to pay your credit card bill? If so, click Yes and Quicken enters the payment for you in the Write Checks window or the register for the bank account that you select.

How will you make the payment? By a Quicken check or a manual check?

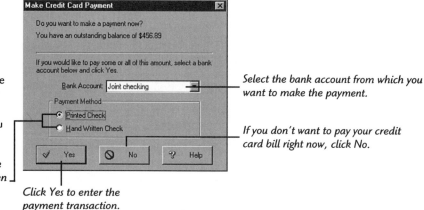

Select the bank account from which you want to make the payment.

If you don't want to pay your credit card bill right now, click No.

Click Yes to enter the payment transaction.

I like to pay the entire balance each month

If you don't want to incur any finance charges, you'll want to pay the entire credit card balance as shown on your statement. Click Yes in the Make Credit Card Payment dialog box that you saw in Figure 13.7. If you selected the Printed Check method, Quicken writes the check for you and displays it next in the Write Checks window (see Figure 13.8). If you selected to write a handwritten check, Quicken enters the transaction in the register.

Fig. 13.8

Quicken writes a check to pay off the balance that your credit card statement says you owe. To pay the entire balance, just record the check as is.

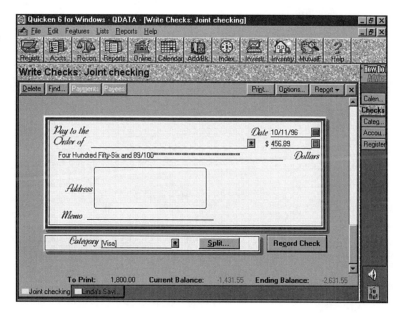

To pay off the balance on your credit card, just record the check in the Write Checks window or the transaction in the register. If you wrote a check in Quicken, all you have to do now is print the check. If Quicken entered a transaction in the register, write your handwritten check for the credit card balance now.

I don't want to pay the whole thing

If money's tight right now, you may not want to pay the entire balance on your credit card. With the exception of the American Express Card, you can make a minimum payment on credit cards. Beware though—if you only pay the minimum payment each month and continue to make credit purchases, you'll never get rid of your credit card debt!

So if you don't want to pay off your balance, decide how much you do want to pay and just edit the amount field in either the Write Checks window (see Figure 13.9) or the register. Then record the check or the transaction; it's that simple.

Fig. 13.9
If you don't want to pay your entire balance on your credit card, just change the amount that Quicken enters in the Amount field.

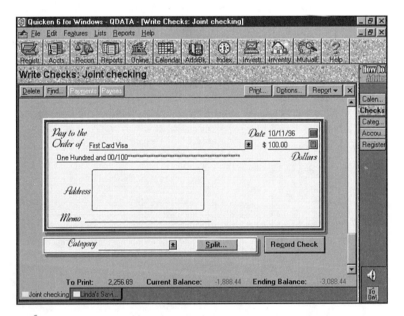

 TIP **If you have a Quicken credit card, be sure to read Chapter 26 to** learn how it works with online banking to download your data by modem.

14

Keeping Track of Your Loans

● **In this chapter:**

- Setting up your loans in Quicken

- Keeping track of loan information in one place

- Time to make a loan payment

- Is it a good time to refinance?

- Calculating loans

- Setting up and using other liability accounts

I've got a car loan, student loan, and a mortgage! How can I keep track of them all? And more importantly, when am I ever going to get them paid off?. . . . . ▶

You've probably figured out by now that if you've got a financial task that needs to be done, Quicken can do it for you. Keeping track of your outstanding loans is no exception. With Quicken, you can set up a loan for all your amortized loans, like your mortgage, car loan, or student loan. Then, Quicken keeps all of your amortized loans in one place so that at any time you can view a loan and its amortization schedule.

Plain English, please!

An **amortized loan** charges you a specified rate of interest on the part of the loan (or outstanding balance) that is unpaid. Each payment that you make on an amortized loan is divided into principal and interest; a certain portion reduces the principal balance of the loan and the remaining portion is the interest charge. When you set up an amortized loan, Quicken creates an amortization schedule that tracks the principal and interest portion of each loan payment.

If you have other types of liabilities that aren't amortized (like maybe a loan from a friend who isn't charging interest on the outstanding balance), you can set up a liability account to track the balance.

I want to set up a loan

Quicken's EasyStep Loan Setup dialog boxes make it easy for you to set up any amortized loan that you have. For each of your outstanding loans, you'll want to set up a separate loan in Quicken. Even though the EasyStep dialog boxes prompt you for the information Quicken needs to set up your loan, here's an overview of what you'll need to enter so that you can have this information ready:

- Original amount that was borrowed. This is the amount that you originally financed. If you borrowed $22,000 for a new car, for example, the original balance of the loan is $22,000.

 When EasyStep asks you for the original balance of your loan, don't make the mistake of entering the amount that you currently owe. If you do, your loan payment schedule will be way off. The amount that you currently owe subtracts all of the payments that you've already made on the loan and will be less than the original loan amount.

- **Date the loan was created.** This is the date that you signed the loan documents and became liable for the loan amount.

- **Balloon payment amount.** Your loan may not have a balloon payment due at the end of the loan term. If the terms of your loan require that you pay the unpaid principal balance at the end of the payment period, then you'll need to enter the balloon payment amount when you set up your loan.

- **Original length of the loan.** This is the period of time over which you make payments on the loan in order to pay off the original balance. Most mortgages are paid over 15 or 30 years. Car loans are usually paid over periods from 3 to 5 years.

- **Payment period for the loan.** This relates to the intervals over which you make payments on your loan, like monthly, semimonthly, and so forth.

- **Compounding period for the loan.** How is the interest calculated on your loan? This is the compounding period. Usually, interest is compounded monthly or semiannually. Contact your lender if you don't know the compounding period.

- **Current balance of the loan and date.** This is the principal amount that you still owe after you've made payments and the date of that balance. For a new loan, the current balance will also be the original loan balance. But, if you've made some payments on a loan, then the current balance will be less. If you don't know the current balance, you don't have to enter it. Quicken can calculate the current balance after you've entered all other loan information.

- **Date of next payment.** When are you supposed to make your next loan payment?

- **Amount of the next payment.** What payment amount will you be making the next time you make one? If you don't know the payment amount, Quicken can calculate it for you.

- **Interest rate of the loan.** This is the rate of interest that's charged on the outstanding principal balance of your loan. If the loan is a fixed rate loan, the interest rate will be constant. If it's a variable rate loan, enter the current rate of interest that's being charged.

- **Escrow amounts.** Portions of your loan payment may be to pay for things like real estate taxes, insurance, and so forth. The bank escrows, or holds, these funds for you until these amounts are due and then pays them for you.

TIP If you need to calculate a loan to find out what the payment amount is or the current interest rate, you can use Quicken's Loan Planner. The Loan Planner is a handy on-screen financial calculator that computes the variables of a loan. Later in this chapter, I show you how to use the Loan Planner.

Setting up your loan

So let's get started setting up your first loan in Quicken. First, you'll need to open the View Loans dialog box (see Figure 14.1) by clicking Home & Car in the Activity Bar and then selecting Set Up or Track an Existing Loan.

Fig. 14.1
In the View Loans window, you can set up a new loan, delete an existing loan, or view a loan that you've already set up.

Click the New button to open the first EasyStep Loan Setup dialog box.

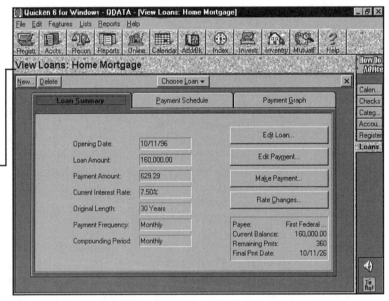

Next, click the New button to open the first EasyStep Loan Setup dialog box that you see in Figure 14.2. Get on your way to setting up a loan in Quicken by clicking the Next button.

Fig. 14.2
Here's the first
EasyStep Loan Setup
dialog box that will put
you on your way to
setting up a loan in
Quicken.

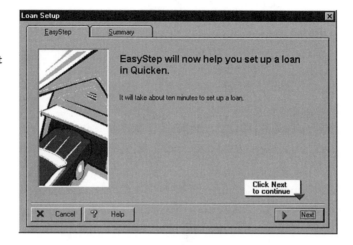

There is quite a bit of information that you'll need to enter to get your loan set up in Quicken. Basically, you'll need to:

- Tell Quicken whether you're setting up a loan for money you've borrowed or money you've lent to others.

- Set up a loan account that Quicken can use to track your loan. Select an existing liability account or, if there isn't an existing account in Quicken that represents this loan, type a name for the loan account using up to 30 characters, but not :] [/ | ^.

- Enter information for your loan, like the amount, loan period, and interest rate.

- Tell Quicken how you'll make payments on the loan.

As you complete each EasyStep Loan Setup dialog box, click the Next button to continue.

TIP **As you know by now, an outstanding loan is a liability. And as I've** advised you in other chapters, you need an account for all of your assets and liabilities if you want Quicken to determine your net worth. When you set up a loan in Quicken, a liability account automatically is set up for you. So, for each loan that you set up, Quicken sets up an associated liability account.

There will be some liability accounts, though, that you need to set up yourself. These are liabilities that aren't amortized, like an interest-free loan from a friend, income taxes payable, insurance premiums payable, accounts payable (for businesses), and so forth. Much later in this chapter, I show you how to set up liability accounts.

Reviewing your loan

Now that you've set up your loan account, entered loan information, and set up your loan payments, you can look through the next few Summary windows to review your loan. If there's some information that's not correct, change it now. When you see the last Summary dialog box (see Figure 14.3), click Done to set up your loan payments in Quicken.

Fig. 14.3
This is the Summary dialog box that shows the balance and payment information for your loan. Click Done when you're sure all loan information is correct.

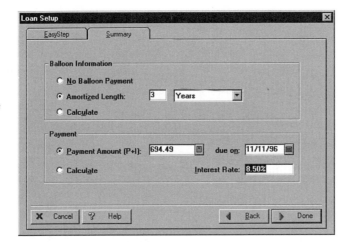

Adding your loan to Quicken

Now that you've entered all the loan and payment information, your loan is added to Quicken and appears in the View Loans window that you see in Figure 14.4.

Setting up loan payments in Quicken

Quicken has all of your loan information, except payment information, which you provide in the Set Up Loan Payment dialog box.

Click the E̲dit button to open a Split Transaction window so that you can enter any escrow amounts included in your loan payment. If you add escrow amounts, Quicken adds them to your total payment amount.

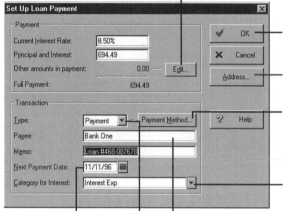

Click OK when you're finished setting up payments on your loan.

If you want to enter the payee's address so that it appears on checks, click the A̲ddress button.

Click the payment M̲ethod button to display the Select Payment Method dialog box where you can schedule the loan payment transaction, memorize it, or repeat it for online payments.

Now, select the category to assign to the interest portion of your loan payments. Here, I've selected to assign the category Interest Exp (Interest Expense) to interest on the car loan.

Your next payment date should already be entered for you; however, you can change it here if you need to.

Type the institution or person's name to whom you make loan payments.

Tell Quicken how you'll be making your loan payment each period. Here, I'm going to have Quicken print a check each time. You can also write a handwritten check and have Quicken enter it in your checking account register each time, or you can make your loan payment online.

Fig. 14.4
After you set up a loan in Quicken, you'll see it in the View Loans window.

Click here to see a list of all the loans you've set up in Quicken.

Click on these tabs to see more information for the current loan.

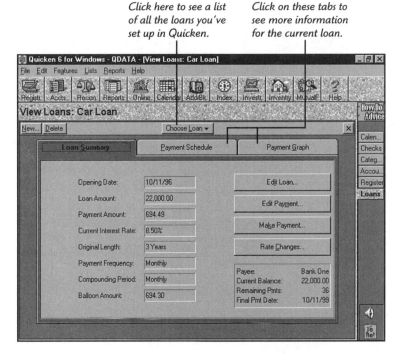

I need to make a change to a loan

Just like most things in Quicken, you can change them after they're entered or set up. So what if you need to change the name of the lender, the interest rate, the payment method, or delete a loan altogether? You can change any of these things from the View Loans window that you saw in Figure 14.4.

To change a loan, it first needs to be the current loan in the View Loans window. To make a loan the current loan, just click the Choose Loan button and select it from the list of loans that appears. In Figure 14.4, the current loan is the Car Loan.

Editing a loan

To change loan information, such as the original loan amount, the date the loan was opened, the length of the loan, and so forth, click the Edit Loan button in the View Loans window (refer to Figure 14.4). When you click this button, Quicken displays one of two Summary dialog boxes with the existing loan information. Just move to the appropriate box to change the information that you need to.

Changing the interest rate

If the loan that you set up in Quicken has a variable interest rate, then at some point the rate will change. So how do you deal with this? Simple. Just click the Rate Changes button in the View Loans window (refer to Figure 14.4) and Quicken displays the Loan Rate Changes dialog box shown in Figure 14.5. Here, you'll see all of the interest rates charged on your loan.

Fig. 14.5

Quicken keeps track of interest rate changes in the Loan Rate Changes dialog box.

To enter a new interest rate, click the New button to see the Insert an Interest Rate Change dialog box as shown in Figure 14.6. Enter the date that the new interest rate is in effect and the new rate. Quicken automatically calculates your new payment based on the changed rate.

Fig. 14.6

Enter a new interest rate on your variable rate loan and the date the new rate is in effect. Click OK to change the interest rate on the current loan.

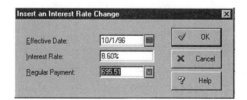

Changing loan payments

Need to change the payee on a loan, the payment method or type, or the category you've assigned to the interest portion of your payments? From the View Loans dialog box (refer to Figure 14.4), click the Edit Payment button. Quicken displays the Edit Loan Payment dialog box with the same information that you saw in the Set Up Loan Payment dialog box. Make your changes here.

Q&A ***What if I want to make a payment on a loan before I've scheduled it in Quicken?***

You can make a payment at any time, regardless of when it's scheduled in Quicken. From the Edit Loan Payment dialog box, there's a Pay Now button that lets you make an early payment. Or, from the View Loans dialog box, you can select the Make Payment button to make a regular payment on your loan now.

Deleting a loan

When do you think you'd delete a loan? Certainly, you'd delete a loan you inadvertently set up (maybe it isn't an amortized loan and should be set up as a liability account—we get to this later). But the time you'll be most happy to delete a loan is when it's paid off!

When you delete a loan, Quicken permanently removes all of the loan and payment information from the View Loans window. If your loan payment was set up as a scheduled transaction, it gets deleted from the Scheduled Transaction List; if it's a memorized payment, it gets removed from the Memorized Transaction List, too. You can select, however, whether or not Quicken deletes the associated liability account for the loan.

To delete a loan, first make the loan that you want to delete the current loan in the View Loans window (refer to Figure 14.4), and then click the Delete button. But not so fast—Quicken doesn't let you make a hasty decision here. You'll first see a confirmation message that tells you you're about to delete an amortized loan. Quicken also asks if you want to save the associated liability account or delete it.

If you want to delete the loan from the View Loans window and also delete the liability account, select Yes. If you want to delete the loan and delete the associated liability account in Quicken, select No. If you really don't want to delete the loan at all, select Cancel.

Time to make a loan payment

Undoubtedly, you'll have to make payments on the loans that you've set up in Quicken. So what happens when it's time to make a payment? Well, remember when you set up loan payments as you were setting up your loan? You selected how payments would be made—by a scheduled transaction, a memorized transaction, or online bill payment.

If you selected a scheduled transaction or to make loan payments online, then your payments are entered automatically by Quicken. Each time a payment is due, Quicken automatically writes a check or enters the transaction in the register for the account that you use to pay bills.

If you're using a memorized transaction to make loan payments, you'll have to recall the transaction each time a payment is due. I showed you how to recall memorized transactions in Chapter 9.

Regardless of how the loan payment is entered, Quicken divides the principal and interest portion of each payment. If part of your payment goes to other charges, like insurance or real estate taxes, Quicken also enters these and assigns the appropriate category to each. And as if Quicken didn't have enough to do when you make a loan payment, the program also updates your loan balance each time. So, you know at any given point how much you still owe on a loan.

You can make regular loan payments when they're due, make extra payments so that you reduce your loan faster, or pay off the entire balance of your loan.

Making a regular loan payment

When it's time to make a loan payment, Quicken will remind you if you've set up the payment as a scheduled transaction or an online payment. For this reason, I strongly urge you to use one of these payment methods so that you never forget to make that all-important loan payment. Lending institutions almost always charge significant late fees for payments that aren't made on time.

When Quicken reminds you to make a payment, it's pretty easy. When you start Quicken, you'll see a Scheduled Transaction Due dialog box, like the one in Figure 14.7, that tells you which payments are due. To select to make the payment now, click Record and Quicken enters the payment for you.

Fig. 14.7
When you start Quicken, you'll see a list of scheduled transactions that are due now. If you've set up payments on your loan as scheduled transactions, you'll see the loan payment in this list.

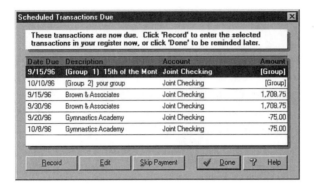

 TIP If you want to make a loan payment before Quicken thinks it's due, just select the loan in the View Loans dialog box and click the Make Payment button. This is helpful if you need to get all of your bills paid ahead of time (like when you go on vacation).

Making extra loan payments

In an amortized loan, payments are scheduled to be made at regular intervals, like every month, week, etc. Part of a loan payment reduces the principal balance of the loan and the other part is an interest charge (you also might have other charges or fees included in your payment).

If you want to make some extra principal payments, though, so that you can pay off your loan sooner, Quicken provides a way for you to do that. Just select the Make Payment button in the View Loans window to see the Loan Payment dialog box (see Figure 14.8). Click the Extra button to tell Quicken that you're not making the usual loan payment, but an extra one.

Fig. 14.8
Click Extra to prepay some of the principal balance on a loan.

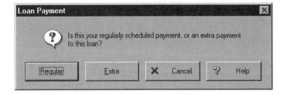

Quicken then shows you the Make Extra Payment dialog box where you can specify how much of the principal you want to pay now (see Figure 14.9). Most of the information in this dialog box is entered for you based on regular loan payments. You'll have to tell Quicken, however, the amount of the extra payment you'd like to make now. Enter this amount in the Amount field and click OK to have Quicken enter the payment for you.

Fig. 14.9
Tell Quicken how much the extra payment is and click OK.

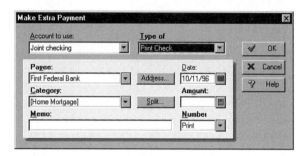

Paying off a loan

It's sure a happy day when you finally get a loan paid off—especially that 30-year mortgage.

If you're making the last payment on a loan, just make it as usual. It will reduce your loan balance to zero. If you're paying off a loan early, get the payoff amount from your lending institution first. Then select the Make Payment button in the View Loans window and change the payment to the payoff amount. When you record the edited payment, the loan balance should be reduced to zero.

After you've paid off a loan, you can delete it from the View Loans window if you want. If you delete the loan account, you can also select to delete the associated liability account, too.

Undoing a loan payment

What if you enter a loan payment inadvertently? Maybe you didn't really make last month's payment. If this happens, just delete the loan payment from the register for the account that you use to make loan payments (probably your checking account).

When you undo, or delete, a loan payment, Quicken removes the payment from the loan's payment schedule in the View Loans window and also deletes the payment from the associated liability account register. The outstanding loan balance will now be correct.

I'm refinancing a loan

With fluctuating interest rates, you might want to refinance a loan to take advantage of a lower interest rate. Refinancing home mortgages is very common because interest rates are otherwise locked in for long periods of time, like 15 or 30 years. If you took out a mortgage in the early-to mid-1980s, the interest rate may be twice the going rate today. If you refinance, your mortgage payments can be reduced significantly.

Before you jump into refinancing a loan, you should carefully evaluate the cost benefits. Many mortgage lenders charge closing costs and points when you refinance. When you take these extra costs into consideration, a lower interest rate may still not save you money in the long run.

 TIP **Don't be fooled into thinking that refinancing is the answer just** because you can secure a lower interest rate. With added closing costs and points to refinance a mortgage, you may not come out ahead at all. If your existing mortgage isn't very old and you incurred closing costs at the time you took out the mortgage, refinancing may not be prudent unless the new interest rate is significantly less than your current rate. And, if you're not planning to stay in your current house many more years, you probably won't be able to recoup the costs of refinancing.

Pay off your loan early!

You'd be surprised what a difference a few days makes on your outstanding loan balance. If you're contemplating paying off a loan early, check with your lending institution first to get the exact payoff amount as of the date that you're going to make the payment. Make sure that you are specific about the date that you'll be paying off the loan. So if you're paying the loan off today, get today's balance. If you're paying it off ten days from now, get the balance for that date. Just one or two days makes a difference in the amount of interest that has accrued on your loan.

Evaluating refinancing options

Quicken can help you determine whether refinancing your current loan makes sense with the Refinance Planner. Open the Refinance Planner (see Figure 14.10) by clicking Planning from the Activity Bar and then selecting the Use Financial Planning Calculators option. Now, from the Financial Planners dialog box, select Refinance and click OK.

In the Refinance Planner, you'll fill in your old payment and any escrow amounts, the amount you'll refinance, the new interest rate, and any closing costs. Instantly, you'll see the cost savings and how many months it will take to break even if you pay closing costs.

Fig. 14.10
The Refinance Planner calculated the payment difference on a $100,000 loan at 8%, refinanced at 6.75% with $2,500 in closing costs. You can see that it will take 29.36 months to break even because of the closing costs involved in refinancing.

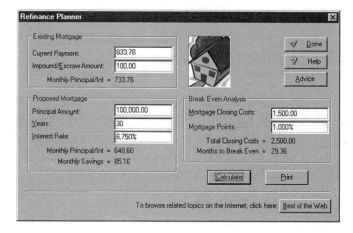

 TIP **If you want to print out the data that the Refinance Planner** just computed for you, click the Print button.

Refinancing a loan

So, you've decided that it makes economic sense to refinance a loan. If this is a loan you've set up in Quicken, you'll have to make some changes to reflect the new interest rate on the loan. Basically, you'll set up a new loan and then pay off—or delete—the old loan.

TIP 6 **Before refinancing, let Quicken help you request and** receive a copy of your credit report. Now, with Quicken 6, you can send a request online and receive a copy of your credit report by mail within five to seven days. To learn more about using Quicken to request a credit report, see Chapter 22.

Set up the new loan first with a name like Refinance or a name other than the name you used for the old loan. Since you're setting up the new loan first and the old loan still exists in Quicken, you can't use the same name.

TIP **If you want to use the same name for your refinanced loan as you** used for your old loan, just edit the new loan to change its name after you've deleted the old loan.

Your new loan should reflect the amount you're refinancing as the Original Balance and the date that you refinance the loan. After you've set up your new loan, Quicken creates a liability account for it.

Now you're ready to pay off the old loan. Remember, you just set up a loan for the amount that you refinanced. This amount should be the same as the outstanding balance of the old loan, right? For example, if your old loan started out at $100,000 but after a few years of payments is now $94,958.81, then the amount you refinance is also $94,958.81.

To pay off the old loan, first go to the register for your new liability account. So, if you called it Refinance, go to the Refinance account register. You should see only one transaction—the Opening Balance transaction. Move to this transaction and replace the words Opening Balance with the name of the lender who refinanced your loan.

Then, in the Category field, select the old account. What happens here is that you're decreasing the old loan account by the outstanding balance.

TIP **If your refinanced loan includes closing costs, enter those in the** Split Transaction dialog box when you're editing the new account register transaction.

Now that the old account has a balance of zero, you can delete the loan account from the View Loans window. When you delete the old account, you can choose whether you want to also delete its associated liability account. If you select to keep the liability account, it will show a zero balance with a complete record of all of your payments.

Calculating loans

If you're contemplating the purchase of a new home, car, or whatever, and want to see what the payments will be if you finance your purchase, use Quicken's Loan Planner. With the Loan Planner, you can enter a loan amount, interest rate, and loan period and instantly see your payments. Or, enter the payment that you can afford, the going interest rate, and a loan period, and the Loan Planner will tell you what purchase price you can afford based on those payments.

To use the Loan Planner, click Planning in the Activity Bar and then select the Use Financial Planning Calculators option. Quicken displays the Financial Planners dialog box where you select Loan to open the Loan Planner that you see in Figure 14.11. Fill in the Loan Planner and tell it what you want to compute—the Loan Amount or the Payment Per Period. Calculations are made instantly as you enter data in the Loan Planner. If you want to see a payment schedule for the loan scenario that you entered, click the Schedule button and Quicken shows you each payment, broken out into principal and interest until the loan's paid off.

 Get some expert financial advice by clicking the Advice button in the Loan Planner. You'll get financial advice, right on your screen, to help you make decisions regarding loans you may be contemplating.

And get quick access to the World Wide Web by clicking the Best of the Web button. Note that Quicken closes the Loan Planner before connecting to the World Wide Web. After you're connected, you can choose Web sites from these categories: College, Dollars & Sense, Investments, and Retirement & Taxes.

Click the <u>A</u>dvice button to get expert
financial counsel right on your screen.

Fig. 14.11
Using the Financial
Planner to calculate
the payment on a
$15,000 loan, at 7.5%,
for five years.

Change data in the Loan
Information section and
then click the <u>C</u>alculate
button to recompute the
loan amount or the
payment per period.

Get quick access to the World
Wide Web by clicking the <u>B</u>est of
the Web button where you can
travel to college, money matters,
investment, retirement, and tax
Web sites.

If you want to see a schedule of payments for the
life of the loan that you're calculating, click the
<u>S</u>chedule button.

What about other liabilities I have?

Up to now, you've been working with loans that are amortized. For amortized
loans, you set up a loan in Quicken that's added to the View Loans dialog box
(and then Quicken sets up an associated liability account for you). But you
won't set up a loan for other kinds of loans that aren't amortized, like an
interest-free loan, income taxes payable, and so forth.

For loans that aren't amortized, you'll set up a liability account only. Liability
accounts have registers just like other accounts in Quicken that track the
activity in the account. So, if you make a payment on a loan that you've set up
a liability account for, you can enter a transaction for the payment that
decreases the outstanding balance.

 Plain English, please!

Liabilities are debts, or the money that you're "liable" for. If you buy a
house and don't have enough money to pay for the whole thing (and who
does!), you pay what you can (that's called a down payment) and borrow
the rest (take out a mortgage). The mortgage is a liability because as long as
you have the house in your possession, you are liable to the mortgage
holder for the amount that you borrowed. 99

Q&A *Let me get this straight. If I have a loan, like my home mortgage, that charges interest on the unpaid balance, then I set up a loan account for it in Quicken, right? But if I want to track the amount that I owe for income taxes this year, even though my taxes aren't due until next April 15th, I set up a liability account for this liability.*

You're absolutely right. Just remember, if you have a loan that charges interest at regular intervals, then you'll track this loan in Quicken in a loan account and set it up in the View Loans dialog box. If you have other types of liabilities that you want to track, like your example of the income taxes payable, you'll set up a liability account for them.

Setting up a liability account

You've probably set up several different types of accounts in Quicken by now. I know that you set up a checking account when you first started using Quicken. Setting up a liability account is very similar. If you need some detailed explanation to the steps for setting up accounts, go back and read Chapter 2.

When you're ready to set up a liability account, click My Accounts from the Activity Bar and then select Create a New Account. When Quicken displays the Create New Account dialog box, click the Liability option to open the first Liability Account Setup dialog box. Then just follow the EasyStep instructions for setting up your liability account. You'll enter a name for the account, the starting date and balance, and other information that you might want to add about the account.

TIP When you set up a liability account, Quicken asks if you want to set up an associated loan account. If you're setting up a liability account for an unamortized loan, don't have Quicken set up a loan account for you. In the first part of this chapter you learned how to set up a loan account for those amortized loans that you have.

Working in the liability account register

After you've set up a liability account, you can begin using its register to track your liability. Figure 14.12 shows the Taxes Payable liability account register with some transactions that affect the outstanding balance in the account. Enter transactions in a liability account the same way that you enter transactions in other Quicken accounts.

Fig. 14.12
Here's a liability account set up to track income taxes that are estimated throughout the year and then paid on April 15th.

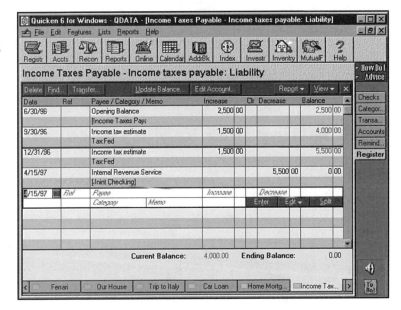

15

Creating Your Budget

● **In this chapter:**

- **Putting together a budget**

- **Save as many budgets as you'd like**

- **Simplify your budget with supercategories**

- **Look at how I'm doing with my budget**

Tired of not being able to eat lunch out at the end of the month? Did you miss that movie last month because you were out of money? Quicken's budget feature could solve these problems and more . . . . ➤

Most of us know we need a budget but don't want to take the time to sit down and put it on paper. We may have an idea in our minds about how much we should be spending, but really don't have an easy way to monitor it. The thought of a budget to many is unpleasant. So budgeting gets an undeserved bad reputation.

Most think of a budget as financial handcuffs, an obstacle to enjoyment, and just a plain drag on their financial freedom. Nothing is farther from the truth. Actually, with a realistic, well-planned budget, you'll feel more comfortable buying that new suit, taking a vacation, or making an investment in the stock market. When you know that you can afford something because it's provided for in your budget, it makes spending money less stressful. Just think of a budget as a game plan for how you're going to make and spend money. You can be as creative as you want, but most importantly, be realistic. With Quicken, budgeting is painless. There are lots of helpful features that make setting up a budget quick and easy. And when you're ready to see how well you're sticking to your budget, Quicken provides some handy tools to take a look.

Do I really need a budget?

If you make and spend money, then you do need a budget to make sure that you don't spend more than you make. And even if you're very financially responsible and would never dream of spending money you don't have, you still need a budget to help you allocate and prioritize your spending.

So I guess the answer to the question on budgeting, is that everyone can benefit by setting up, and living within, a budget. And now that you're using Quicken, setting up a budget couldn't be easier.

Setting up a budget is easy

You're about to find out how easy creating a budget is in Quicken. Here's an overview of the simple steps you'll go through to set up your budget:

1 Open the Budget window.

2 Change the layout of the Budget window, if necessary.

3 Enter your budget amounts.

4 Save your budget.

First, open the budget window

Budgeting starts in (where else?) the Budget window. The Budget window is like a spreadsheet with rows for each category that you use and columns for each period in which you want to budget.

When you're ready to set up your budget, click Planning from the Activity Bar and then select the Budget by Spending option to open the Budget window.

Changing the layout in the Budget window

Notice that the Budget window is set up to budget on a monthly basis. Each column in the Budget window represents a month in the year. But what if you don't want to budget monthly? Maybe you want to budget on a quarterly or annual basis instead. Or, maybe you want to budget for transfers from one account to another.

You may need to change the layout of the Budget window so that it meets your needs before you start entering budget amounts. Just click the View button in the button bar to open the View menu (see Figure 15.1) and select what you want shown in columns and in rows in the Budget window. In Figure 15.2, you see that I changed the Budget window to budget on a quarterly basis and to include rows for transfers.

A close look at the Budget window

All your budget information is entered in the Budget window.

Fig. 15.1
The View menu lets you change what Quicken shows in columns and in rows in the Budget window.

The Budget Window

Edit button
Is used to enter data in the Budget window.

Save button
Saves the data entered in the current Budget window.

Print button
When you're ready to print your budget, click this button.

New button
Lets you create a whole new budget.

View button
If you want to change what appears in the Budget window, click this button.

Restore button
Click Restore to change the current budget back to the way it was the last time you saved it.

Close button
Closes the current Budget window.

Cells
The intersection of a column and a row is called a cell. Budget amounts are entered into cells in the Budget window.

Scroll bars
Use the scroll bars to move up and down or right and left in the Budget window. As you move through the Budget window with the scroll bar, Quicken shows you where you are in the window by displaying the category name in a box to the left of the scroll bar.

Categories
Each of these rows represent the categories that you use in Quicken.

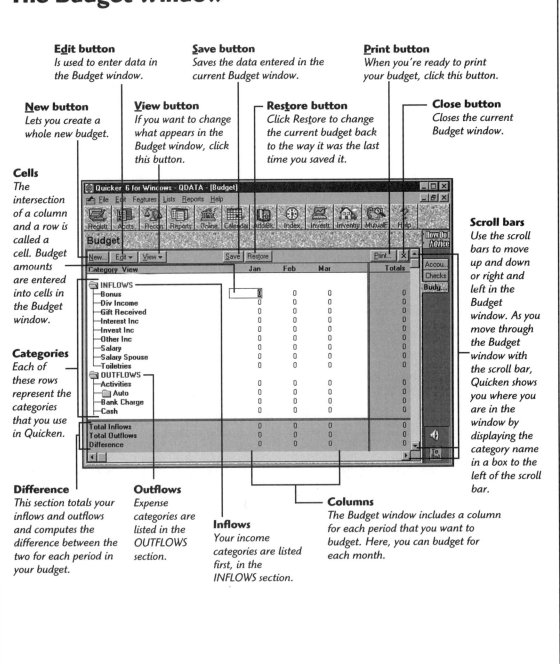

Difference
This section totals your inflows and outflows and computes the difference between the two for each period in your budget.

Outflows
Expense categories are listed in the OUTFLOWS section.

Inflows
Your income categories are listed first, in the INFLOWS section.

Columns
The Budget window includes a column for each period that you want to budget. Here, you can budget for each month.

Fig. 15.2
In this Budget window,
I can budget on a
quarterly basis.

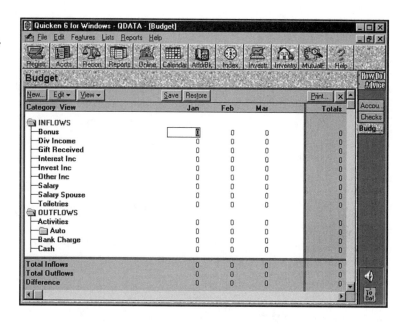

After the Budget window is laid out the way you want it, you're ready to enter
budget amounts.

Q&A   ***I see from Figure 15.1 that I can select to show
supercategories in the Budget window. What are
supercategories and how are they used?***

Supercategories group categories into broad levels for budgeting purposes. When you have several categories that are similar, you can group
them together so that you don't have to enter a separate budget amount
for each. For example, you may have several entertainment categories that
you use, like Movies, Sporting Events, Videos, and Theater. Instead of setting
up budget amounts for each category, you can set up a supercategory called
Entertainment and set up one budget amount for all entertainment
expenses. Later in this chapter, I show you how to set up supercategories
and assign categories to them.

Entering budget amounts

So now you're ready to start entering budget amounts in the Budget window.
You can enter budget amounts in one of two ways—automatically with
previous Quicken data, or by entering amounts yourself in each cell within
the Budget window.

Quicken can enter amounts automatically

When you enter budget amounts automatically, Quicken looks at data from a prior period and copies those amounts in the appropriate column and row in the Budget window. For example, if you used Quicken last year you'll have a year's worth of income and expenses entered in account registers. You can have Quicken look at your actual income and expenses from the prior year and base this year's budget on those amounts. So, if you earned $50 per month in interest income last year, Quicken will enter $50 for each month in the Interest Inc category in this year's budget.

You can select to have Quicken enter the actual amounts from the prior period into the same month in this year's budget. Or, Quicken can average the actual amounts from the prior period and enter an equal amount into each month that you're budgeting.

Q&A ***If I have Quicken enter amounts in my budget automatically, can I make any changes?***

Yes. No matter how budget amounts are entered in the Budget window, you can change any of the amounts at any time. Just move to the cell with the budget amount that you want to change and type in the new amount. You can change just one amount or all budget amounts.

To enter budget amounts automatically, click the Edit button in the Budget window button bar to open the Edit menu. From here, you can select Autocreate to have Quicken enter budget amounts automatically from previous data.

Select the Autocreate option to open the Automatically Create Budget dialog box (see Figure 15.3). Give Quicken some instructions for creating your budget and click OK.

How do you want the values that Quicken finds from the previous period to be rounded? By $1, $10, or $100?

Here's where you tell Quicken which period to base your current budget on. Type in the From and To dates or use the mini-calendar to select the dates.

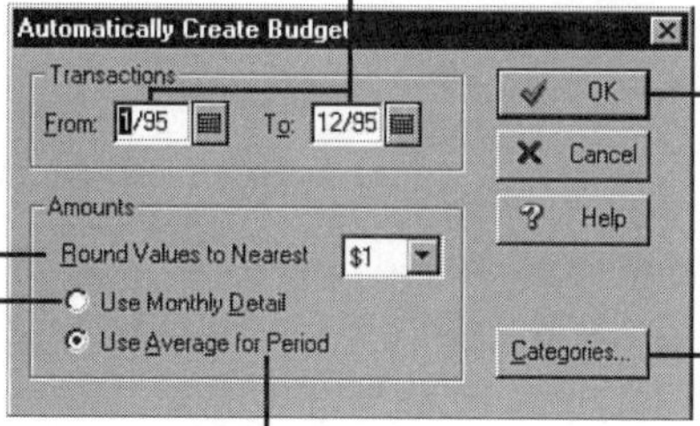

Fig. 15.3
Although Quicken creates your budget automatically, you still need to provide a few instructions first.

Click OK and Quicken automatically enters budget amounts in the Budget window.

If you want to have Quicken enter budget amounts automatically for only selected categories, click the Categories button. Quicken shows you all your categories so that you can select the ones that you want Quicken to enter budget amounts for.

Do you want Quicken to use the actual amounts from the previous period and enter them in the same months in your current budget? So, if you spent $250 last year in March for groceries, Quicken will enter $250 as this year's budget amount for the category Groceries in March.

You can have Quicken calculate average amounts from the previous period and enter them in the current budget. If you spent $2,400 last year (12 months) on utilities, Quicken averages the $2,400 over the number of months in the previous period and enters that amount into the current year budget. So Quicken would enter $200 in each month for the category Utilities.

Or, you can enter amounts manually

If you just started using Quicken, then you won't have any previous data that Quicken can look at to automatically enter your budget amounts this year. In this case, you'll need to enter your budget amounts yourself. This is not as difficult as it may sound. Just think of the Budget window as a spreadsheet with columns and rows for you to enter data. Enter amounts just as you would in a spreadsheet, like Excel or 1-2-3.

To enter a budget amount for a category, first move to the row for that category; then, decide in which period you want to enter the amount. If you're budgeting monthly, you probably first want to enter a budget amount for January, then February, and so forth. Use the Tab key or your mouse to move to the correct column. After you enter a budget amount, press the down arrow key to move down one row at a time.

TIP You don't have to enter budget amounts for expenses as a negative number. When you type an amount in an expense category cell, Quicken automatically converts the amount to a negative when you press Enter or Tab.

Quicken gives me lots of budget shortcuts

If you have a lot of categories that you use in Quicken, entering your budget amounts may become tedious and time-consuming. Quicken provides several shortcuts for entering budget amounts quickly and easily. These shortcuts are all found in the Edit menu that you see in Figure 15.4. Here is how these handy timesavers work:

Fig. 15.4
Click the Edit button in the Budget window button bar to open the Edit menu.

- **2-Week.** Select 2-Week to budget for items that you receive or pay on a biweekly basis. Use this to budget your paycheck if you receive it every two weeks.

- **Copy All.** This option is really not used for entering budget amounts in the Budget window. Use the Copy All option to copy the current budget amounts to the Windows Clipboard. You can then paste your budget into a spreadsheet program.

- **Clear Row.** The Clear Row option erases all of the budget amounts in the current row. This saves you time if there are amounts entered for a category and you later decide the budget amounts should be zero.

- **Clear All.** If you need to erase the current Budget window so that you can start, select the Clear All option.

- **Fill Row Right.** If there's an amount that you want to copy to every cell in the current row, select Fill Row Right. Quicken copies the amount from the current cell to each cell to the right in the entire row. To fill in $100 in each month for the category Charity, enter $100 in the January cell and then select Edit, Fill Row Right, and then select Yes.

- **Fill Columns.** To fill in columns to the right with the same budget amounts from the current column, select E̲dit, Fill C̲olumns and then select Y̲es.

Saving your budget

Just click the S̲ave button in the button bar and Quicken saves your current budget. The next time that you open the Budget window, the budget you just saved will appear.

If you forget to save your budget and try to close the Budget window or even exit Quicken, you'll be reminded that you've just made some changes that need to be saved. If you want to save the changes, click Y̲es. If you want the budget to remain the way it was before you made changes, select not to save the budget by clicking N̲o.

Q&A *I just made some changes to my budget that I don't want to keep. Is there a way to get back to my original budget?*

Yes. Click the Re̲store button in the Budget window button bar and you'll see the budget as it was the last time that you saved it. If you made your changes, however, and then saved them, you won't be able to get back to your original budget.

TIP **With Quicken, you can save multiple budgets. You may want to** create more than one budget based on different scenarios. Use one budget if you stay in your current job, and another if you decide to take that new job with the 20 percent pay increase. Later in this chapter, I show you how to create more than one budget.

Here's what supercategories are all about

In a Q & A earlier in this chapter, I told you a little about supercategories. Supercategories are used to group similar categories to make budgeting less burdensome. When the categories in your Budget window are grouped into supercategories, your budget becomes much easier to set up and work with.

You don't have to micromanage those smaller categories because they'll be lumped into a larger supercategory. You'll find four supercategories already set up in Quicken: Discretionary, Non-Discretionary, Other Income, and Salary Income. These are common supercategories that everyone can use.

 Plain English, please!

Some of your income and expenses is considered **discretionary** and some is considered **non-discretionary**. Discretionary items are those that you can make choices about or control the amounts of. Examples of discretionary items are entertainment, clothing, dining, and so forth. These are discretionary because you can make a conscious choice about how much you'll spend in these areas. Non-discretionary items, however, are those that you have little control over, like your mortgage payment, rent payment, child care fees, insurance premiums, and so forth.

You can set up other supercategories, if you'd like. Then, you can assign categories to each supercategory that you set up. After you've set up the supercategories that you want to use in your budget, you can change the Budget window to show categories grouped by supercategory so that you can enter budget amounts for each supercategory.

Setting up supercategories

Before you set up supercategories, review your category list and maybe even your actual amounts for last year. This review will help you decide which categories should be grouped into supercategories.

When you're ready to set up a supercategory, select Edit, Supercategories to open the Manage Supercategories window shown in Figure 15.5. Set up a new supercategory by clicking the New button. Then give your supercategory a name using as many as 19 characters.

Quicken has already assigned one of the predefined supercategories to each of your categories.

All of the supercategories that have been set up are in this list.

Fig. 15.5
Set up a new supercategory or assign categories to supercategories in the Manage Supercategories dialog box.

Here's the list of all the categories that you currently use.

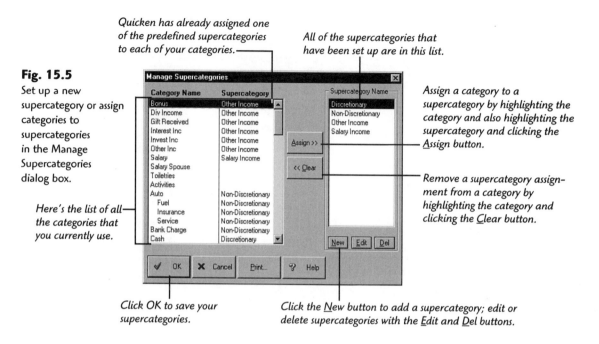

Assign a category to a supercategory by highlighting the category and also highlighting the supercategory and clicking the Assign button.

Remove a supercategory assignment from a category by highlighting the category and clicking the Clear button.

Click OK to save your supercategories.

Click the New button to add a supercategory; edit or delete supercategories with the Edit and Del buttons.

After you've set up a supercategory, assign categories to it by highlighting the supercategory and the category that you want to assign and clicking the Assign button. Figure 15.5 shows that the category Bonus is assigned to the Other Income supercategory.

Showing supercategories in the Budget window

After your supercategories are set up and you've assigned the appropriate categories to them, you'll want to change the Budget window to include a row for supercategories. Do this by selecting View, Supercategories.

Figure 15.6 shows the Budget window after the view has been changed to include a row for supercategories. Notice that the Budget window is in Supercategory View. When you saw the Budget window earlier in this chapter, it was shown in Category View.

Fig. 15.6
Showing the
Budget window in
Supercategory
View.

*Click the folder button
for a supercategory to
show each category
assigned to it.*

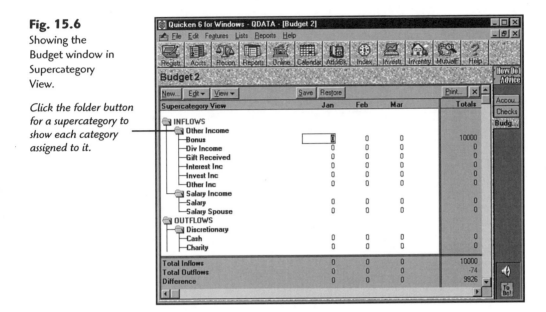

I want to create more than one budget

Even though there's only one Budget window, you can create more than one budget in Quicken. This feature in Quicken works great if you'd like to create multiple budgets to take into consideration different scenarios, like a job change, college expenses for your son, or retirement.

To create another budget, select View, Other Budgets to open the Manage Budgets dialog box that you see in Figure 15.7.

Fig. 15.7
Click the Create
button if you want to
set up another budget.
If you want to work
with a budget that
you've already set up,
highlight the budget
and click Done.

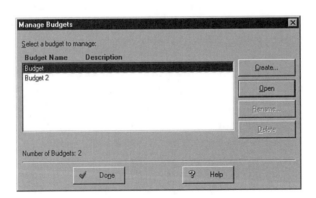

From the Manage Budgets dialog box you can either create a new budget or, if you've already set up more than one budget, select the budget that you want to work in.

If you've already created another budget, you'll see it in the Manage Budgets dialog box. To work in that budget, highlight it and click Done.

If you're creating a new budget, click the Create button to see the Create Budget dialog box shown in Figure 15.8. Here, you assign a name to your budget, a description (if you want), and tell Quicken how to create the budget. Click OK to open a new Budget window

Enter a name for your new budget.

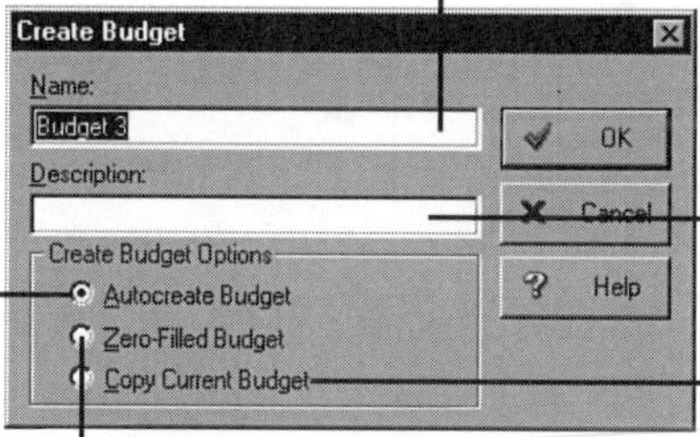

Fig. 15.8
Assign a name to your new budget and tell Quicken how to create it.

If you want to add a description of the new budget, enter it here.

You can create the new budget automatically based on previous data in Quicken.

Copy the budget amounts from the Budget window in which you're currently working.

Or open a new Budget window without budget amounts. You'll start from zero and create your budget from there.

I want to see how well I'm sticking to my budget

You set up a budget in Quicken and have been diligent about entering all of your financial activity and now you're anxious to see how well (or not so well) you're doing. Or, maybe you're not anxious at all. Assessing your budget can be like stepping on the scale in the morning. It's tough to do when you know you just had that caramel torte the night before; it also may not be pleasant looking at your budget after a recent splurge at the shopping mall. In either case, you know it ain't gonna look good! But you have to face up to it so that you can get back on track (with your eating and your spending).

Quicken provides a few tools that you can use to quickly assess the progress you're making with your budget. You can create a Monthly Budget Report that shows your budgeted amounts right alongside your actual amounts.

Then there's the Budget Variance Graph that charts budget variances in a bar graph. And finally, you can monitor your budget using the Progress Bar that shows your actual income or expenses for a single category compared to budgeted amounts through the current month, quarter, or year.

 Plain English, please!

> A **variance**, when talking about budgets, is the difference between actual amounts and budgeted amounts. There are positive and negative variances. A positive variance occurs when actual income exceeds budgeted income or actual expenses are less than budgeted expenses. You have a negative variance when actual income is less than budgeted income and actual expenses exceed budgeted expenses.

Creating a budget report

You're going to learn the ins and outs of Quicken's reports in Chapter 18, but for now, I'd like to show you how you can quickly create a Budget Report so that you can see how well you're doing with your budget.

Create a Budget Report by clicking Reports from the Activity bar and then selecting Show Me a Graph or Report of My Finances. Quicken shows you the EasyAnswer Reports & Graphs dialog box (see Figure 15.9) with the reports that you can create to answer some basic personal finance questions. See the one that says, "Did I meet my budget?" This is the one you'll want to select. Decide which period you want to assess, like Did I meet my budget last month, last quarter, last year, and so forth, by making a selection from the drop-down list. Then click the Show Report button to see the report on your screen (see Figure 15.10).

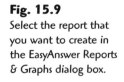

Fig. 15.9
Select the report that you want to create in the EasyAnswer Reports & Graphs dialog box.

Select the Did I meet my budget? question to create a budget report.

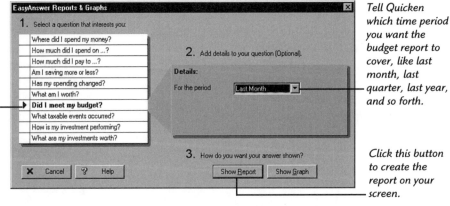

Tell Quicken which time period you want the budget report to cover, like last month, last quarter, last year, and so forth.

Click this button to create the report on your screen.

Fig. 15.10
Here's a Budget Report for the month of September as shown on your screen. As you can see, Quicken lists each category, its actual amount, budgeted amount, and the difference between actual and budget.

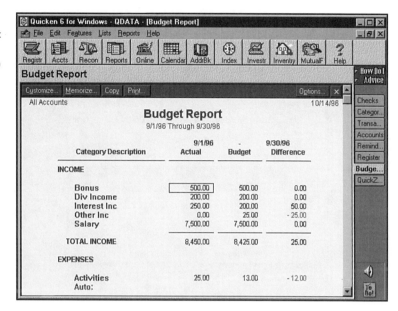

Use the scroll bar to move up and down the report to see all categories. If you want to print your Budget Report, click the Pri_n_t button while the report is displayed on your screen. To remove the Budget Report from your screen, click the close (X) button.

Looking at a budget graph

Quicken has some really neat graphing features that help you assess your financial situation, but more specifically, the progress you're making with your budget. You're not going to learn everything you need to know about graphing in Quicken from this chapter (read Chapter 19 for the unabridged discussion of graphs). Like with the Budget Report, I want to show you how you can create a graph that shows you how you're doing with your budget.

Here's how you can create a graph that compares your actual and budgeted data. Go to the EasyAnswer Reports & Graphs dialog box that you saw in Figure 15.9. Be sure that you've selected the Did I meet my budget? report option, as well as the time period that you want the graph to cover. Now, instead of choosing to show a report, click the Show Graph button. Quicken creates a graph on your screen, similar to the one you see in Figure 15.11.

Fig. 15.11
The Budget Variance Graph compares actual and budgeted amounts in two bar graphs—one for income and one for expenses.

This graph shows your actual vs. budget variances by month.

Here, the actual amount and the budgeted amount are graphed for five categories.

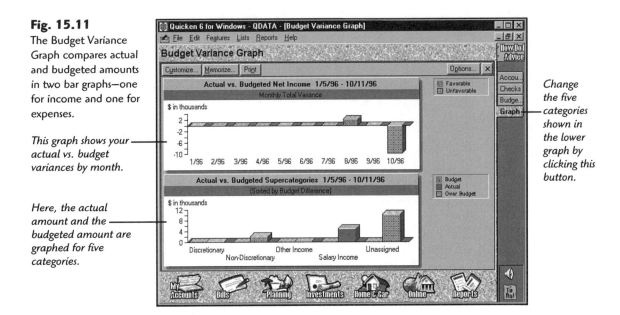

Change the five categories shown in the lower graph by clicking this button.

You can print the Budget Variance Graph by clicking the Print button or remove it from your screen by clicking the Close button.

Monitoring your budget with the Progress Bar

Quicken's Progress Bar is one more handy tool that you can use to monitor your budget. The Progress Bar (when you select to use it) is displayed at the bottom of your screen and monitors two categories or supercategories for you. Let's say that you're really worried about how much you've been spending on dining out and entertainment, both of which are discretionary expenses that you could easily cut back on. You can select to have your Dining category and your Entertainment category monitored by the Progress Bar so that you can see your actual dining and entertainment expenses as compared to your budgeted expenses for the current month, quarter, or year.

Here's how you get the Progress Bar to appear on your screen. Choose Features, Planning, Progress Bar.

Now you're probably wondering how I selected the two categories that I wanted to monitor with the Progress Bar. See the Cust button on the right end of the Progress Bar? Click this button to see the Customize Progress Bar dialog box. From here, you can select the category for the left gauge by clicking the Choose Category button; click the other Choose Category button to select the category for the right gauge. Notice that you also can select which time period is monitored by selecting one from the Date Range drop-down list. When you've made your selections in the Choose Category dialog box, click OK to begin monitoring the category that you selected.

TIP **Want a quick peek at the budget amount for a monitored cat-egory?** Just point to the gauge in the Progress Bar (the mouse pointer changes to a magnifying glass) and double-click. Quicken opens the Budget window and highlights the budget amount for the category being monitored.

Q&A *I like using the Progress Bar to monitor my budget, but it's just so darned big that it gets in my way. Is there any way to make it smaller?*

Yes. You can choose to not show the labels above the gauges. Do this by clicking the Cust button and then clicking the Show Labels option to turn it off. The absence of labels reduces the size of the Progress Bar by about half.

Part IV: Analyzing Your Finances

16

Staying on Top of Your Investments

● **In this chapter:**

- ● **Set up your investments in Quicken**

- ● **Use Quicken to track your investments**

- ● **Use mutual fund investment accounts**

- ● **Analyze investments with reports**

- ● **Use online services to update investments**

- ● **One-click access to the Quicken Web site**

Keep track of that stock certificate your grandfather gave you when you were born, or manage a diverse portfolio. Either way, you can use Quicken to monitor your investments and to keep you informed of changes and trends. . . . . ▶

One of the main reasons people purchase programs like Quicken is to monitor their investments. Keep all your investment records in one place with Quicken and you always can be assured of getting a complete, up-to-the-minute summary of all your investment activities.

What types of investment accounts can I set up?

Quicken lets you choose between two types of investment accounts:

- Regular investment accounts keep track of the market value of multiple securities, the number of shares you own, and the cash balance.

- Mutual fund investment accounts keep track of the number of shares you own and the market value of individual mutual funds.

Create a separate account for each mutual fund you own, and set up one regular investment account to track all your other investments. If you prefer, you can create more than one regular investment account to group investments. For example, you may want all the investments held by one broker in one account. Or you may want to track one investment in an account by itself.

I want to set up a regular investment account

Keep track of one or more securities in a regular investment account. Much like your check register, the register for your regular investment account keeps track of increases and decreases in the value of your investment and presents a balance showing the amount in the account.

To set up a regular investment account, click Investments from the Activity Bar and then choose the Enter a New Investment option. Then click OK to see the first in a series of EasyStep Investment Account Setup dialog boxes (see Figure 16.1). Here, you enter a name for your new investment account (as many as 30 characters, excluding] [/ | ^ :) and an account description. Click the Next button to continue.

TIP **Notice in the Investment Account Setup dialog box that there's an** EasyStep tab and a Summary tab. If you want Quicken to walk you through the investment account setup, just keep clicking the Next button at the bottom of each dialog box. If you'd rather not go through all these steps, you can click the Summary tab to go straight to the Summary dialog box where you can enter all the investment account information and save yourself some time.

Fig. 16.1

Assign an account name and description to your new investment account.

In the next Investment Account Setup dialog box, click the Yes option if your investment account works like a checking account—in other words, if you write checks and withdraw cash from your investment account just like in your checking account. If not, click the No option. Click Next again to keep going.

The next dialog box is where you tell Quicken the kind of securities you'll be tracking in your new investment account. So, because you're setting up a regular investment account, click the Stocks, bonds, or several mutual funds option. If you select the One mutual fund option, Quicken makes this a mutual fund account. Now, click Next again.

In the next Investment Account Setup dialog box, you are asked whether this is a tax-deferred account. An account is tax-deferred if its income is not currently subject to taxation. So, if you will be using your new investment account to track 401(k), IRA, Keogh, 403(b), or SEP-IRA investments, choose Yes. If the income you earn is taxable, choose No.

When you click Next, Quicken shows you the Summary dialog box with all of the information that you just entered for your new investment account (see Figure 16.2). In the Summary dialog box, make sure the information entered agrees with your expectations for this account. If you want, you can click the Info button to enter some additional information about this account such as the name and telephone number of your broker or other comments. You can also click the Tax button to designate with which part of your tax return the income from this account is associated. You then have the capability to merge your information from Quicken with a tax software program, such as TurboTax.

Click Done to finish setting up your new investment account. In the next section Quicken can help you set up the securities in your account.

Fig. 16.2
Here's the information that you entered for your new investment account. Look over it carefully to make sure it's correct.

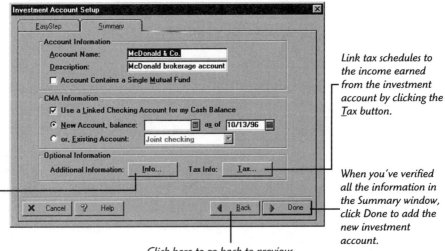

Link tax schedules to the income earned from the investment account by clicking the Tax button.

If you want to enter additional information about the investment account, click here.

When you've verified all the information in the Summary window, click Done to add the new investment account.

Click here to go back to previous Investment Account Setup windows.

I'm ready to enter my securities

If you've just set up a new investment account, Quicken displays a series of Investment Setup dialog boxes that help you set up securities in your account. Click the Next button at the first dialog box to proceed. You'll see another Investment Setup dialog box where you enter information about the security (see Figure 16.3). Here, you enter the security name (using as many as 30 characters), ticker symbol (the symbol used in the stock exchange columns of a newspaper), and indicate the type of security (<u>S</u>tock, <u>M</u>utual Fund, <u>B</u>ond). As with other EasyStep windows, click the Next button to continue.

Fig. 16.3
After you set up a new investment account, Quicken helps you set up your securities. Enter the name and ticker symbol of the security and tell Quicken what kind of security it is.

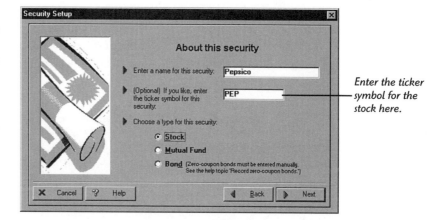

Enter the ticker symbol for the stock here.

Next, there's some optional information that you can tell Quicken. In the Investment <u>G</u>oal box, select your long-range goal for the investment. Options include: College Fund, Growth, High Risk, Income, and Low Risk.

In Quicken 6, you can organize your securities by a preset list of asset classes. Then, when you create reports or graphs, you can sort and subtotal your investments by asset class. For example, you can group bonds together into global or domestic asset classes. Investment reports and graphs that you create in Quicken will subtotal the value of bonds into these two classes. To assign a security to an asset class, click the arrow in the Asset Class drop-down list and select from these options: Domestic Bonds, Large Cap Stocks, Small Cap Stocks, Global Bonds, International Stocks, Money Market, and Other.

Now, you need to choose a start date for tracking the security that you're setting up. Choose to start tracking today, the end of last year, or the date you purchased the security.

You're almost finished entering the security. Quicken now needs to know how many shares you own, the cost per share, and any commissions you paid when you purchased the security. Now, in Quicken 6, you can enter share and cost per share numbers up to six decimal places. So, if you own 200.123456 shares of a security, you can enter that precisely. Or, if you paid $25.567855 per share, Quicken will accept this price without rounding.

You're finished entering information about the security that you're adding to your new investment account. If you have other securities to add, click the Yes option when Quicken asks if you'd like to add more securities to this account. Otherwise, click No.

If you're not adding other securities, Quicken shows you the Summary window, like in Figure 16.4, with the security name, type, number of shares, and total value. You also see the name of the investment account that the security will be added to. Click Done to add the security to your investment account.

Fig. 16.4
Here's a recap of the security that you just entered. Click Done and this security is added to the investment account shown in the Account Name box.

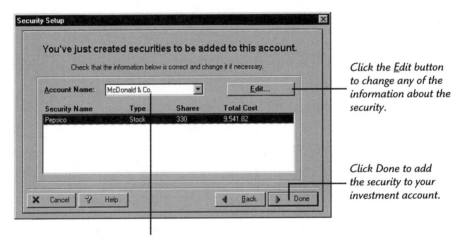

Click the Edit button to change any of the information about the security.

Click Done to add the security to your investment account.

Here's the investment account where the security will be added.

TIP **You've just entered a security after you set up your first investment account. But what about entering securities if you've already set up investment accounts in Quicken?**

Just click Investments in the Activity Bar and then select Enter a New Investment. Quicken will ask you if you want to set up a new security or a new investment account. Tell Quicken that you want to set up a new security in an existing account and you'll see the same Investment Setup windows that you saw when you set up your first investment account (see Figures 16.1, 16.2, and 16.3).

And, you can always just enter a new security name in an investment account register as you're entering a transaction. When Quicken doesn't find the security in the Security List, a Set Up Security window will open so that you can enter information about the security.

Here's the difference in a mutual fund investment account

With a mutual fund account, you record your starting balance in the fund, then you periodically record changes in your fund balance based on the purchase of additional shares or the redemption of shares. When you get a statement in the mail from your mutual fund, you can update your Quicken account register as well.

Set up a mutual fund investment account in much the same way you set up a regular investment account: click the One mutual fund option when asked what kind of securities will be included in the investment account. After you've finished setting up the mutual fund account, Quicken gives you an opportunity to enter the number of shares you own in the mutual fund, and the price per share in the Create Opening Share Balance dialog box (see Figure 16.5). Enter this information, then click OK. Your new money market account register is displayed.

Fig. 16.5
Enter the number of shares and cost per share of your mutual fund in this dialog box.

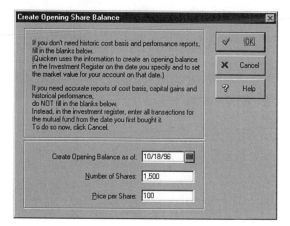

The Quicken investment register looks familiar

The register for tracking investments looks like the Quicken check register (see Figure 16.6). Entries in the investment register are made in much the same way as they are in the check register.

Fig. 16.6
The Quicken invest-
ment register looks a
lot like the check
register.

Click Easy Actions to select the
transaction that you want to
enter in the investment register.

Enter the name of
the security here.

The date is entered
in this column.

Use the transaction
buttons to enter or
edit a transaction, or
go to the EasyStep
form to edit transac-
tion information.

Enter the
number of
shares here.

The price of
the security
goes here.

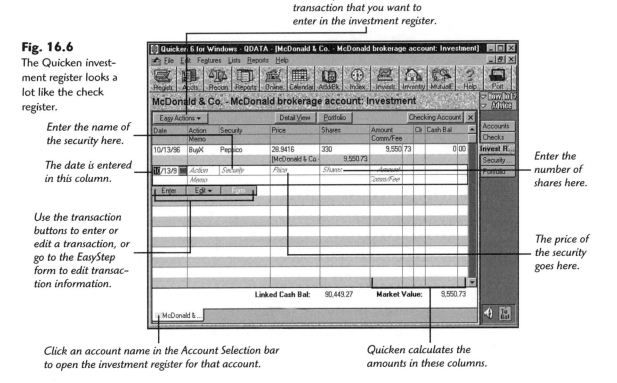

Click an account name in the Account Selection bar
to open the investment register for that account.

Quicken calculates the
amounts in these columns.

I need to enter my investment transactions now

When you're ready to enter investment transactions in an investment account, it's important that you first select the appropriate account so that its
register is open. To open the register for an investment account, click
Investments from the Activity Bar and then select the Use My Investment
Register option. Quicken opens the investment register for the first investment account listed in the Account List (investment accounts are listed in
alphabetical order, after bank, credit, cash, asset, and liability accounts). If
this isn't the investment account that you want to use, click the investment
account name from the Account Selection Bar at the bottom of the investment register. With the investment register open, you're ready to enter an
investment transaction.

I bought a security

When you open the register for an investment account, the cursor should be blinking on the first blank transaction line in the register, right under the last transaction that you entered. Today's date is already entered for you. Follow these directions to enter a new transaction:

1 Click the Easy Actions button to see a list of transactions that you can enter in the investment register. Select Buy/Add Shares. Quicken displays the Buy/Add Shares EasyStep dialog box.

2 Enter the name of the security using the QuickFill feature. Either drop down a list of securities currently in the system or begin typing and Quicken fills in the name. Click Next.

3 Now tell Quicken how you are paying for the security that you're buying. Choose to debit the cash balance from your investment account or use funds from another Quicken account. Note that if you're adding shares to an investment account, you can choose to deposit the shares without affecting the cash balance.

4 Next, in the Acquire box, enter the number of shares you purchased, followed by the price per share of the security.

5 Enter the date of the purchase and then the broker's commission, if you paid one.

6 Now, click the Next button and Quicken shows you a summary of the purchase that you just entered (see Figure 16.7).

7 Click Done and Quicken enters the transaction for the purchased security in the register.

You can edit or delete transactions in the investment register just as you do any other Quicken register. Use the Edit button in a transaction to restore, delete, memorize, copy, or paste investment transactions. Use the Form in a transaction to go back to the EasyStep form to edit information.

Fig. 16.7
Here's the information that you entered to buy a security. Make changes to the information, if necessary, and then click Done to record the transaction in the investment register.

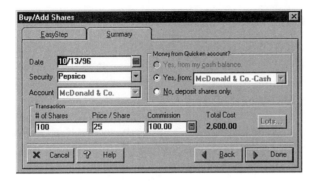

I sold a security

To record the sale of a security, follow the steps in the "I bought a security" section changing step one to select Sell/Remove Shares from the Easy Actions list.

After you enter the information for the sale of a security, Quicken shows you the Summary window (see Figure 16.8) with a Lots button. Click the Lots button if you want to identify specific lots of the security that you're selling. What this means is, if you purchased the shares of stock you are now selling on different dates (not all on the same date), you may want to specify which shares you are selling today.

If you click Lots in the Summary window, Quicken opens the Specify Lots For (*your security*) dialog box (see Figure 16.9), which shows all the purchases you made on the stock you are now selling. You can click on one of the purchases, then choose Use All to specify that all shares you sold are from this lot, or Use Part to indicate that some shares are from this lot and some are from another lot.

Fig. 16.8
The Summary dialog box shows you the information that you entered for the sale of a security.

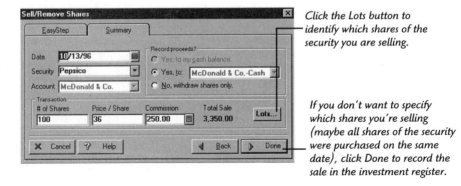

Click the Lots button to identify which shares of the security you are selling.

If you don't want to specify which shares you're selling (maybe all shares of the security were purchased on the same date), click Done to record the sale in the investment register.

Fig. 16.9

Use this dialog box to identify from which lot(s) of securities you are selling.

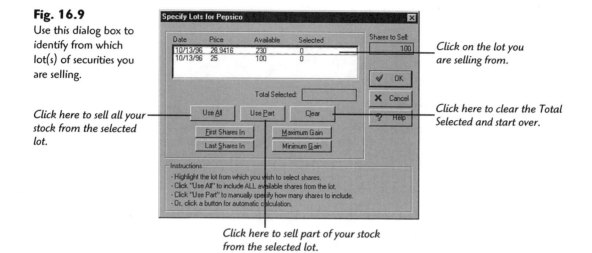

Click on the lot you are selling from.

Click here to sell all your stock from the selected lot.

Click here to clear the Total Selected and start over.

Click here to sell part of your stock from the selected lot.

I received income from my investments

Your investment account should reflect all the activity of your investments, not just purchases and sales. So whenever there is a stock split, whenever you receive a dividend, when you reinvest a dividend, whenever anything transpires that affects your investments, make an entry in the investment account register. That way you will always have the most up-to-date image of your portfolio.

To enter income into your investment account, open the investment account register and select Record an Income Event from the Easy Actions list. Quicken opens the Record Income dialog box (see Figure 16.10) where you can enter dividends, interest, capital gains (both short-term and long-term), and miscellaneous income. Select the name of the security, then enter the amount in the appropriate box. Enter cash dividends at actual cash value.

If you are entering a reinvested dividend, interest, or capital gain, select Reinvest Income from the Easy Actions list. You must know the price per share of the stock and the number of shares you acquired on reinvestment. This information should be available on your statement. If you don't have a statement, contact your broker.

Fig. 16.10
In the Record Income
dialog box, you can
enter dividends,
interest, capital gains,
and miscellaneous
income earned on a
security.

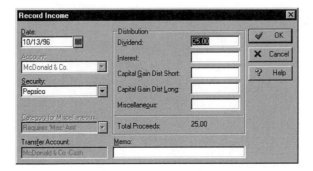

Dealing with stock splits and stock dividends

Sometimes, instead of paying cash dividends, companies pay their shareholders in additional shares of stock, known as stock dividends. If you receive a stock dividend, record it by following these steps:

1 Open the investment register for the account.

2 Click the Easy Actions button.

3 Select Advanced and then Stock Dividend from the Easy Actions list. Quicken opens the Stock Dividend dialog box like the one in Figure 16.11.

Fig. 16.11
In this example, the
shareholder received a
stock dividend of 1
new share for every
share owned previ-
ously.

Quicken fills in the quantity of shares you received and updates your stock records.

If you receive a stock split, select Stock Split from the Easy Actions list. In the Stock Split dialog box, Quicken prompts you to enter both the old number of shares you owned and the new number you now own.

I can memorize an investment transaction

Some people repeat their investments transactions regularly. If you have a stock purchase plan at your job, for example, and with each paycheck you purchase a share of your company's stock, you would like to be able to enter this purchase quickly from a memorized transaction list rather than having to enter all the details every time you get paid.

Quicken provides you with the opportunity to create a memorized transaction in the investment register. Memorized transactions in your investment register work in the same way as they do in a regular register.

To memorize an investment transaction, highlight the transaction and press Ctrl+M. Then click OK to memorize the transaction.

Quicken stores memorized investment transactions in a separate list from other transactions (say, in your check register) that you have memorized. Open the Investment Transaction List by selecting Lists, Investment, Memorized Investment Trans.

To use a memorized investment transaction, go to a blank transaction line in the investment register. Then select Lists, Investment, Memorized Investment Trans. to open the Investment Transaction List. Double-click the transaction that you want to use and Quicken automatically enters it in the investment register. Click Enter to record the memorized transaction.

I'd like Quicken to remind me about my investments

You can rely on Quicken to remind you of forthcoming investment events. For example, you may want a reminder of the maturity date of a CD, or you may want to remind yourself to make a deposit to your IRA account before the tax return deadline.

Make notes in the investment register that will appear in the Quicken Billminder and Reminder windows. To enter an investment reminder:

1 In the investment register, click the Ea_s_y Actions button to display the list of investment transactions. Choose Advanced, Reminder Transaction to display the Reminder dialog box seen in Figure 16.12.

2 Enter the date on which you want to be reminded.

3 Type the text of your reminder in the D_e_scription box.

4 The account that you're currently in is already selected in the _A_ccount drop-down list box.

5 In the _M_emo box, type any additional information that you want to be reminded of.

6 Click OK when you are finished entering the reminder.

You can keep the reminder in the investment register, even after you're finished being reminded, in case you want to use it again. Click twice in the Clr (Cleared) field to place an "R" in that field. That turns off the reminder without deleting it.

Fig. 16.12
Here's where you enter an investment reminder that will show up in the Billminder or Reminder windows.

Summarize your investments in the Portfolio view

So far, you've only seen your securities in the investment register. But the register doesn't really show you all of the data that you need to analyze your investments. The Portfolio view of an investment account, however, lists your securities (by name and ticker symbol), market price, number of shares, market value (number of shares times market price), cost basis, and any gain or loss realized on the security. Switch to Portfolio view (see Figure 16.13) by clicking on the Portfolio button at the top of your investment register.

Fig. 16.13
You can see all your investments at a glance in Portfolio view.

Click the Update Prices button to get online quotes or see a window detailing the price history of the selected security.

Click on a security then click on this Report button for a report of all the transactions involving that security.

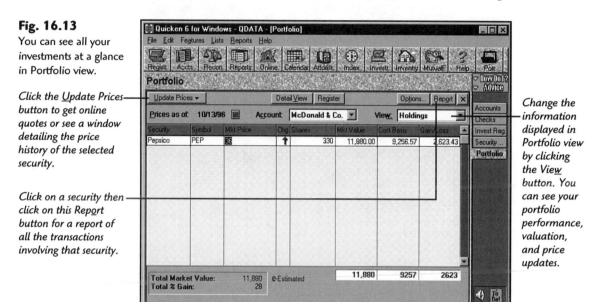

Change the information displayed in Portfolio view by clicking the View button. You can see your portfolio performance, valuation, and price updates.

Give me a detailed view of a security

New in Quicken 6 is the Security Detail View that gives you transaction and price data for a single security (see Figure 16.14). Here, you see a summary of your holdings in a specific security, a complete history of transactions involving the security, and a graph of the security's price over a specified time period.

To switch to the Security Detail View, from the investment register or Portfolio view, click the Detail View button.

Click here to
go back to
Portfolio view.

Click here to go
back to the
investment register.

Need to make a change to this
security? Just click the Edit
Security button.

Fig. 16.14
In the Security Detail
View, you can see a
complete history of a
specific security that
you own.

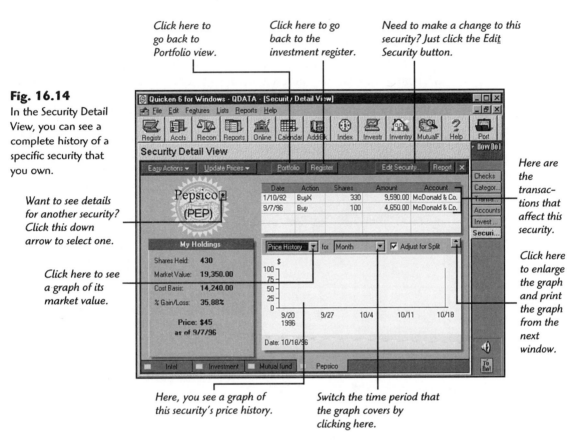

*Want to see details
for another security?
Click this down
arrow to select one.*

*Click here to see
a graph of its
market value.*

Here are
the
transac-
tions that
affect this
security.

Click here
to enlarge
the graph
and print
the graph
from the
next
window.

*Here, you see a graph of
this security's price history.*

*Switch the time period that
the graph covers by
clicking here.*

I want to update my stock prices

You can read the stock section of the daily newspaper and get the closing
stock prices for the previous day. Quicken lets you update the market value
of your securities in the Portfolio view window by following these steps:

1 Click the Portfolio button if you're not already in Portfolio view.

2 Click the View box at the top right corner of the Portfolio view window
and choose Price Update from the drop-down list.

3 Select the security you want to update.

4 Enter the latest market price in the Mkt Price column.

Alternatively, you can let Quicken update your stock prices for you online. In previous versions of Quicken you could also update your security prices online. So what's new here? Well, Quicken no longer uses the Portfolio Price Update service. Instead, through Quicken Live, you'll use Online Quotes to update prices. The best thing about it, though, is that for the first 12 months, you get this service FREE! Only one condition: you must register your Quicken software with Intuit to receive this freebie. I'd say it's a small price to pay.

To use the Online Quotes, follow these steps:

1 Make sure your modem is hooked up and your telephone line is free. Quicken connects you via modem to Online Quotes.

2 Click the Update Prices button at the top of the Portfolio view window and then select Get Online Quotes.

3 Quicken displays the Online Quotes dialog box (see Figure 16.15) with the list of securities that you can update. Note that if you haven't entered the ticker symbol for a security, Online Quotes will not be able to update that security. You can, however, have Quicken look up a ticker symbol by selecting the security and clicking the Lookup Symbol button. Click the Missing tab in the Online Quotes dialog box to see a list of securities with missing ticker symbols.

4 If there are securities that you don't want to update, enter an asterisk (*) in the symbol column for that security. Click the Excluded tab to see a list of securities you've excluded from the online update.

5 Click the Continue button to view the Update Quicken Live Features dialog box (see Figure 16.16). Click Online Quotes to select it for updating.

6 Now, click the Update Now button and sit back and watch as Online Quotes updates all your stock prices to the current market value.

Fig. 16.15
Quicken lists all of
your securities in the
Online Quotes dialog
box. You can choose
to update all securities
or only one or two.

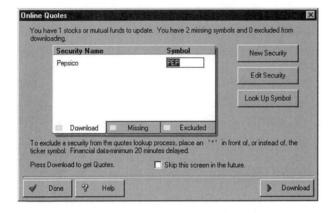

Fig. 16.16
Select Online Quotes
and then click the
Update Now button
to begin updating
security prices to the
current market value.

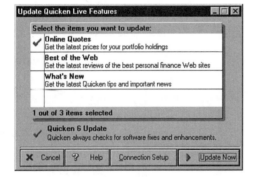

Quicken can help me choose a mutual fund

Are you considering investing in a mutual fund? Quicken's Mutual Fund
Finder can help you select from many mutual funds based on the performance of the funds and your tolerance for risk. Using data from Morningstar,
Mutual Fund Finder shows you a detailed summary of each fund's performance, traces its history, and shows you a fund's fee structure.

Now, in Quicken 6, you can go online with Mutual Fund Finder and view
mutual fund prospectuses for free! And you can update your mutual fund
data online anytime.

You can use Mutual Fund Finder while you're in Quicken, or if you're not
using Quicken right now, you can open it from the Windows 95 taskbar.

To open Mutual Fund Finder while in Quicken, click Investments from the Activity Bar and then select Research Mutual Funds. To open Mutual Fund Finder from another program, click the Start button from the Windows 95 taskbar, click Programs, select the Quicken file folder, and then select Mutual Fund Finder. When you first open Mutual Fund Finder, the Search by EasyStep dialog box opens (see Figure 16.17) so that you can select how you want to find a mutual fund, by name or other specific criteria. Click the Next button to enter the fund name or the other criteria that you want to base your search on.

Fig. 16.17
Select how you want to search for a mutual fund: by name or other specific criteria.

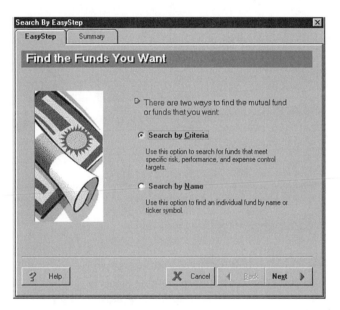

To select a fund by name, just enter the name of the fund and its symbol. To select a fund by other criteria, choose from various criteria options that Mutual Fund Finder presents.

When you have finished considering the criteria that seem appropriate for your needs (and you always can go back and make changes in the criteria), the Mutual Fund Finder presents a list of mutual funds that meet the criteria that you selected (see Figure 16.18). To start another search, click the Criteria, Name, or EasyStep buttons in the Mutual Fund Finder window.

Fig. 16.18
You are presented with
a list of funds that
currently meet your
criteria.

*View and sort the list of mutual funds that meet your needs in
a variety of ways by clicking on the Sort By and View buttons.*

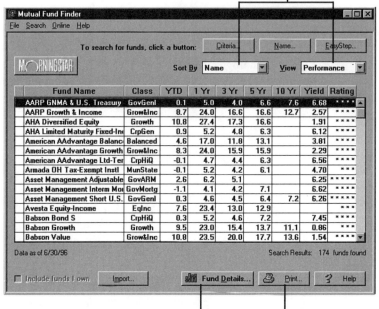

*See the details of any of the funds in the list, including
the minimum investment fee, and the phone number
and address where you can contact the fund for further
information, by clicking on the Fund Details button.*

*Print a copy of the summary screen
by clicking on the Print button.*

To get additional information on a mutual fund through the Internet, select a
fund from the Mutual Fund Finder window (refer to Figure 16.18), click the
Fund Details button, and then click the Prospectus tab. To view a prospectus,
for free, on the Internet via the World Wide Web, click the Prospectus button.

When you're finished evaluating mutual funds, close the Mutual Fund Finder
by clicking the Close (X) button or choose Exit from the Mutual Fund Finder
File menu.

Hey, I can really visit the Internet from Quicken!

Quicken Live provides immediate access to the Quicken Web site on the
Internet as well as other popular financial Web sites. Get notifications of
Quicken releases and news and special offers from Intuit. This is a free

service to all Quicken users; however, you must have a modem connected to a phone line to access this service. Once connected, browse through information offered by the many financial institutions that are working with Quicken to provide online banking services. You also can read personal finance tips and place orders for Intuit software.

Just click Online from the Activity Bar and see your Internet options. Select the Download Quotes and Update My Quicken 6 option to get updated security prices and any minor Quicken releases. Select Check Out the Best Financial Web Sites to see the Quicken Live window in Figure 16.19. From here, you can explore College, Dollars & Sense, Investments, Retirement, and Taxes Web sites as well as browse other Web sites.

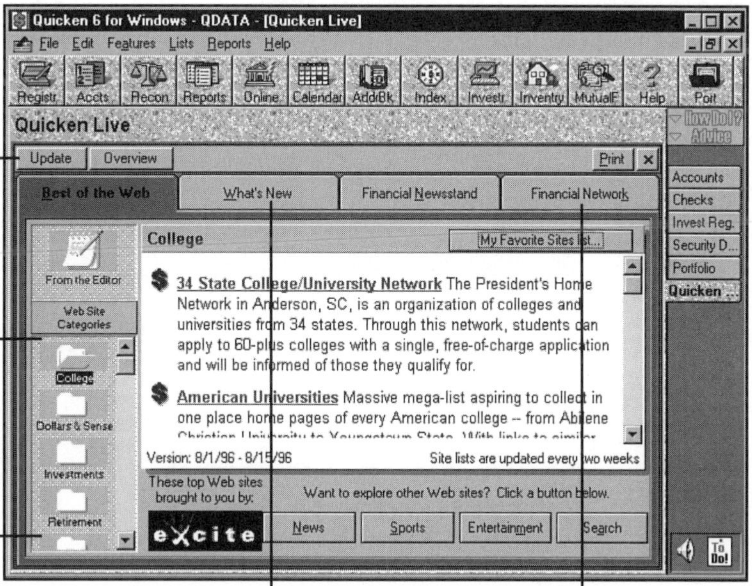

Fig. 16.19

From the Quicken Live window, update security prices, browse financial Web sites, see what's new from Quicken, and access the Quicken Financial Network.

Click here to update security prices.

Limit your Web site exploration by clicking one of these financial categories.

Want to see what's new in Quicken? Click here.

Click here to access the Quicken Financial Network.

17

Getting Ready for Tax Time

● **In this chapter:**

- **Match a tax form to a category**

- **Get help from the Tax Link Assistant to assign tax form lines to categories**

- **Find tax deductions**

- **Put together some tax reports**

- **It's tax time again!**

- **Don't let Uncle Sam catch you with your pants down—estimate your tax liability ahead of time**

Now that you're using Quicken, tax time's going to be a breeze. There will be no more worrying when the April 15th deadline nears. . . . . ➤

You've been entering transactions in Quicken all year to stay on top of your finances. So why not take it one step further and use those same transactions to get ready for taxes? As April 15th approaches, Quicken can summarize all of your tax-related transactions and put them in one place. With Quicken, you can even export your data to a tax preparation software program so that you don't have to reenter anything.

And look what's new in Quicken 6! A tax deduction finding feature that prevents you from overlooking the most inconspicuous expenses that you may be able to deduct!

Also use Quicken to estimate your taxes so that you don't have any big surprises at tax time. With Quicken's Tax Planner, you can forecast your income tax liability at any time.

I first need to designate tax categories

As you know, when you enter a transaction in Quicken, you assign a category to it so that you can track your income and expenses by type. You can go one step further by designating some of your categories as tax-related.

66 *Plain English, please!*

A category is **tax-related** if the transactions that are going to be assigned to it are associated with taxable income or tax-deductible expenses. For example, the category Salary is tax-related because your salary is considered taxable income. The category Charity is also tax-related because charitable contributions are tax-deductible. 99

Designating categories as tax-related can be done while you're adding a new category or by editing an existing one. Whether you're adding a new tax-related category or editing an existing category, start from the Category & Transfer List (press Ctrl+C). Click the New button to add a new category, or edit a category by highlighting it and clicking the Edit button. You'll see the Set Up Category (see Figure 17.1) or Edit Category dialog box next (depending on which button you click). The same information is included in each dialog box.

Move to the Ta<u>x</u>-related check box and click to select. This tells Quicken that this category is tax-related and all transactions that have this category assigned to them should be summarized and included in tax reports. Those categories that you've designated as tax-related are shown in the Category & Transfer List (see Figure 17.2).

Fig. 17.1
When you add a new category, you can designate it as tax-related by selecting the <u>T</u>ax-related check box. Then select the tax form or schedule where transactions for this category should be reported.

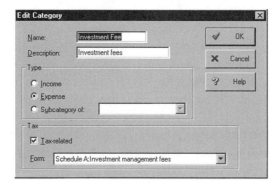

Click the Tax Lin<u>k</u> button to use Quicken's Tax Link Assistant.

Fig. 17.2
The categories that you designate as tax-related appear with the word Tax in the Tax column of the Category & Transfer List.

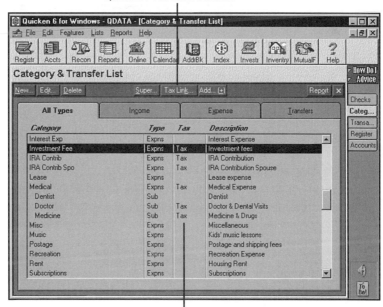

These categories are tax-related.

Now, if you want, you can assign a tax form or schedule to the category.

TIP **If you are using one of Quicken's predefined category lists, tax-** related categories are already designated for you. If you add another category, however, you'll have to select whether it's tax-related. Or, you can edit one of Quicken's categories to change its tax-related status.

Assigning tax forms to categories

After you've designated a category as tax-related, you can assign a tax form or schedule where transactions for the category should be reported. Just click the drop-down list and select the form or schedule. The Salary category, for example, is reported on the W-2 Salary or wages schedule. The Investment Fee category that is shown in Figure 17.1 is reported on Schedule A.

Q&A ***What if there's not a drop-down list to select the tax form or schedule in the Set Up Category or Edit Category dialog boxes on my screen?***

If you don't see the Form drop-down list box in either of these dialog boxes, then you don't have the tax schedule option in Quicken turned on. To turn on this option, select Edit, Options, Quicken Program to open the General Options window. Then click the General Tab to see the list of general options that you can change. In the General Tab window, select the Use Tax Schedules with Categories option. Chapter 24 explains in more detail how to set general options in Quicken.

Assigning tax form lines with the Quicken Tax Link Assistant

Now you've got your categories set up as tax-related and selected the forms or schedules where they should be reported. Track your tax-related transactions even closer by designating the line on the form or schedule where they should be reported. With Quicken's Tax Link Assistant, you can select tax form lines all from one place.

Clicking the Tax Link button from the Category & Transfer List (refer to Figure 17.2) opens the Tax Link Assistant dialog box that you see in Figure 17.3. Use the scroll bar and click in the Category list to highlight the category to which you want to assign a tax form line. Then highlight the line that you want to assign and click the Assign Line Item to Category button. Continue assigning lines to categories and then click OK when you're finished.

Fig. 17.3
Assign specific tax form
lines to categories in
the Tax Link Assistant
dialog box.

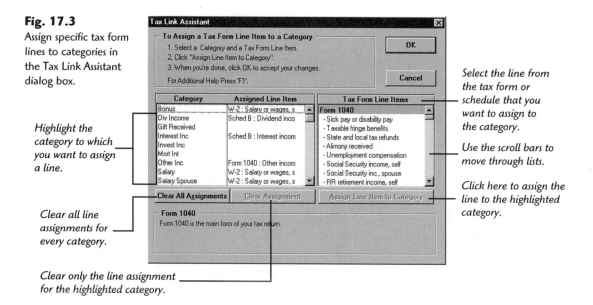

*Highlight the
category to which
you want to assign
a line.*

*Clear all line
assignments for
every category.*

*Clear only the line assignment
for the highlighted category.*

*Select the line from
the tax form or
schedule that you
want to assign to
the category.*

*Use the scroll bars to
move through lists.*

*Click here to assign the
line to the highlighted
category.*

Great! Quicken can help me find tax deductions

Quicken 6 has a great new feature that almost makes it impossible for you to miss out on deducting any eligible expense. The new Deduction Finder works sort of like an online interviewer, asking you questions about different types of deductions. Based on your answers, the Deduction Finder determines whether you are eligible to tax a deduction. You can even print an Action Plan that lists your eligible deductions and steps you may need to take. Of course, I always recommend that you consult with your tax advisor before taking an aggressive position on tax deductions.

To use the Deduction Finder, click Planning from the Activity Bar and then select the Identify Possible Tax Deductions option. Quicken displays an introduction to the Deduction Finder. After you've read this information, click OK to open the Deduction Finder (see Figure 17.4).

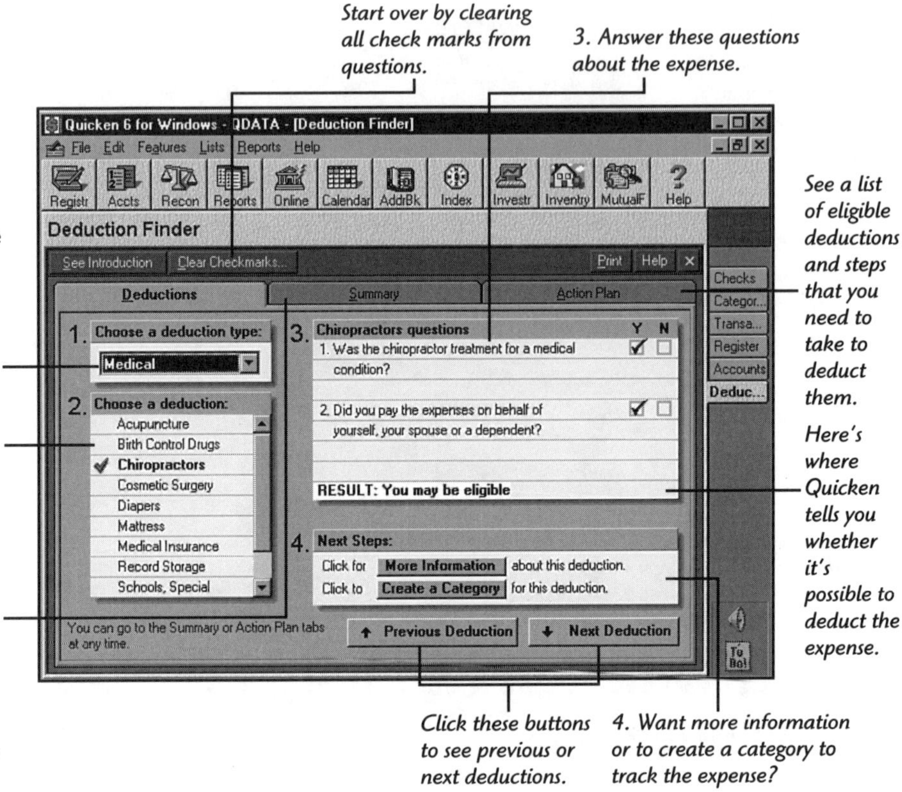

Fig. 17.4
The Deduction Finder interviews you and determines which expenses you're eligible to deduct for tax purposes.

1. Select from a list of deduction types.

2. What kind of expense do you want to evaluate?

Click here to see a summary of the tax deductions that are available, the number of questions you've answered in each tax deduction category, and the number of tax deductions (by category) for which you are eligible.

Start over by clearing all check marks from questions.

3. Answer these questions about the expense.

See a list of eligible deductions and steps that you need to take to deduct them.

Here's where Quicken tells you whether it's possible to deduct the expense.

Click these buttons to see previous or next deductions.

4. Want more information or to create a category to track the expense?

Using the Deduction Finder is easy. Click the Deductions tab and just follow the steps in the Deduction Finder window, (refer to Figure 17.4). First, select the deduction type. For example, if you want to determine whether medical expenses you paid during the year are tax-deductible, select Medical in Step 1. In Step 2, pinpoint the specific medical expense. For example, if you paid for chiropractor visits and want to determine whether they're deductible as medical expenses, select Chiropractors.

Now, go to Step 3 and answer the questions that relate to the type of deduction and expense that you selected in the first two steps. To answer yes to a question, click the Y box. To answer no, click the N box. After you've answered all of the questions in Step 3, the RESULT: line tells you whether you can deduct the expense. In Figure 17.4, you see that my chiropractic expenses are probably eligible for deduction.

In Step 4, you can click the More Information button to see additional information about the deduction. For example, Quicken will suggest a category to set up to track the expense, any IRS limits placed on the tax deduction, the type of receipts you should keep to document the deduction, the tax form or schedule where the deduction is shown on your tax return, and the IRS definition of the tax deduction.

Also in Step 4, you can have Quicken automatically set up a category for you to track the expense. Click the Create a Category button and the expense category is added.

Look at a summary of available deductions, those you've answered questions for, and those that you're eligible for by clicking the Summary tab. Click the Action Plan tab to see a summary of those expenses that you're eligible to deduct (see Figure 17.5).

Fig. 17.5
Here's an Action Plan with all of the expenses that you're eligible to deduct and some steps you should take before you actually deduct the expenses on your income tax return. It's a good idea to consult with your tax advisor before you show these expenses as tax-deductible.

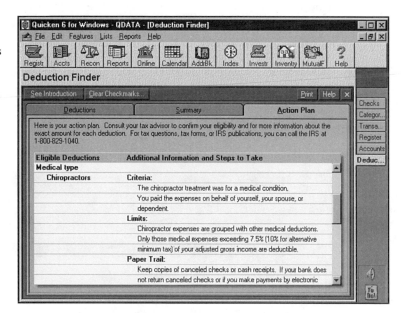

Quicken summarizes my tax data in reports

During the year, as you've assigned tax-related categories to transactions, your tax data is being accumulated by Quicken. At any time, you can generate tax reports that extract the information that you need to complete your tax return (either manually or using tax preparation software).

There are two reports that you can generate to summarize your tax data:

- **Tax Summary Report.** Groups and subtotals your tax-related transactions by category, starting with taxable income categories first, and then tax-deductible expense categories.

- **Tax Schedule Report.** Groups and subtotals your tax-related transactions by tax form or schedule line.

I need a Tax Summary Report to prepare my return manually

If you're preparing your income tax return yourself, or you need to accumulate your tax data to give to a paid preparer, the Tax Summary Report provides all the information you'll need. This report groups all tax-related transactions by category. For instance, it will total all Salary income, all Dividend income, and all Charity donations. With this information, you can easily transfer the totals to the tax forms and schedules in your return.

Here's how to generate a Tax Summary Report. First, click the Reports icon to open the Create Report dialog box. Click the <u>H</u>ome tab to display the list of reports for home use. Then double-click the Tax Summary report option. Figure 17.6 shows you what the Tax Summary Report looks like when it's displayed on your screen.

Fig. 17.6
This report groups and subtotals transactions assigned to your tax-related categories.

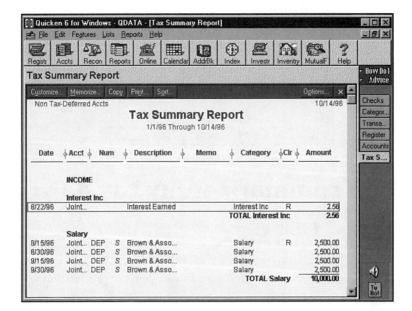

Click the Print button and change options as needed in the Print Report dialog box. Then click OK to get a printed copy of the Tax Summary Report.

 TIP **If you want to change the dates that the Tax Summary Report** covers or exclude some of the accounts included in the report, click the Customize button and make your changes. Chapter 18 tells you all about customizing reports so that they give you the information you need in the format that you want.

I also need a Tax Schedule Report because I use tax preparation software

If you're using tax preparation software to prepare your income tax return, then you'll need to create a Tax Schedule Report. This report not only subtotals your tax-related transactions by income and expense, but groups and subtotals them by form or schedule and then again by line. After you've created a Tax Schedule Report, you can then transfer the data in the report to a tax program.

 Create a Tax Schedule Report by clicking the Reports icon to open the Create Report window, where you click the Home tab to see the list of home reports that you can create. Then double-click the Tax Schedule report option. Figure 17.7 shows you what the Tax Schedule Report looks like.

Fig. 17.7
This report groups and subtotals transactions assigned to your tax-related categories by tax form or schedule line.

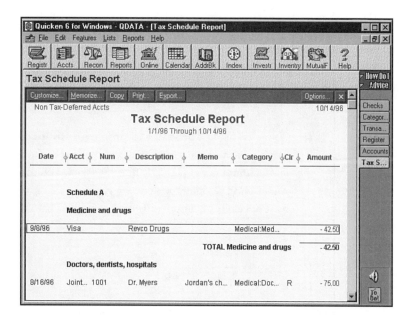

You can choose to print a copy of your Tax Schedule Report to your printer (click the Print button) or export it to a file that can be transferred to a tax preparation program. (You'll learn about exporting files in the next section.)

Time to prepare my return

When you're ready to prepare your income tax return, create the appropriate report. You just learned how to create a Tax Summary report that groups your tax-related transactions by category and then how to create the Tax Schedule Report that groups transactions by tax form line.

Just print a copy of either report to use in preparing your return manually or give the report to your CPA as part of your tax information.

If you're using a tax program, however, you'll export the Tax Schedule Report to a TXF file for transfer.

 Plain English, please!

TXF (Tax Exchange Format) refers to the extension that's given to the file for the tax report that you're exporting. Files must be saved in the tax exchange format to be exported and read by tax preparation programs. **99**

Create the Tax Schedule Report as explained in the previous section. Then, click the Export button to open the Create Tax Export File dialog box. Here is where you'll give a name to your report file and include TXF as the extension. So, provide a file name (using Windows 95 naming rules) and the location where you want the file stored. Then click OK to export the data in the Tax Schedule Report to a TXF file.

 TIP **If you're using TurboTax to prepare your income tax return, you** won't need to create the Tax Schedule Report. TurboTax can read and import your tax data directly from Quicken. You can start TurboTax while you're using Quicken by selecting Features, Taxes, TurboTax. (Of course, you must have already installed TurboTax on your hard drive.)

Because all tax preparation programs are different, I'll refer you to the documentation for the program that you're using to learn how to import the TXF file into the program.

CAUTION　　**Make sure that the dates covered by the Tax Schedule Report are** appropriate for your return. If you're preparing your tax return for 1996, the dates should include 1/1/96 to 12/31/96. To change the date range in the report, click the Customize button and then change the Report Dates in the Customize Tax Schedule Report dialog box.

I want to estimate my taxes for next year

Want to know how much tax you're going to owe for this year? Or what about next year? And how much will your tax liability go up if you take that new job with the nice pay increase? These are all questions you can get answers to with Quicken's Tax Planner. The Tax Planner lets you estimate the amount of tax you'll owe on that dreaded day (April 15th) so you're not caught by surprise.

To use the Tax Planner to estimate your taxes, first gather your tax information together. You'll need tax items, like paycheck stubs, medical and dental receipts, tax receipts, interest payment records, child care receipts, charitable contributions, and perhaps your prior year's tax return. Then, open the Tax Planner by clicking Planning in the Activity Bar and then selecting the Plan for Taxes option (see Figure 17.8). From here, you'll change the tax rate (if necessary), enter data, and then analyze the results.

What if the tax rates change?

You know how Congress is—continually changing the tax code and rates, especially around election time. Quicken's Tax Planner incorporates the tax rates based on the most recent tax legislation. However, if these rates increase or decrease, you can easily change them in the Tax Planner so that your tax calculations are up-to-date.

Before you change the tax rate, be sure that the appropriate filing status and year are shown in the Tax Planner. In Figure 17.8, the rates in effect are for Single filing status in 1996. If you want to change the rates for next year, select 1997 in the Year drop-down list box. Now you can click the Rates button at the top of the Tax Planner to open the Tax Rates dialog box shown in Figure 17.9. Type over any of the existing rates with the new rates, or modify the AMT exemptions or the inflation rate and click OK.

Use your Quicken data in the Tax Planner.

Print a tax estimate.

Calculate tax amounts to enter in fields.

Reset values in tax scenarios to zero.

Fig. 17.8
Quicken's Tax Planner estimates your tax liability for the current year or next year.

Close the Tax Planner.

Compare different tax scenarios.

Modify 1996 and 1997 tax rates.

Click these buttons to enter data manually in fields that are recessed.

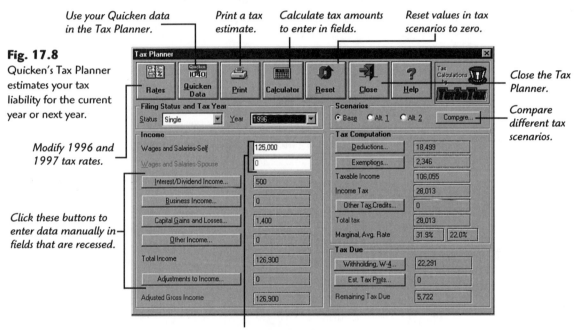

You can have Quicken enter data automatically in these fields.

Entering data in the Tax Planner

The Tax Planner needs a little information before it can estimate your taxes, like how much your income will be and the amount of your tax-deductible expenses. You can use your Quicken data in the Tax Planner, or you can manually enter data. You might use a combination of both, however, if you're estimating taxes for the current year (Quicken for year-to-date data and manual entries for the remainder of the year). Quicken can, however, annualize any year-to-date information so that you don't have to enter anything manually.

Fig. 17.9

If Congress decides to change the income tax rates, you can modify the rates that the Tax Planner uses to make its calculations so that you can get an up-to-date tax estimate.

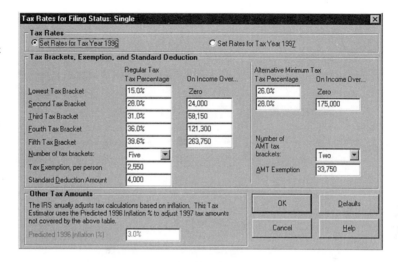

If you want to use the tax-related information that you already have in Quicken, click the Quicken Data button in the Tax Planner to open the Preview Quicken Tax Data dialog box (see Figure 17.10). Quicken summarizes all of your transactions through the end of the last full month completed. If the period that Quicken uses is not a full year, you can select to have Quicken annualize any or all of the amounts in the Preview Quicken Tax Data window. Click OK to use the data in the Tax Planner.

Here's the year-to-date amounts from your Quicken data.

Fig. 17.10

Here's all of your tax-related items summarized by tax form or schedule. If you want, you can annualize any or all of these amounts.

Double-click an item to annualize it.

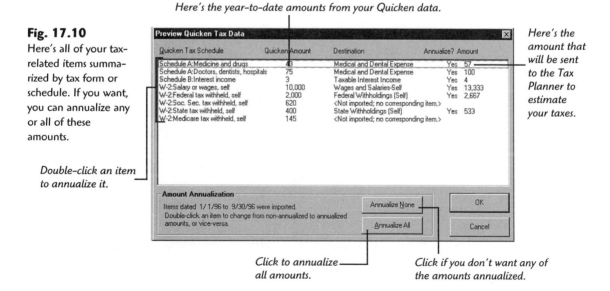

Here's the amount that will be sent to the Tax Planner to estimate your taxes.

Click to annualize all amounts.

Click if you don't want any of the amounts annualized.

If you want to enter information directly into the Tax Planner, click the appropriate button to display its related dialog box for you to enter data. For example, to enter interest or dividend income, click the Interest/Dividend Income button; to enter tax deductions, click the Deductions button.

Analyzing tax estimates

The Tax Planner makes instant tax calculations as you enter data. So, you'll see what your taxable income is, the total tax, marginal and average tax rates, and how much tax you still owe. Figure 17.11 shows a completed tax estimate in the Tax Planner window.

 Plain English, please!

> Your **marginal tax rate** is the rate of tax on the highest range of your taxable income. If you are married, filing jointly, with a taxable income of $40,000 in 1996, for example, your marginal tax rate on the last dollar of income is 28 percent. Your marginal tax rate is determined by the specified tax rates set forth by the Internal Revenue Code. In 1996, this rate for joint filers was 28 percent for taxable income between $39,000 and $94,250.
>
> The average tax rate that the Tax Planner computes is the overall rate of tax on your adjusted gross income. If your adjusted gross income is $50,000 and your tax liability is $10,000, for example, your average tax rate is 20 percent ($10,000/$50,000). **"**

Fig. 17.11
Here's your tax estimate for 1997. Looks like you'll be cutting a check to the IRS for $1,336 unless you increase your withholding or make an estimated tax payment before the end of the year.

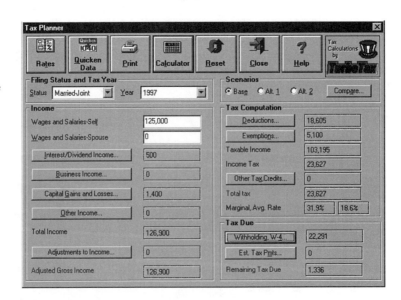

If you want a printed copy of your tax estimate, click the Print button. Then complete the Print dialog box and click OK to print your tax estimate.

See different tax scenarios at the same time

The Tax Planner not only estimates your current tax liability, but also can compare two more tax scenarios and show the results side by side. Let's say that you're contemplating selling a stock at a gain and you want to see what the tax effect will be. Or, you're paying off the mortgage on your house this year and you want to see what how your tax liability will be affected when you no longer have the mortgage interest deduction. You can compare all of these scenarios without affecting any of the data in Quicken.

Your current scenario is the Base scenario and uses the data from the Tax Planner dialog box. You can create two other scenarios: Alt. 1 and Alt. 2. To create and compare scenarios, click one of these buttons in the Tax Planner dialog box. Quicken asks whether you want to copy the current scenario. If you're comparing similar scenarios, it's probably easiest to copy the current one and then make one or two changes to it. After you've made changes to either Alt. 1 or Alt. 2, or entered new data, click the Compare button in the Tax Planner dialog box to see a side-by-side comparison as shown in Figure 17.12.

Fig. 17.12
Here's how your tax scenarios compare. The Tax Scenario Comparisons window shows you the total tax and marginal and average tax rates for each scenario so that you can make an apples-to-apples comparison.

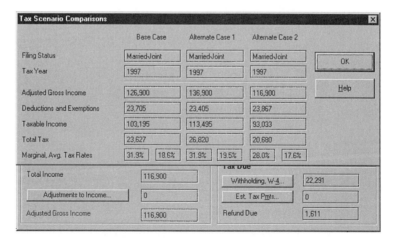

Tax Scenario Comparisons	Base Case	Alternate Case 1	Alternate Case 2	
Filing Status	Married-Joint	Married-Joint	Married-Joint	OK
Tax Year	1997	1997	1997	
Adjusted Gross Income	126,900	136,900	116,900	Help
Deductions and Exemptions	23,705	23,405	23,867	
Taxable Income	103,195	113,495	93,033	
Total Tax	23,627	26,820	20,680	
Marginal, Avg. Tax Rates	31.9% 18.6%	31.9% 19.5%	28.0% 17.6%	

Total Income	116,900	Tax Due	
Adjustments to Income...	0	Withholding, W-4...	22,291
		Est. Tax Pmts...	0
Adjusted Gross Income	116,900	Refund Due	1,611

18

Printing Reports

● In this chapter:

- Create many different types of reports in Quicken

- The ins and outs of creating a report

- How to print reports

The world has come a long way from scratching with rocks on cave walls to printing spiffy reports on computers! . . . . . . ❯

When I began working as an accountant, I had to write up reports on wide sheets of ledger paper. Column after column of numbers, adding down and adding across, making sure everything was accurate. If a number changed on the report, all the columns had to be re-added and the totals double-checked for accuracy. And if someone wanted the report presented in a different way, maybe organizing numbers by month instead of by week, or sorting accounts alphabetically instead of by dollar amount, I'd have to start over, get a clean sheet of ledger paper, and begin the process again. I logged many hours over those big sheets of paper filled with columns of numbers, my trusty 10-key calculator by my side.

Now computer programs and printers have made all that work I used to do obsolete. Click a button with the mouse to display a report on-screen, click a few more buttons to change the order of the display, one more click and the report is sent to my printer, and there's never any question at all about the accuracy of the totals.

What kind of reports can I create with Quicken?

You can create many different types of reports from the numbers in your Quicken registers. Among Quicken's standard reports are those for cash flow, budget, net worth, transaction summary, tax, investment performance, profit and loss statement, and income and expense comparison.

This is just a partial list of the standard reports from which you can choose, reports that are already designed for you and ready to be displayed when you request them. Each of these standard reports can be customized in many different ways, so that you can retrieve just about any information you may want from the amounts you have entered into your registers.

I sure like Quicken's EasyAnswer reports

If accounting terms like Cash Flow and Net Worth throw you for a loop, then you'll enjoy working with Quicken's EasyAnswer reports. These reports are geared to answer the questions that you may have regarding the amounts you've entered in your registers. EasyAnswer reports provide answers to the following questions:

- Where did I spend my money?

- How much did I spend on (fill in the category)?

- How much did I pay to (fill in the payee)?

- How much did I save in a particular time period compared to a prior time period?

- How much did I spend in a particular time period compared to a prior time period?

- What am I worth?

- Did I meet my budget?

- What taxable events occurred during a particular time period?

- How are my investments doing?

- What are my investments worth?

To display the EasyAnswer questions, click Reports in the Activity Bar and then select Show Me a Graph or Report of My Finances. Quicken opens the EasyAnswer Reports & Graphs dialog box as shown in Figure 18.1.

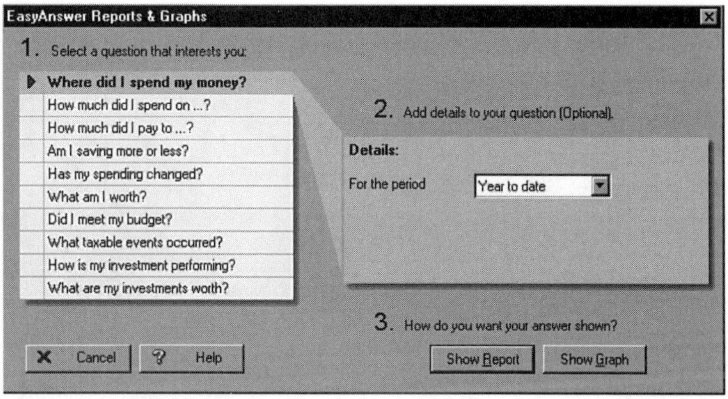

Fig. 18.1
It's quick and easy to create a report by following the steps in the EasyAnswer Reports & Graphs dialog box. Just select a question, the time period, and whether you want a to create a report or a graph.

Follow the steps in the EasyAnswer Reports & Graphs dialog box to display the answer to your question. In Step 1, you select the question. For example, the first question is, "Where did I spend my money?"

Then, in Step 2, you choose the time period that you want to cover by clicking the down-arrow and selecting from the drop-down list. You can select

Year to date, Current Month, Last Year, Last Month, or any number of other choices.

 Last, you tell Quicken whether you want to display the data in report or graph format. Click the Show Report button to display the report on your screen. And now, in Quicken 6, you can display EasyAnswer data as graphs. So, to display a graph, click the Show Graph button.

Click the Close (X) button to remove a report from your screen, or see the section "Okay, let's print!" later in this chapter for printing options.

Also click the Close (X) button to remove a graph from your screen. Check out the next chapter to learn how to print graphs.

I want to see a "snapshot" of my finances

Snapshots are miniature reports that give you different perspectives on your financial position. A page of snapshots can contain as many as six reports and can include a graph, a budget-to-actual comparison, a cash flow report, a monthly income statement, calendar notes, and more.

To display snapshots on your screen (see Figure 18.2), click Reports from the Activity Bar and then select View All My Finances at a Glance. Or, select Snapshots from the Reports menu.

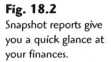

Fig. 18.2
Snapshot reports give you a quick glance at your finances.

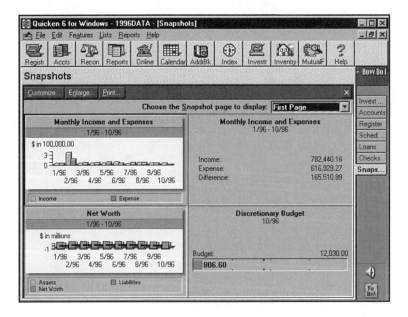

Choose how many snapshots you want to display and what type of information you would like to see summarized by clicking the Customize button in the Snapshots dialog box. When snapshots are displayed on your screen, you can point (the mouse pointer changes to a magnifying glass) to the graph images to see the actual number represented in the graph. Also, you can double-click many of the snapshot images to enlarge the graph and see the detail that makes up the amount in the snapshot.

Click the Close (X) button when you are finished displaying snapshots.

 TIP You can create multiple pages of snapshot reports by clicking the Customize button and then clicking the New button in the Snapshot Page box. Then choose the snapshot reports that you want to include in the new page.

QuickReports give you instant feedback

Throughout your Quicken registers and lists you will often see a Report button (see Figure 18.3) that represents Quicken's QuickReport feature. QuickReport provides you with an instant summary of the information you are currently viewing. For example, if your check register is displayed on-screen, clicking the Report button in the register button bar and then selecting Register Report gives you a report that summarizes all the transactions in your register, arranged chronologically by date.

There are QuickReports available from the following locations in Quicken:

- **Category & Transfer List.** When the Category and Transfer list is displayed, you can select a particular category, then click the Report button to see a detail of all the transactions from all your registers assigned to that category.

- **Class List.** If you are using classes in Quicken, you can display the Class List and click the Report button to see a list of transactions from a selected class.

- **Memorized Transaction List.** While displaying the Memorized Transaction list, select a memorized transaction, and then click Report to see a detail of all the occurrences of that transaction.

- **Registers.** While displaying a register, select a particular transaction, then click the Report button to display all the transactions in your register with that same payee.

- **Write Checks window.** While displaying a check that you've written, click the Rep<u>o</u>rt button to display all the checks written to the same payee.

- **Portfolio or Security Detail View.** Select one of your securities in either view, then click the Rep<u>o</u>rt button to see all the transactions involving that security.

- **Security List.** Select one of the securities in the list, then click the Rep<u>o</u>rt button to see all the transactions involving that security.

From any QuickReport you can double-click a transaction line in the report to see the detail of that transaction.

Fig. 18.3
Display a QuickReport by clicking the Report button.

Click the Report button to create a QuickReport.

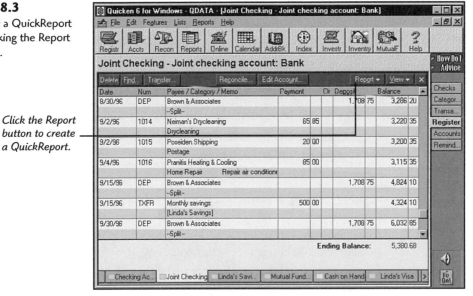

I'm ready to create a report

Quicken has so many standard reports available, it's sometimes hard to know which one to choose. With time, you'll get used to the reports that come with the program and you'll learn to customize your own reports as well. This section discusses the steps for creating standard reports in Quicken. Later you'll learn how to adapt those reports to meet specific needs.

Let's see which report I want

Click the Reports icon from the iconbar to display the Create Reports dialog box with all the available standard reports in Quicken.

TIP **If the iconbar is not currently displayed on your Quicken screen,** select Edit, Options, Iconbar and then click the Show Icons checkbox. To show labels for icons, click the Show Text checkbox.

From the Create Reports dialog box, click the tab for the category of report that you want to create:

- Home
- Investment
- Business
- Other
- Memorized

Within each report category there are several choices of reports. Notice that on some of the tabs you can't see all the report choices.There is a scrollbar at the right side of the screen that you can use to advance the report list.

First, choose a date range for the report or choose a specific date. For some reports, you'll choose a date range; for others, you'll choose just one date (the value of your investments as of today, for example). Click the icon next to the report that you want to create and, voilà, it's displayed on your screen!

Getting more information from your on-screen report

The report you display on-screen is just a starting point. You can take the standard report that you chose and massage it until it more appropriately meets your needs. Use the buttons at the top of the report window (see Figure 18.4) to change your report.

Fig. 18.4
One of Quicken's
many standard reports.

*Click here to change
your report settings.*

*Click here to
memorize the report
(save the settings).*

*Click here to copy
your report to the
Windows Clipboard.*

*Double-click any
transaction in
the report to see
the source of the
transaction.*

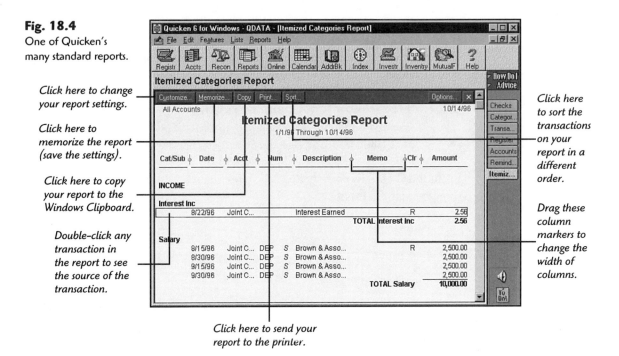

*Click here
to sort the
transactions
on your
report in a
different
order.*

*Drag these
column
markers to
change the
width of
columns.*

*Click here to send your
report to the printer.*

Okay, let's print!

There are separate print settings in Quicken for printing reports and for printing checks. Before you attempt to print, be sure the settings for your printer are correct.

Tell Quicken about your printer

To set up your printer for printing reports, follow these steps:

1 Choose File, Printer Setup, then click Reports/Graphs. The Report Printer Setup dialog box opens (see Figure 18.5). Check to see that your printer is named in the Printer box. If it isn't, click the drop-down arrow and select your printer.

Fig. 18.5
Adjust your printer
settings in this dialog
box.

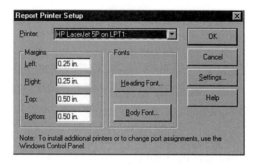

2 Click the Settings button to select particular printer options such as orientation and paper size. Click OK to accept your settings.

3 In the Report Printer Setup dialog box you can select Heading Font or Body Font to customize the typeface of the header and the body text of your reports.

4 You can change the default margins by typing in new measurements in the Left, Right, Top, and Bottom boxes.

5 Click OK to save your print settings for all future reports.

The settings you make in this dialog box become your defaults. You can still select individual print options on your specific reports, overriding the defaults. For information on setting up your printer for printing graphs, see Chapter 19, "Looking at Data Through Graphs."

Ready to print

Click the Print button from the report displayed on-screen, or choose File, Print Report. The Print dialog box is displayed (see Figure 18.6). You can also press Ctrl+P to display the Print dialog box.

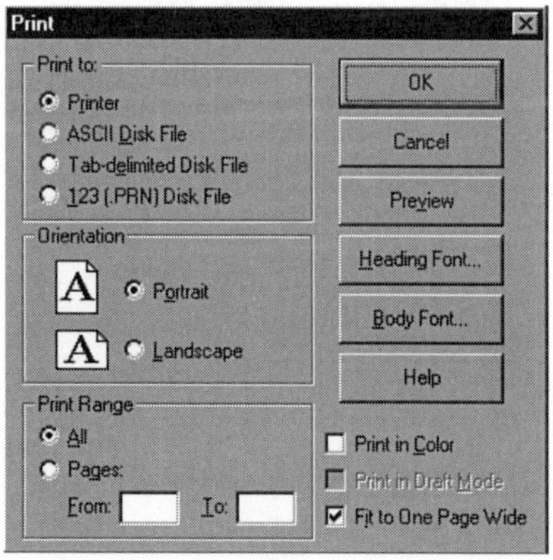

Fig. 18.6
Last chance to pick
your printer settings!

Select the print options you want for your report from this dialog box. The options are:

- Print to the Printer or select a file format for printing your report to a file on disk for use in another program.

- Choose Portrait or Landscape orientation.

- Print All pages of your report, or select a range of pages by filling in the From and To boxes.

- Select a typeface and size for your report heading with the Heading Font button, or choose a typeface and size for the body of your report with the Body Font button.

You can preview your report from this Print dialog box to make sure it's going to look the way you want it to before you actually print it. Click the Preview button to examine the printed format of your report on-screen.

When you're ready to print, just click OK from the Print dialog box or click the Print button from the Print Preview window.

I want to save a report to a disk file

You can retrieve your Quicken files in other programs by saving your reports to disk files. For example, you may want to pull your register summary into a spreadsheet program like Lotus, Excel, or Quattro Pro to perform some what-if projections or some more advanced calculations.

To save a report for use in a different program, choose one of the following print options from the Print dialog box:

- **ASCII Disk File.** Use this choice if you want to import your Quicken report to a word processing program.

- **Tab-delimited Disk File.** A file saved in this format can be read by most word processing and spreadsheet programs.

- **123 (.PRN) Disk File.** This format can be read by most spreadsheet programs.

Neat! I can memorize reports

Don't work hard at creating a report that looks the way you want it to and provides the information you need, just to print it once, click the Close button, and have to do it all over again next month. You have better things to do with your time than re-create the same report over and over again.

Let Quicken save your report, just as it saves transactions that you perform repeatedly. While your report is displayed on the screen, press Ctrl+M, just like you would if you were memorizing a transaction, or you can click the Memorize button at the top of the report window. The Memorize Report dialog box appears (see Figure 18.7).

Fig. 18.7
Don't look now, but you're about to save yourself lots of time by memorizing a report.

Select the date for your report.

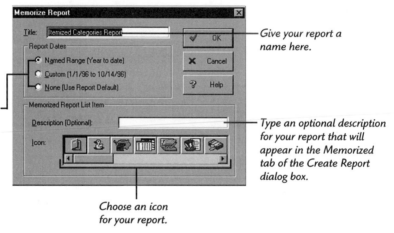

Give your report a name here.

Type an optional description for your report that will appear in the Memorized tab of the Create Report dialog box.

Choose an icon for your report.

Your memorized report gets saved and appears when you click the Memorized tab in the Create Report dialog box (see Figure 18.8). Just click the Reports icon in the iconbar to open the Create Report dialog box. Click the Memorized tab, then click the icon for the memorized report you want to use.

Fig. 18.8
Your memorized report
is added to the
Memorized tab in
the Create Report
dialog box.

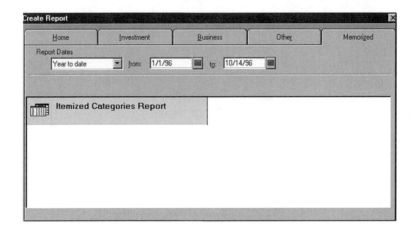

19

Looking at Data Through Graphs

● In this chapter:

- You can create lots of different kinds of graphs in Quicken

- Before you print, display a graph on-screen

- What makes up this graph?

- Don't be satisfied with defaults; customize your graphs!

- Once you've designed a graph, memorize it so you don't have to create it all over again

- How do I print graphs?

Why not take your reports one step further? Produce full-color, three-dimensional graphs and let your numbers tell their story visually . . . .

When I first learned to draw graphs, it was a process of joining a vertical line (the Y-axis) and a horizontal line (the X-axis), plotting points in the space around the lines, then connecting my points like a dot-to-dot picture. If I wanted to get fancy, I'd use a different colored pencil for connecting the dots, but that's about as innovative as I got.

With Quicken, I can create graphs that are as eye-appealing as they are informative—graphs that tell a visual story of my finances, that make trends easy to spot, and that constantly remind me of just one more reason why I spent my money on a computer instead of, well, whatever else I might have spent my money on.

What types of graphs can you display in Quicken?

There are five types of graphs that you can display in Quicken, and then there are lots of variations on these five types. The Quicken graph types are:

- **Income and Expense**. These graphs help you understand where your money is going. They help you determine trends in spending, compare the amount of cash coming in (income) to that going out (expense), and compare current income and spending with earlier periods.

- **Budget Variance**. These graphs provide a comparison between what you thought you would earn and spend and what you actually earned and spent. You can use these graphs to help you keep tabs on how close you are to meeting your budget goals.

- **Net Worth**. These graphs compare account balances from one period to the next. Is the month-end balance in your investment register decreasing every month? It may be time to reconsider how your money is invested.

- **Investment Performance**. These graphs plot the trends in individual investments and show you how you are progressing toward meeting your investment goals such as retirement and college planning.

- **Investment Asset Allocation**. These graphs show you the composition of your investments by the asset class you've assigned to securities. Asset classes are a new feature in Quicken 6, so now you can gauge how diversified your portfolio is.

I want to display a graph

So, I got your attention, huh? Displaying graphs in Quicken is only a few mouse-clicks away. In fact, you already got a glimpse of some graphs in Chapter 18 when you looked at EasyAnswer Reports & Graphs and Snapshot Reports.

To create a graph in Quicken, choose Reports, Graphs and then select any graph type from the Graphs menu. The Create Graph dialog box you see in Figure 19.1 opens. From this dialog box you can choose the type of graph you want to display, select the time period that the graph should cover, and customize a graph by choosing specific accounts and/or categories to include in or exclude from the graph.

Fig. 19.1
Creating a graph starts right here.

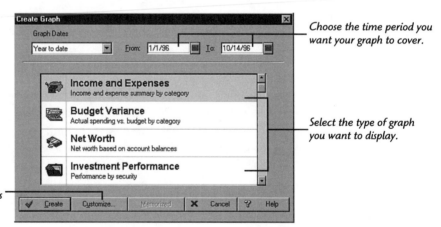

Choose the time period you want your graph to cover.

Select the type of graph you want to display.

Click here to include or exclude specific accounts and/or categories.

Now, click the Create button and your graph appears on-screen. The graph in Figure 19.2 is an Income and Expense graph.

Fig. 19.2
This graph compares
income and expenses.

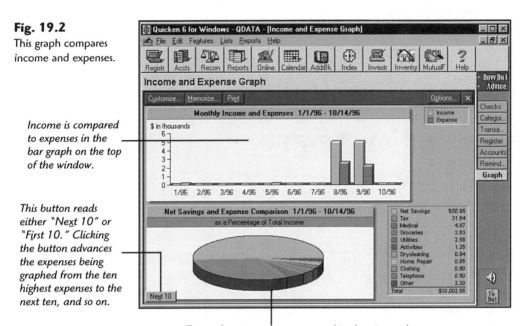

Income is compared to expenses in the bar graph on the top of the window.

This button reads either "Next 10" or "First 10." Clicking the button advances the expenses being graphed from the ten highest expenses to the next ten, and so on.

Types of expenses are represented in the pie graph and the percent each expense is to the whole.

Getting more detail behind an item in a graph

All of the bars, lines, and pie pieces on your graphs represent numbers from your account registers. You don't have to go back to the register or produce reports to see what the actual amounts are behind the graphs. Just point to an area of the graph you want to investigate to see the amount that makes up the piece of the graph displayed on the screen.

For even more detail, place your mouse over any bar or pie piece on the graph and double-click. A QuickZoom graph appears, breaking out the pieces that make up the item on which you double-clicked. For example, if you double-click on one of the bars representing income in the top graph, a QuickZoom graph appears showing what is included in that first income bar (see Figure 19.3).

The legend shows you the details that make up the graph image.

Fig. 19.3

Double-click on a piece of your graph and you get a QuickZoom graph like this one, giving you a close-up of the original piece.

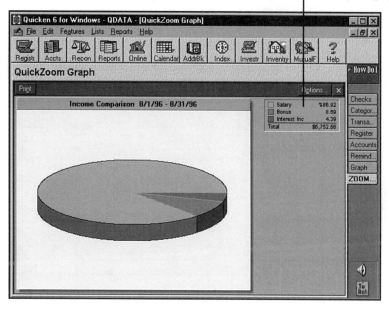

If that's not enough detail for you, when you display a QuickZoom graph on-screen, you can put your mouse on any piece of the graph and your mouse pointer changes to a magnifying glass with a "Z" inside. With this symbol showing you can double-click on a portion of the QuickZoom graph and see exactly which transactions make up the piece of the graph on which you clicked. Figure 19.4 shows an Income Comparison report that gives you the detail of a piece of the pie from Figure 19.3.

Click the Close (X) button in the Income Comparison report to return to the QuickZoom graph. Click the Close (X) button in the QuickZoom graph and you're back at the original Income and Expense graph.

Fig. 19.4
This report shows the
detail after you
double-click a piece of
the QuickZoom graph.

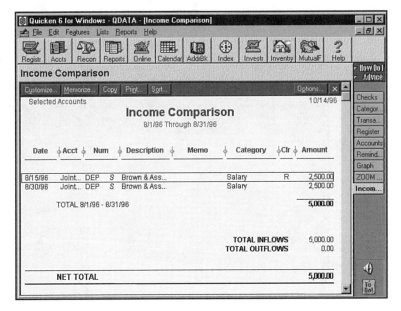

Neat! I can customize my graphs

You don't have to settle for the graph settings Quicken has chosen for you.
You can set the dates to be covered in your graph, pick and choose what
accounts you want to include, and select which transactions will appear in
your graph.

When you first create the graph you have the options for customizing graph
settings, but sometimes you don't know what you want to change until you
actually see the graph. Unless you know exactly what you want to see, go
ahead and create a graph, select the type of graph you want, and click Create.
This puts a graph on your screen which you can examine and then decide
how you want to change it.

I don't want this item in my graph

After your graph is displayed on-screen you can decide what you do and
don't want included in the graph. Say, for example, in an Income and Expense graph, you want to include amounts only from your checking account
and not any other accounts. Click on the Customize button at the top of the
graph window, click on the Accounts tab in the Customize Graph dialog box
that appears, and click on the accounts you don't want to include,
unchecking them in the process.

Then click C̲reate to create the graph with only the accounts you included.

I want to select specific transactions

Perhaps you don't want to show certain expenses in your graph. Click on the C̲ustomize button at the top of the graph window and then click on the Cate̲gories tab to see a list of all categories (income and expense). Scroll down until you find the expense categories. You can click on each expense that you want to exclude from your graph, unchecking each one as you click on it.

TIP **When unchecking items in the account and/or category list for** purposes of customizing your graphs, you can drag your mouse through several items, unchecking them all at once instead of clicking individually on each one.

A graph can be memorized too!

After you've figured out exactly how you want your graph to appear, you don't have to worry about remembering all the steps you went through to create that graph so that you can re-create it in the future. Just click the M̲emorize button at the top of the graph window.

When you click M̲emorize, Quicken displays a Memorize Graph dialog box (see Figure 19.5) in which you can name your graph. Give your memorized graph a meaningful name so that when you search for it in the future the name will lead you to the graph you want.

Fig. 19.5
Give your graph a name before memoriz–ing it.

To use a memorized graph, select R̲eports, G̲raphs, Memoriz̲ed Graphs to open the Memorized Graphs dialog box (see Figure 19.6). Select a memorized graph from the list and then click U̲se to display that graph.

Fig. 19.6
Choose a memorized graph from this window.

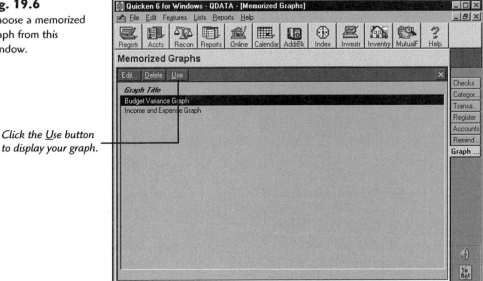

Click the <u>U</u>se button to display your graph.

I want to change the way graphs appear

Your graphs appear in 3-D with color display by default, but you can change that appearance.

With a graph on your screen, click the O<u>p</u>tions button at the top of the graph window to open the Graph Options dialog box displayed in Figure 19.7. In the Graph Options dialog box you can select any of the following options:

- **<u>U</u>se Patterns Instead of Colors**. Instead of color bars, you can choose to display black and white patterns. Sometimes this makes the different pieces of the graph easier to discern, especially when printing the graph on a black-and-white printer.

- **<u>C</u>reate All Graphs in Separate Windows.** Your graphs are really two graphs, one above the other. By checking this box you can display your graphs in separate windows and, therefore, have the option to print only one and not both.

- **<u>D</u>raw in 2D (faster).** Your three-dimensional graph looks nice, but two-dimensions may do the job and both the screen display and the printing will be faster.

Fig. 19.7
Click any of these options to change the appearance of your graph.

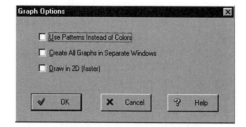

Let's print this graph

If your graph appears on the screen the way you want it to look, you're just about ready to print. Before you print your graph, you should check the printer settings by choosing File, Printer Setup, then select For Reports/ Graphs. For information about the particular printer setup options, see Chapter 18, "Printing Reports." The printer options for reports and graphs are the same.

TIP **Remember, you can customize the typeface for your graph**
headings by selecting Heading Font in the Report Printer Setup dialog box.

When you know your print settings are correct, click the Print button in the graph window, choose File, Print Graph, or press Ctrl+P. Quicken sends your graph to the printer.

Part V: Planning for the Future

20

Forecasting Your Cash Flow

● **In this chapter:**

● **What's a cash forecast and how do I get one?**

● **Customizing your cash forecast**

● **Creating multiple forecasts**

● **Comparing forecasts**

Look into your financial future with Quicken's crystal ball . . . . ▶

Nobody really knows what the future holds, but we frequently have the opportunity to make intelligent guesses. Quicken's cash forecasting feature gives you an opportunity to make intelligent guesses about the future. Using financial information from your registers, working with the actual numbers you've entered, Quicken estimates your future income and expenses for a period of up to two years.

Quicken creates a cash forecast out of existing numbers in your registers, but you can fine-tune that forecast, making changes in the estimates based on your knowledge of your financial situation. For example, if you anticipate receiving a raise next year at your job, or if you're about to start paying college tuition for your son or daughter, you can anticipate the changes that will occur in your cash flow, and make adjustments in your forecast accordingly.

I want to see my cash forecast

When creating a forecast, Quicken works with data that it already has—the amounts in your registers, and any future transactions you may have scheduled in your financial calendar, like future loan payments, tax payments, and so on (see Chapter 10, "Scheduling Future Transactions," for information about scheduling transactions on the Financial Calendar). Quicken then extends your data into the future, similar to the way in which you might design a budget, except that instead of the wishful thinking that sometimes goes into a budget, the forecast is based on real expectations.

The forecast is kind of like a financial timeline on which Quicken places the transactions of which it is aware. For example, if you get paid semimonthly at your job, Quicken assumes this trend will continue and plots out semimonthly payroll deposits in your forecast. Quicken also takes the bills you pay regularly and assumes that those payments will continue.

Quicken looks for trends when searching through your registers. For example, if your utility bills have increased by five percent for each of the past eight months, Quicken assumes that increase will continue as it forecasts your utility expenses for the future. If you have a loan payment that is the same every month, Quicken keeps that payment constant in your forecast.

In addition, you can tell Quicken to consider additional amounts that aren't in your register or the Financial Calendar in its forecast. You can experiment with the forecast, changing projections to see what your forecast might look like if you get an increase in salary or you make that last mortgage payment.

Use the forecast to help you plan for future expenditures and figure out your savings options.

To create a forecast, follow these steps:

1 Choose Features, Planning, Forecasting to open the Forecasting window. The first time that you create a forecast, the Automatically Create Forecast dialog box appears (see Figure 20.1). From this point forward, the dates you set in the next step will enable Quicken to bypass opening this dialog box.

Fig. 20.1
Quicken considers financial transactions from the time period you designate when creating your forecast.

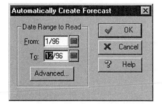

2 Set the range of dates for Quicken to examine in creating your forecast.

Designate a range of dates that contains illustrative deposits and expenditures. For example, say it's October 1, 1996, and you've entered income, expenses, and investments into your Quicken registers since January 1, 1995. Furthermore, say you feel the transactions from the current year (1996) closely resemble those you anticipate having in the future. Your range of dates would be January 1, 1996, to the present. Quicken would then consider only your 1996 transactions when making its estimates about your future financial activity, and not transactions from 1995.

3 Click OK to create your forecast and display it on the screen (see Figure 20.2).

Click here to return to the Automatically Create
Forecast dialog box and change the dates used in
gathering information for your forecast.

With your mouse, point anywhere on the
forecast graph line to see the projected
balance in your accounts as of that date.

Click the *Track* button to assign
categories to unassigned forecast
items. Click the unassigned item,
then click the Assigned Category
drop-down list to select a category.

Fig. 20.2
A sample forecast
based on data in your
Quicken registers.

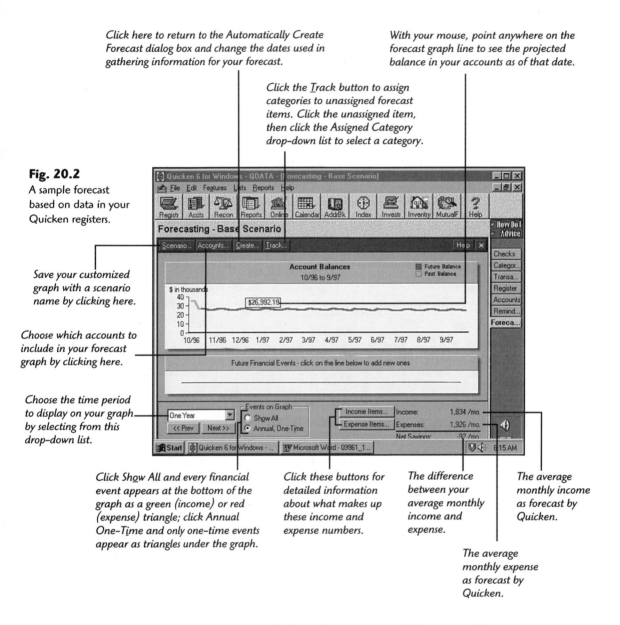

Save your customized
graph with a scenario
name by clicking here.

Choose which accounts to
include in your forecast
graph by clicking here.

Choose the time period
to display on your graph
by selecting from this
drop-down list.

Click Sh*o*w All and every financial
event appears at the bottom of the
graph as a green (income) or red
(expense) triangle; click Annual
One-T*i*me and only one-time events
appear as triangles under the graph.

Click these buttons for
detailed information
about what makes up
these income and
expense numbers.

The difference
between your
average monthly
income and
expense.

The average
monthly income
as forecast by
Quicken.

The average
monthly expense
as forecast by
Quicken.

What you see is a projection of your account balances—all your accounts
combined. At the bottom of the screen on the right you can see the monthly
projected average income and expense and the net increase (or decrease) to
savings (Net Savings). You can move the forecast forward or backward by
clicking the arrows in the bottom left corner of the graph. Choose to advance
the forecast one month, six months, one year, or two years at a time.

Print your forecast if you want a hard copy by selecting Print Forecast from the File menu (or press Ctrl+P). With your mouse, point anywhere on the forecast graph line to see the projected balance in your accounts as of that date.

My cash forecast can be fine-tuned

The graph you get the first time you click OK in the Automatically Create Forecast dialog box is really just a starting point. There are several ways you can customize your forecast so it provides you with useful information.

- Click either the Show All option to include all the transactions and estimates in the forecast, or the Annual, One-Time option to include just yearly figures in the forecast.

- Click the Scenario button to choose or create a new forecast scenario.

- Click the Create button to open the Automatically Create Forecast dialog box (refer to Figure 20.1) and change the dates used in analyzing data for your forecast. You also can click the Advanced button in this dialog box and designate whether you want to draw information From Register Data or From Budget Data.

I only want certain accounts included in my forecast

Your forecast, by default, includes all your accounts—bank, cash, credit card, savings, investment, and so on. To exclude certain accounts and build your forecast just on the projections of particular accounts, click the Accounts button in the Forecasting window. The Select Accounts to Include dialog box opens. From this dialog box you can select the accounts you want to exclude, removing the checkmark from alongside the account name. Alternatively, if accounts that you want to include in your forecast are unchecked, just click them to include those accounts in the forecast.

I want to change a forecast amount

In the Forecasting window, you can change projected income and expenses by clicking either the Income Items or Expense Items button at the bottom right side of the Forecasting window. Clicking either one opens a dialog box in which you can, first of all, see what amounts make up those items, and second, you can add to the list of projected items (click <u>N</u>ew) or edit the existing numbers (click <u>E</u>dit). A sample Forecast Expense Items dialog box is shown in Figure 20.3.

Fig. 20.3
Look at all these expenses—both actual and estimated—that go into my expense forecast!

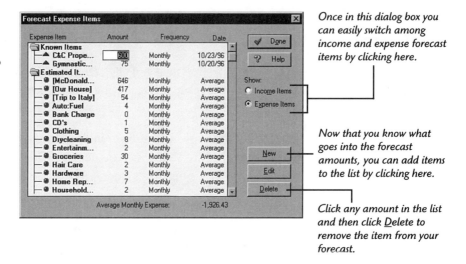

Once in this dialog box you can easily switch among income and expense forecast items by clicking here.

Now that you know what goes into the forecast amounts, you can add items to the list by clicking here.

Click any amount in the list and then click <u>D</u>elete to remove the item from your forecast.

Can I create more than one forecast?

Create as many forecasts as you like. To create a new forecast (called a Forecast Scenario), click the <u>S</u>cenario button in the Forecasting window. Creating a Forecast Scenario is a lot like creating a Memorized Transaction. You choose the setting you want to save, then give it a name. Then in the future you can recall those same forecast settings without having to re-create them.

When you click the <u>S</u>cenario button, the Manage Forecast Scenarios dialog box opens (see Figure 20.4). To save the changes you have made in your forecast into a new, named, recallable scenario, click <u>N</u>ew, type the name of your new scenario, and then click OK.

TIP **After you've saved a scenario by name, you can change the name** of the scenario by clicking the <u>S</u>cenario button on the forecast screen, and then clicking <u>E</u>dit. Also, you can delete an existing scenario if you don't think you'll ever use it again by clicking <u>D</u>elete in the Manage Forecast Scenarios dialog box.

Fig. 20.4
Creating a new
Forecast Scenario is
similar to memorizing
transactions.

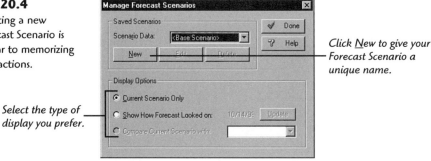

*Click New to give your
Forecast Scenario a
unique name.*

*Select the type of
display you prefer.*

Choose the display option you prefer for your scenario:

- Current Scenario Only displays just your newly named scenario.

- Show How Forecast Looked on [*date*] lets you display your scenario as of a particular date as opposed to the current date which is the default.

- Compare Current Scenario with [*fill in name of another scenario*] lets you display two forecasts on the same graph and compare them.

When you have selected the options you want, click Done to save the scenario.

How to compare two forecasts

As previously mentioned, after you've created more than one forecast scenario, you can compare two forecasts in the same window. To pull up a forecast and compare it with another, follow these steps:

1 Select Features, Planning, Forecasting to open the Forecasting window.

2 Click the Scenario button.

3 In the Manage Forecast Scenarios dialog box that appears, choose Compare Current Scenario with, and choose the scenario you want to compare with in the drop-down list at the right.

4 Click the Done button to bring both scenarios into the Forecasting window at once.

21

Saving for College, Retirement, and Everything Else

● **In this chapter:**

- Looking college, weddings, and other big expenses in the eye

- Help make retirement a reality with Quicken

- Watching your investment (garden) grow

- How can I use Quicken to track my savings?

How much do you need to save to reach your goals? Quicken to the rescue! . . . . ▶

I f your daughter came up to you tomorrow and said, "Dad, I need $25,000. Will you write me a check?" Would you say, "Sure, honey!"? Or are you more likely to come back with, "In your dreams!"?

Usually, when big expenses are coming due, we like to know a little bit in advance, so we can do some planning for those events. Not many people can write a check on the spur of the moment for $25,000 (at least not a good check), and even if you could, you wouldn't want to do it if you weren't prepared.

Quicken's special planning features help you save for college and retirement, and help you track your savings and investments.

I don't want college to sneak up on me

Unfortunately, no one is going to take you aside and tell you exactly how much you need to project for your child's college education and how you should save to meet that goal. It's all up to you, and the last thing you want to do is come up short. So start saving today.

Start saving now even if your child is an infant and it seems like you'll have forever to put aside money. Start now, even if your child is in high school and it seems like it's too late to put aside money. No matter which end of the college planning spectrum you're at (or even if you have both young and old children that put you at both ends of the spectrum), every step you take toward saving will benefit you and your children when college time comes.

 TIP   **It doesn't just have to be college that you start saving for early.** There are cars, weddings, vacations, homes, trips, home additions—whatever your needs or dreams are.

Estimate your needs

To start planning for college, or any major expenditure, you first need to have a handle on how much you'll need. For college costs, investigate today's tuition costs at several colleges of varying size, both in-state and out-of-state, both state-funded and private. Figure out a range of potential costs. Don't forget to include housing, food, books, pizza money, trips home, bus passes, fraternal organizations, football tickets (or basketball, if the school is in Indiana)—all the things that can make the tuition alone pale in significance.

Next, you need to get a feel for how much those costs are going to rise between now and the time little Jordan and Ali are ready for college. Do a little research. There are published reports on the projected rise in college costs. Also, talk to the financial aid offices at some colleges. The people who advise parents about paying for college can give you some guidance on planning for future college costs.

Okay, let's say you've arrived at a projected dollar amount for how much you think four years of college is going to cost. The next step is to estimate how much of that you expect to pay yourself. I'm not talking about scholarships, financial aid, or bank loans that you may have to rely on for part of the cost. I'm talking about how much is going to come out of your pocket.

For purposes of this example, I'm going to use $15,000 per year as the estimated cost of college for your student who is going to start college in the fall, five years from now. In five years, you're going to need $15,000 per year for four years and you haven't yet begun to save.

Figure out how much to save

Start planning for college with Quicken's College Planner. To use the College Planner, follow these steps:

1 Click Planning in the Activity Bar and then select the Use Financial Planning Calculators option. Now, select College and click OK to open the College Planner dialog box (see Figure 21.1).

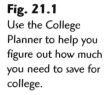

Fig. 21.1
Use the College Planner to help you figure out how much you need to save for college.

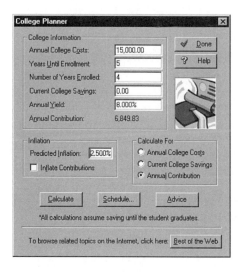

2 In the Calculate For section of the College Planner dialog box, choose the calculation that you want Quicken to perform:

- **Annual College Costs.** If you know how much you can afford to contribute regularly to a college savings fund, choose this option and Quicken calculates how much you will be able to afford to spend on college.

- **Current College Savings.** If you know the amount you plan to spend on college and the amount you can afford to contribute regularly to a college savings fund, choose this option and Quicken tells you how much you will have to add from your current savings to reach your goal.

- **Annual Contribution.** Tell Quicken how much college is going to cost and Quicken calculates how much you need to contribute regularly to a college savings fund.

3 Fill in the amounts in the College Information section to provide Quicken with the information it needs to make its calculations:

- **Annual College Costs.** Enter the total amount you expect to spend each year for college. Include in this amount not just tuition, but room and board, books, fees, and all other related college costs.

- **Years Until Enrollment.** How many years is it from right now until your child begins the first year of college?

- **Number of Years Enrolled.** For how many years will your child be a college student? Typically, this number will be four, but if you are planning on paying tuition for the next Dr. Kildare, this number will increase.

  One of the following three items will be left blank, depending on which one you expect Quicken to calculate for you.

- **Current College Savings.** If you've already got a head start on saving for college, enter the amount of your college savings here.

- **Annual Yield.** Enter the annual rate of interest you expect to earn on your savings as they accumulate.

- **Annual Contribution.** Enter the amount you are able to contribute for college savings. Quicken assumes that the amount you enter is for the entire year's contribution.

4 In the Inflation section of the College Planner, enter the current rate of inflation (by default, Quicken uses four percent) and check the Inflate Contributions check box if you want to have Quicken increase your required annual contribution by the expected rate of inflation.

5 Click the Calculate button and the College Planner performs its calculations. In my example, in order to have $15,000 per year for college five years from now, I need to save $6,849.83 each year (as well as each of the four years my daughter's in college)!

6 Now, click the Schedule button and Quicken provides you with a yearly schedule of the amount of contribution you need to make. You can print this schedule by clicking the Print button in the Deposit Schedule dialog box (see Figure 21.2). Notice that you are still expected to make contributions the four years while your child is in college.

Fig. 21.2

You can print this deposit schedule and refer to it each year as you make college fund deposits. Notice the withdrawals for actual college costs in the final four years have been increased from your original estimate due to inflation.

Year	Deposit	Tuition	Balance
0	0.00	0.00	0.00
1996	6,849.83	0.00	6,849.83
1997	6,849.83	0.00	14,247.65
1998	6,849.83	0.00	22,237.29
1999	6,849.83	0.00	30,866.10
2000	6,849.83	0.00	40,185.22
2001	6,849.83	16,971.12	31,921.05
2002	6,849.83	17,395.40	22,537.53
2003	6,849.83	17,830.29	11,933.66
2004	6,342.39	18,276.04	0.00

TIP **Use the Annual Contribution amount calculated by the College** Planner in your Quicken budget (see Chapter 15, "Creating Your Budget," for more information). In your budget you can separate your contributions into monthly or quarterly deposits to spread the cost throughout the year.

7 Click the Close button to close the Deposit Schedule dialog box; then click the Done button to close the College Planner dialog box.

TIP **6** **In each of the Financial Planners in Quicken, you can** access the Internet to browse financial Web sites. Just click the <u>B</u>est of the Web button, and Quicken takes you directly to Quicken Live where you can choose to explore College, Dollars & Sense, Retirement, Investment and Tax Web sites. Note that when you access the Internet from a Financial Planner, Quicken closes the planner. So, make sure that you've performed all of your calculations and printed a schedule before you access the Internet.

I want to make sure I can afford to retire

Dreams of retirement seem farther and farther out of reach these days as our society gets older and stays healthy longer. But most people like to think that someday they will be able to stop working, rest, and enjoy their later years without worrying about having to earn a living.

Getting ready for retirement takes planning, just like any other long-term goal. If you wait until you're ready to retire to start thinking about how you're going to support yourself, you'd better hope you have lots of good friends and children who will care for you, because you won't be able to do it yourself. Start now—plan for the future as if it were a necessity, not just something that you'll deal with "later."

Quicken's Retirement Planner can help you figure out how much your current savings will earn and how you can add to those savings so that you will be able to retire in comfort. Work for your retirement now so that you can enjoy it later.

The Retirement Planner is one of Quicken's Financial Planners. To use the Retirement Planner, follow these steps:

1 Click Planning in the Activity Bar and then select the Use Financial Planning Calculators option. Now, select <u>R</u>etirement and click OK to open the Retirement Planner dialog box, as shown in Figure 21.3.

2 First, determine what kind of information you want Quicken to calculate for you. In the Calculate For section of the Retirement Planner dialog box you can choose between the following options:

  • **Current Savings.** If you know how much you can contribute each year and how much you want to withdraw annually when you retire, let Quicken calculate how much of your current savings should be designated as retirement savings.

- **Annual Contribution.** If you know how much you would like to withdraw annually from your retirement account and how much you can designate as retirement savings from your current savings, let Quicken calculate how much you must contribute each year to meet your goals.

- **Annual Retirement Income.** If you know how much you can contribute each year and how much you can designate as retirement savings from your current savings, Quicken will tell you how much you are going to be able to withdraw from your retirement account when you retire.

 TIP **Take advantage of Quicken's ability to quickly calculate several** scenarios for you. Experiment with the numbers, trying different combinations while you try to work out the plan that best fits your financial needs and your ability to meet the annual contribution amount.

Fig. 21.3
Make a financial plan for your retirement using Quicken's Retirement Planner.

Retirement Planner

Retirement Information

Current Savings:	29,999.98
Annual Yield:	8.000%
Annual Contribution:	2,000.00
Current Age:	39
Retirement Age:	65
Withdraw Until Age:	85
Other Income (SSI, etc.):	20,000.00
Annual Income After Taxes:	28,181.46

Inflation
Predicted Inflation: 4.000%
☐ Inflate Contributions
☑ Annual Income in Today's $

Calculate For
○ Current Savings
○ Annual Contribution
● Annual Retirement Income

Tax Information
● Tax Sheltered Investment   Current Tax Rate: 28.000%
○ Non-Sheltered Investment   Retirement Tax Rate: 15.000%

✓ Done
? Help
Calculate
Schedule...
Advice

To develop a complete retirement plan, see Quicken Financial Planner in the Intuit Marketplace.

To browse related topics on the Internet, click here: Best of the Web

3 Filling in the amounts in the Retirement Information section will provide Quicken with the information it needs to make its calculations. (One of the three, Current Savings, Annual Contribution, and Annual Income After Taxes, will be left blank, depending on which amount you want Quicken to calculate for you.)

- **Current Savings.** Enter the amount of your savings you have designated as being set aside for retirement.

- **Annual Yield.** Enter the annual amount of interest or dividends your retirement savings can earn.

- **Annual Contribution.** Enter the amount you plan to contribute annually toward your retirement.

- **Current Age.** How old are you today?

- **Retirement Age.** At what age do you plan to retire?

- **Withdraw Until Age.** This is the toughest one. You have to guess how old you're going to be when you stop withdrawing money from your retirement fund. I know—it's a shot in the dark. Just give it your best guess. You can always experiment with these numbers and try different ages.

- **Other Income.** What other sources of retirement income do you expect to have besides the amount you're putting away yourself. Social Security? Retirement fund from your job? Inheritance? Enter the annual amount you expect to receive beyond your retirement savings.

- **Annual Income After Taxes.** How much do you want to be able to withdraw from your retirement account each year?

As you fill in the answers to these questions, Quicken fills in the amount you requested it to calculate.

4 In the Tax Information section of the Retirement Planner dialog box, check whether your retirement fund is tax-sheltered. In other words, if your retirement fund is currently tax-deferred, like an Individual Retirement Account (IRA), but you'll have to pay tax on the amounts from the fund when you withdraw the funds, check Tax Sheltered Investment. Then enter the estimated tax rate when you retire. If you pay tax currently on the money you put in your retirement fund, check Non-Sheltered Investment. Then enter your current tax rate, as well as the estimated tax rate when you retire.

5 In the Inflation section of the Retirement Planner, enter the current rate of inflation (by default, Quicken uses four percent) and check the Inflate Contributions check box if you want to have Quicken increase your required annual contribution by the expected rate of inflation. Check the Annual Income in Today's $ check box if you want Quicken to incorporate the effects of inflation into your retirement income. If you leave this box blank, Quicken will not adjust your retirement income for inflation.

6 Click Calculate to perform calculations in the Retirement Planner.

7 Now, click the Schedule button and Quicken provides you with a yearly schedule of the amount of contribution you need to make and the annual increase in the balance of your retirement fund. The contribution schedule starts with your retirement savings already in place in the first year. You can print this schedule by clicking the Print button in the Deposit Schedule dialog box.

 TIP **Use the Annual Contribution amount calculated by the Retire-** ment Planner in your Quicken budget (see Chapter 15, "Creating Your Budget," for more information). In your budget you can separate your contributions into monthly or quarterly deposits to spread the cost out through the year.

8 Click the Close button to close the Deposit Schedule dialog box and click Done to close the Retirement Planner dialog box.

Watching my investments grow

Using the same concepts applied in the College Planner and the Retirement Planner, you can track the savings in any account or fund with Quicken's Investment Savings Planner. Indicate your opening balance and regular contributions and Quicken will calculate how those savings will grow. Alternatively, tell Quicken how much you want to have saved after a certain period of time has passed and Quicken will let you know what you have to do to reach that goal.

To use the Investment Savings Planner, follow these steps:

1 Click Planning in the Activity Bar and then select the Use Financial Planning Calculators option. Now, select Savings and click OK to open the Investment Savings Planner dialog box, as shown in Figure 21.4.

Fig. 21.4
Use the Investment
Savings Planner to
determine how quickly
your investments will
grow.

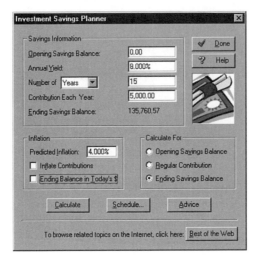

2 First, determine what kind of information you want Quicken to calculate for you. In the Calculate For section of the Investment Savings Planner dialog box you can choose between the following options:

- **Opening Savings Balance.** If you know how much you can contribute each month (or quarter or year) and you know how much you eventually want to accrue, let Quicken tell you how much you need to start with to meet your goal.

- **Regular Contribution.** You know how much you're starting with and you know how much you plan on ending with; Quicken will calculate how much you need to contribute regularly to achieve your goal.

- **Ending Savings Balance.** If you know how much you're starting with and you know how much you can contribute regularly, Quicken will calculate the amount you will have in the end.

3 Filling in the amounts in the Savings Information section will provide Quicken with the information it needs to make its calculations:

- **Opening Savings Balance.** Enter the amount in your investment account at the start of this investment program, unless this is the amount you plan to have Quicken calculate.

- **Annual Yield.** Enter the annual amount of interest or dividends your investment savings can earn.

- **Number of (fill in a choice of a time interval—Weeks, Months, Quarters, Years).** Enter the time interval during which you plan to make contributions and then enter how many contributions you plan to make in this investment account.

- **Contribution Each (time interval).** The entry of a time interval here is automatic based on the entry at the line above. Unless you are letting Quicken calculate your periodic contribution, fill in the amount you plan to contribute regularly to your investment.

- **Ending Savings Balance.** Enter the desired ending balance of your investment account, unless this is the amount you plan to have Quicken calculate.

4 In the Inflation section of the Investment Savings Planner, enter the current rate of inflation (by default, Quicken uses four percent) and check the Inflate Contributions check box if you want to have Quicken increase your required annual contribution by the expected rate of inflation. Check the Ending Balance in Today's $ check box if you want Quicken to incorporate the effects of inflation into your investment income. If you leave this box blank, Quicken will not adjust your investment income for inflation.

5 Click the Calculate button to perform calculations in the Investment Savings Planner. In Figure 21.4, you see an investment of $5,000 per year for 15 years, at an eight percent annual yield, grows to $135,760.57!

6 Click the Schedule button and Quicken provides you with a periodic schedule of the amount of contribution you need to make and the periodic increase in the balance of your investment savings account. The contribution schedule starts with any investment savings you may already have in place in the first year. You can print this schedule by clicking on the Print button in the Deposit Schedule dialog box.

7 Click the Close button to close the Deposit Schedule dialog box, and click Done to close the Investment Savings Planner dialog box.

Quicken can help me track my savings

Quicken offers a nifty little feature called the Savings Goal Account. A Savings Goal Account is like having a savings account without the trouble of setting up a separate account. For example, say you want to put aside $50 from every paycheck to save for your next vacation.

You wouldn't go to the bank and open a new savings account just to hold your savings for your trip. With Quicken you don't have to add a new account either. Instead, Quicken lets you pretend you're withdrawing $50 from your checking account each pay period. Hide the money away so it will seem like that much has been removed from your checkbook, even though the money really hasn't left your checkbook at all. You can then peek to see how your secret savings are doing and keep track of how close you are to meeting your vacation goal.

CAUTION **After you set up a savings goal, your checking account balance in** your Quicken check register will no longer match your real balance. Since you really have more than the register shows, you don't run the risk of writing a check you can't cover. You may feel uncomfortable, however, knowing the balance isn't right. Consider displaying your savings goals on-screen (see the section "How do I monitor my progress?" for instructions) so that you'll know how much you've really got in your account.

I need a Savings Goal Account!

To set up a Savings Goal Account, follow these steps:

1 Click Planning in the Activity bar and then select the Save for an Upcoming Expense option. Quicken displays the Savings Goals window, as shown in Figure 21.5.

2 To begin a new savings goal, click the New button. The Create New Savings Goal dialog box opens (see Figure 21.6).

3 In the Create New Savings Goal dialog box, enter the name of your savings goal, the amount you want to save, and the date by which you want to have accomplished your goal. Click OK when this information has been entered.

Fig. 21.5
You can track your savings progress in this Savings Goals window.

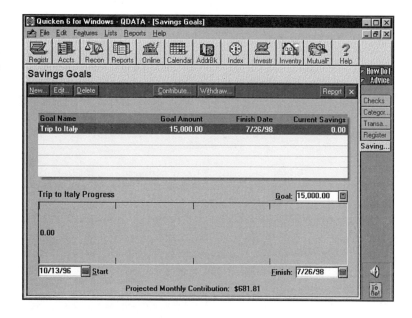

Fig. 21.6
Arrivederci! We're going to Italy!

The setup is finished. Now you're ready to start saving for your goal.

I want to enter a savings contribution

Setting up your savings goal is a good start, but now for the hard part. You have to actually put the money aside. Here's how:

1 To make a contribution to your savings goal, display the Savings Goals window on your screen. If you have more than one savings goal listed, click the one to which you want to contribute.

2 Click the Contribute button in the Savings Goals window. The Contribute to Goal dialog box opens (see Figure 21.7). Today's date and the amount of contribution appear, but you can change either of these if you want to.

Fig. 21.7
Click the Contribute
button and you can
deduct your savings
contribution from any
Quicken account.

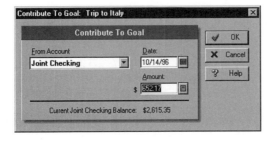

3 Select the account from which you want to make your imaginary
withdrawal.

4 Click the OK button to execute the withdrawal from your account.

Quicken deducts the savings goal transaction from your account. Not really—the money is just being set aside with the hope that you won't spend it
between now and your planned goal date. If an emergency arises, or if you
change your mind about your goal, you can always have access to your
money. The contribution to the savings goal is shown in Figure 21.8.

Quicken calculates your savings contribution amount based on your savings
goal and the length of time until you want to reach your goal.

Fig. 21.8
Quicken entered your
savings goal contribu-
tion just like a normal
withdrawal transaction.

This is the savings
goal transaction.

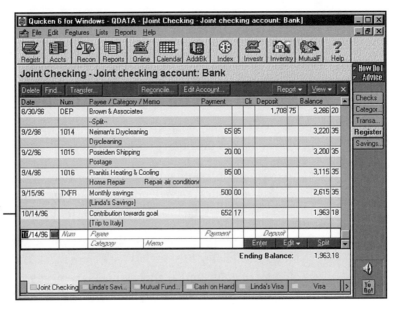

If you need some of the money you have put aside for your savings goal, you can "withdraw" funds from the savings goal by opening the Savings Goal dialog box and clicking the Withdraw button. In the Withdraw from Goal dialog box that appears, enter the amount you want to withdraw. That amount gets added back into your register as a deposit.

 Use the skills you learned in Chapter 10, "Scheduling Future Transactions," to schedule your savings goal contributions. That way you don't have to think about it at all—just let that money pile up until you're ready to cash it in and achieve your goal.

 If you want to see the account activity without the savings goal contributions, click the View button in the register button bar and then select Hide Savings Goals. Quicken hides all savings goal contributions and withdrawals. To see them again, select Hide Savings Goals from the View menu again.

How do I monitor my progress?

There are two ways in which you can monitor your savings goal progress.

First, you can return to the Savings Goals window at any time and see a bar gauge that indicates how much you have saved and how close you are to meeting your goal (see Figure 21.9).

Fig. 21.9
The Savings Goals window uses a bar gauge to monitor your progress toward saving for a particular goal.

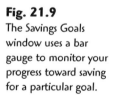
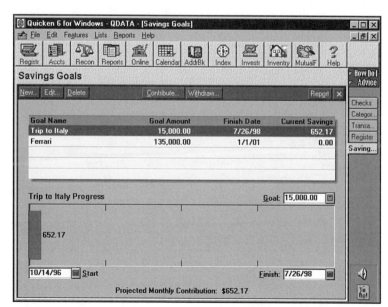

Also, you can display a Progress Bar on the bottom of your screen in Quicken. The Progress Bar monitors your savings goal amount for the time period that you specify. Display the Progress Bar by following these steps:

1 Select Features, Planning, Progress Bar. The Progress Bar appears on the bottom of the screen. You can monitor two items in the Progress Bar and you get to choose what those items are.

2 Click the Cust button on the right side of the Progress Bar to display the Customize Progress Bar window. This is where you can tell Quicken what you want to monitor in the Progress Bar.

3 Click the drop-down list in the Left Gauge Type or the Right Gauge Type to select the item on which you want to monitor progress. Select Savings Goal from the list of available items.

4 Click the Choose Goal button to select the savings goal that you want to monitor.

5 Click OK to display the Progress Bar at the bottom of your screen (see Figure 21.10).

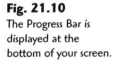

Fig. 21.10
The Progress Bar is displayed at the bottom of your screen.

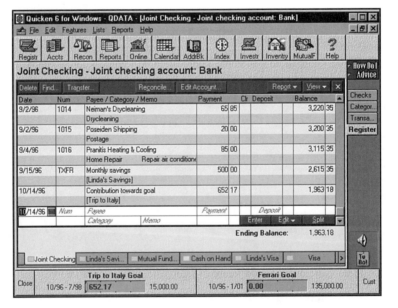

22

Getting Out of Debt

● **In this chapter:**

● **List your debts**

● **Create an action plan to reduce your debts**

● **Use Quicken to request a credit report**

Tired of feeling like you're never going to get ahead? When are you ever going to get out of debt? Has Quicken got a treat for you! You'll get an action plan to reduce your debts and feel like you can breathe again . . . . ➤

Now that you've got Quicken 6, you can develop a plan for paying off your debt quicker with the least amount of interest. With Quicken's new Debt Reduction feature, you can devise a plan to finally get out from under those annoying debt payments and make some headway toward being debt-free.

And speaking of debts, wouldn't you like to know, firsthand, how your credit stacks up? Perhaps you're thinking of buying a new home or refinancing an existing mortgage. You can now use Quicken 6 to request and receive a copy of your credit report.

Starting your debt reduction plan

Putting together a plan to reduce your debt doesn't sound much like the way you'd like to spend a Sunday afternoon. But with Quicken, it's quick, it's easy, and it's going to make you feel like you've got the horse by the reins, the boots by the bootstraps, or maybe just a better handle on your finances!

Quicken's new Debt Reduction feature does all the work for you. Quicken finds all of your outstanding debts (those that you've entered in Quicken) and lists them in the order in which they should be paid off (highest interest rate to lowest rate). Starting with the most expensive debt, Quicken calculates a new payment so that you can get it paid off as soon as possible, while still making the minimum payments on all your other debts. Then, when you've paid off the first debt, Quicken factors in the freed up cash from that debt and applies it to the second debt, and so forth.

Before you know it, you'll be out from under those pesky credit card debts and able to focus on your long term debts (like your mortgage).

Listing your outstanding debts

First things first. Let's put a list together of all your outstanding debts, like your car loan, mortgage, credit card debts, or even a loan from a friend. If you've entered all these debts in Quicken, then with the click of a button, you'll see all those debts listed in one place. Here's how to begin:

1 Click the Planning icon in the Activity Bar and then select Create a Debt Reduction Plan. Quicken opens the Debt Reduction dialog box that you see in Figure 22.1.

Fig. 22.1
Here's where you begin to formulate a plan to reduce your debts!

2 Now, click the Next button to start. If your Quicken CD is still in your CD-ROM drive, you'll see a short Show Me video that gives you an overview of the debt reduction plan process. If you're not interested in watching, click the Next button to move to the Debts tab.

3 Here's where Quicken lists the debts that were found in your Quicken file (see Figure 22.2). If there are debts that aren't entered in your Quicken file, click the Add button to open the Edit Debt Reduction dialog box where you can enter the lender, loan balance, interest rate, and minimum payment required on the loan. You can also make changes to a debt in the debt list by selecting the debt and then clicking the Edit button. Delete a debt from the list by selecting the debt and then clicking the Remove button. Click the Update Debts button to have Quicken look through your file again and re-enter all debts it finds.

Fig. 22.2
Quicken looks through your accounts and finds all of your outstanding debts.

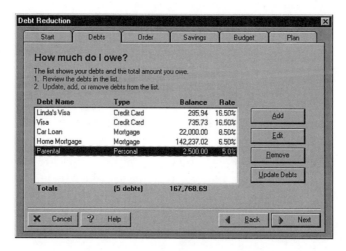

4 Click the Next button to see what your current debt situation is (see Figure 22.3). Quicken tells you when you'll be debt-free and how much interest you will have paid at that time. (It's usually a scary number!)

Fig. 22.3
Want to know how long it's going to take you to pay off your debts making the payments you're currently making? And look at all that interest you're paying!

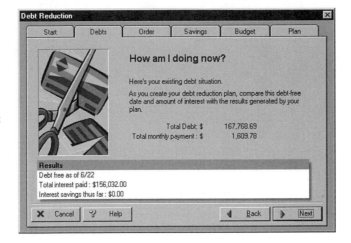

5 Click Next again to see the order in which Quicken recommends you pay off your debts (see Figure 22.4). Change the order by clicking the Change Payment Order option box and click Next.

Fig. 22.4
Here's the order in which Quicken suggests you pay off debts.

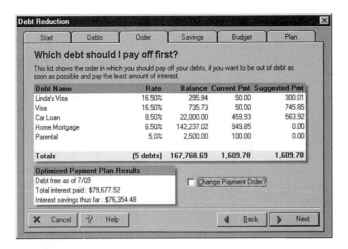

Now your debts are in order (at least listed that way), and you're ready to get resourceful about how you're going to reduce them.

Applying some of your savings to reduce debts

There are basically two ways to reduce your debts quicker: Make a lump-sum payment to reduce or pay off some of your debts or reduce some of your expenses so that you can step up the payments you make each period. In the next steps, you can decide which you'd like to do.

So now you're at the Savings tab in the Debt Reduction dialog box (see Figure 22.5). Here, you can enter an amount that you'd like to take from savings (whether it be an actual savings account, investment account, money market fund, and so forth) to apply to your outstanding debts. Quicken shows you how much you have in savings accounts and investments accounts so that you can make an informed choice about the amount you'd like to apply. Enter the amount and then click the Recalculate button.

Fig. 22.5
If you have got a nice nest egg, take a little from it to pay down your debts.

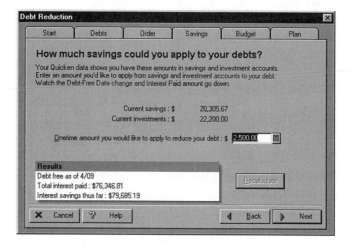

Based on the amount of savings you applied to your debts, Quicken calculates the new pay-off date, the amount of interest paid, and how much interest you'll save by making this lump-sum payment.

Click Next to look at the Budget tab (see Figure 22.6). Here's where you decide in which areas of spending you can cut back so that you can free up some cash to make extra debt payments. Quicken identifies some of the most common discretionary categories where you could possibly cut spending. In Figure 22.6, Quicken suggests cutting back on vacations, federal tax withholding, home repair, and dentist expenses. Of course, you can display other categories by clicking the drop-down arrow and selecting another category.

Fig. 22.6
Reducing your spending is a must if you hope to reduce your debts!

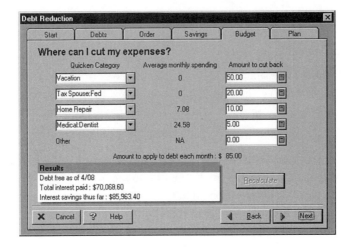

Quicken also shows you your average monthly spending in each of these discretionary categories. Enter an amount by which you think you can cut back. As you enter cut-back amounts, Quicken calculates your new pay-off date, interest payments, and interest savings.

Following your action plan

Now you're ready to see your action plan to reduce your debts. Click the Next button after you've entered your savings and budget contributions. What you see now is your Action Plan to Get Out of Debt (see Figure 22.7). You'll see how long it will take you and how much you'll save in interest charges to get out of debt.

The Action Plan takes a step-by-step approach to move you closer to being debt-free. Use the scroll bar on the right side of the Plan tab to move down the Action Plan, or better yet, click the Print this Action Plan to send it to your printer so it's easier to read.

Click the Done button to see a summary and graph of your debt situation (see Figure 22.8).

Fig. 22.7
Here's your Action
Plan to get out of
debt. Follow the
recommended steps
and you'll find yourself
debt-free sooner than
you would be if you
stick to your current
payment schedule.

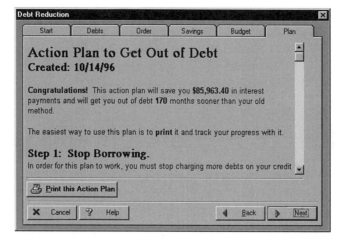

Here's a schedule of payments to reduce your debts.

Start over to create a new Action Plan by clicking this button.

Fig. 22.8
Here's a summary of
your debt situation
before and after you
implement your Action
Plan.

Click here to change your minimum payment or debt balances.

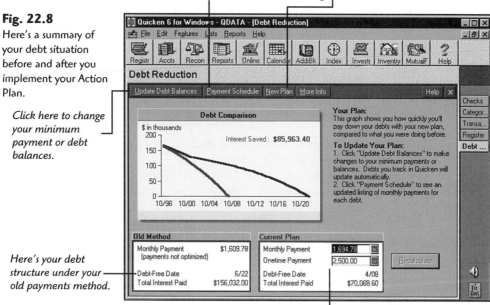

Here's your debt structure under your old payments method.

Here's your debt structure if you take the steps that Quicken recommends to reduce your debts.

TIP   **Don't forget that the interest you pay on your home mortgage is** tax deductible. (There are limitations on mortgages in excess of $1 million, however). So, be sure to take into consideration the lost tax deduction when you're deciding to pay down your home mortgage.

Use Quicken to request a credit report

Thinking about buying a house? Or maybe you'd like to refinance your existing mortgage with a more favorable interest rate? Time to fill out those college loan applications? This can be an anxious time because you're not quite sure how your credit rating stacks up.

Let Quicken help you request and receive a copy of your credit report. With Quicken, you can send a request online and receive a copy of your credit report by mail within five to seven days. The charge for your credit report is $6.00. You'll need to enter a credit card name, account number, and expiration date so that you can be billed for this charge.

If you prefer, you can use Quicken to print out a letter that includes all the information needed to order your credit report. Just sign and mail the letter to the appropriate credit bureau. You'll receive a copy of your credit report in three to five weeks, but there's no charge.

To request a credit report, follow these steps:

1 Click the Planning icon in the Activity Bar and then select Check My Credit Online to open the Credit Check dialog box.

2 There's a lot of information in the Welcome tab dialog boxes that tell you about credit reports. Click the Next button until you get to the dialog box that asks what you want to order. If ordering your credit report by mail, click the Order credit report by mail option. To order online, click the Order credit report online.

3 Click the Next button to get to the Info tab (see Figure 22.9). Now, you're ready to start filling in your personal information. Click Next as you complete each Action tab dialog box.

4 If you're requesting your report online, you'll need to enter a credit card name, account number, and the expiration date so that you can be billed for the $6.00 fee.

5 For online requests, click the Send button in the last Action tab dialog box. For mail requests, click the Print button to print out a request letter with your personal information.

Fig. 22.9
Carefully fill in your personal information. Make sure all the information that you enter is accurate.

TIP **Did you know that if you're denied credit, federal law requires** that credit bureaus provide you with a copy of your credit report if you request it within 30 days of the date you're turned down? Ask the lender which credit bureau supplied your credit report. Then, request a copy of your credit report from that bureau.

Part VI: Managing Quicken

23

Doing Some General Housekeeping in Quicken

● **In this chapter:**

- **Create a new Quicken file**

- **Open and close files**

- **Copy and rename a file**

- **Delete a file**

- **Play it safe and back up your Quicken data**

- **Restore a file**

- **What's your secret password?**

Here are some helpful housekeeping tips that keep your Quicken data files in order and keep you from losing important data (and subsequently pulling your hair out!) . . . . . ▶

Y ou may have only worked with one file in Quicken, the one you established when you installed the program. But did you know that you can create multiple Quicken files to track related accounts? I'll show you how to create new files, open existing files, and do some other neat things with your Quicken files.

By now, you've entered a lot of information in Quicken, so you want your data to be safe. I'm going to show you how to safeguard your data from power shortages or hard disk crashes and also how to keep unauthorized eyes from looking at your Quicken files.

Where is Quicken storing my data?

You've been working in a Quicken file all along and probably didn't know it. When you install Quicken, a file named QDATA.QDB is automatically set up for you to store your accounts, categories, and all transactions. Each Quicken file consists of several data files with the same filename, but different extensions. You really don't even need to concern yourself with files other than the QDATA.QDB file.

Most likely, you won't need more than one Quicken file. A separate Quicken file is needed only to store related accounts together. For example, if you and your spouse keep your finances separate, you'll want to create a different Quicken file for each of you. Or, if you want to use Quicken to handle the finances from your small business, you can create a business file that's separate from your personal file.

 CAUTION If you create separate Quicken files to store data, you cannot make transfers between two files. For example, if you have one file for your personal finances and one for your business finances, you cannot make a transfer from one of your business accounts in your business file to a personal account in your personal file. If you need to record these kinds of transfers, you can keep both your personal and business finances in the same Quicken file. Just tell Quicken you'll be tracking both when you set up your file so that it can handle both types of transactions.

Creating a new file

If you decide that you do need another Quicken file, here's how you add one. Select File, New to open the Creating new file: Are you sure? dialog box (which may seem a little strange to you). Quicken wants to make sure that you really want to create a new file, and not a new account. Remember from Chapter 3 that accounts are used to store your transactions; files, on the other hand, are used to store accounts. So, select the New Quicken File option and then click OK.

What you see next is the Create Quicken File dialog box (see Figure 23.1) where you assign a name to your new file, tell Quicken where to store it, and select categories for use in your new file. Fill in the Create Quicken File dialog box and then click the Categories button to make your category selections. Click OK to get back to the Create Quicken File dialog box and then click OK again to create the new file. Quicken closes the last file that you were working in and opens the new file. Remember that to work in a Quicken file, you have to have at least one account set up. So, Quicken displays the Create New Account dialog box so that you can set up an account to use.

Fig. 23.1
Assign a name to the new file that you're creating and tell Quicken where to store it. Also, click the Categories button to select the categories that you want to use in your new file.

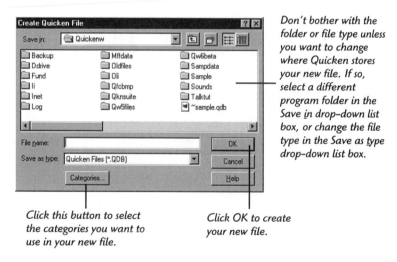

Don't bother with the folder or file type unless you want to change where Quicken stores your new file. If so, select a different program folder in the Save in drop-down list box, or change the file type in the Save as type drop-down list box.

Click this button to select the categories you want to use in your new file.

Click OK to create your new file.

Q&A *Can I use my Quicken data in other programs?*

Yes. You can export your Quicken data into database programs, spreadsheet programs, word processing programs, and so forth. When you export data from a Quicken file, an ASCII text file is copied to a file that another program can read. You also can import data from another program into your Quicken file. Both the Export and Import commands are found in the File Operations submenu of the File menu.

How to open and close a file

If you have more than one Quicken file, you'll need to know how to open the one you want to work in. When you open another Quicken file, the file that you're currently working in is closed automatically, so you really don't ever have to close a Quicken file.

When you're ready to switch to another Quicken file, select File, Open (or press Ctrl+O) to display the Open Quicken File dialog box (see Figure 23.2). All of the Quicken files that are stored in the current folder (Quickenw) are listed for you. Double-click the name of the file you want to open or enter the filename in the File name text box.

Fig. 23.2
Select the file that you want to open from the Open Quicken File dialog box. When you open another Quicken file, the current file that you are working in is automatically closed.

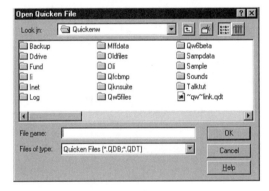

Want to see which Quicken files you've worked in recently?
Quicken shows you the last four files that you opened in the File menu (click on File to open the File menu).

I need to copy a file

You can copy the data in your Quicken file to a new file. This may be helpful if you need to give your accountant a copy of your file at the end of the year or at tax time.

When you copy a file, Quicken copies the current file to another file. So, make sure that the file that you want to copy is the current file. If it's not, open it now.

Then, choose File, File Operations, Copy to open the Copy File dialog box (see Figure 23.3). Assign a name for the new file to copy your data to and tell Quicken which transactions to copy. Then, click OK to copy your file. After Quicken has copied your file, you can select to return to the original file or go directly to the new file.

Fig. 23.3
Quicken copies all or selected transactions from the current file to a new file. Then, you can choose whether to keep the current file open or open the new file.

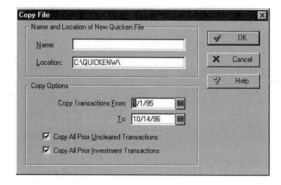

 TIP **If the power went out while you were working in Quicken, you** may experience some difficulties when you restart your computer and Quicken. To check the integrity of your Quicken file, select File, File Operations, Validate and then select the file that you want to check.

I don't like this file's name

Want to change a file's name? Go ahead—Quicken lets you rename a file without changing any of the data in it. Rename a file by selecting File, File Operations, Rename. In the Rename Quicken File dialog box that appears (see Figure 23.4), select the file that you want to rename and then enter the new filename. Click OK and the file's got a new name.

Fig. 23.4
Select the file that you
want to rename and
then enter the new
name using Windows
95 naming rules.

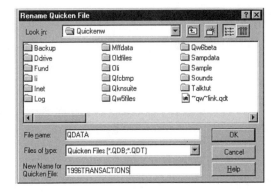

 TIP **I like to rename my Quicken files for each year that they**
represent. For example, for my 1996 financial activity, I name the file
1996DATA. For the following year, I create a file and call it 1997DATA.

Can I risk deleting a file?

If you want to get rid of an old file that you no longer need, you can delete it.
However, delete files with caution because when you delete a file, all accounts and transactions in the file are permanently removed.

 CAUTION **Because Quicken permanently removes your file when you choose**
to delete it, take a little precaution first by backing up the file. Even if
you're sure that you don't need the file anymore, it can't hurt to make a
backup copy before you delete it.

If you're using Windows 95, however, when you delete a Quicken file, it
goes to the Recycle Bin. If you decide that you need it later, you can
retrieve it from there.

Delete an unneeded file by selecting File, File Operations, Delete. Quicken
opens the Delete Quicken File dialog box that looks just like the Open
Quicken File dialog box you saw in Figure 23.2. Select the file that you want
to delete and click OK. You know by now that Quicken won't let you make
any rash decisions, so a confirmation dialog box is displayed so that you can
affirm the deletion. Type YES in the confirmation dialog box and click OK to
delete the selected file.

Q&A *Is there any way to get a file back that I've deleted?*

If you made a backup copy of your file before you deleted it, you can get your file back by restoring it. I'll show you how to restore Quicken files a little later.

Also, if you're using Windows 95, you can retrieve a deleted Quicken file from the Recycle Bin.

I don't want to lose my Quicken data

No matter how careful you are, inevitably you're going to lose some of your data. Reduce this possibility by faithfully and diligently backing up your Quicken data. It only takes a few seconds (or minutes, if you have a large data file) to back up your file, and the time it saves you in the long run if you lose data makes backing up well worth it.

If you've made backups of your Quicken files, losing data isn't that cata-strophic. You can easily restore your file using the backup copies.

TIP **There's an option in Quicken that is turned on by default, so that** you get reminders to back up your files. When you exit the program or open another file, Quicken reminds you that you haven't backed up your current file in a while. You then can choose to back up before you leave the current file; just follow the on-screen instructions.

If you're not getting these reminders, make sure the option is turned on. Choose Edit, Options, Quicken Program to open the General Options dialog box. Then click the General tab and make sure that the Prompt to Backup Files on Shutdown option is checked.

Backing up is critical!

You know how important it is to back up your Quicken files, and you're ready to do it. First, you'll need at least one formatted disk. If your Quicken file is large, you may need more than one disk to back up to, so have more than one ready.

Next, choose File, Backup (or press Ctrl+B) to open the Select Backup Drive dialog box (see Figure 23.5). Select the drive where you've inserted your backup disk and then tell Quicken whether to back up the current file or another file that you can select. Usually, you'll back up the current file.

Fig. 23.5
You can back up the current file or select another Quicken file to back up.

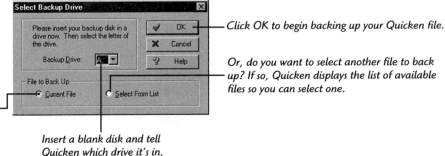

— *Click OK to begin backing up your Quicken file.*

Or, do you want to select another file to back up? If so, Quicken displays the list of available files so you can select one.

Do you want to back up the file that you're currently working in?

Insert a blank disk and tell Quicken which drive it's in.

You can choose to back up to your hard disk drive, but you should always back up to a floppy disk to avoid the risk of losing your original data and your backup data in the case of a hard disk crash.

Click OK to begin the backup procedure, which takes only a few moments. If your data file is large, Quicken will prompt you to insert another formatted disk. Click OK to continue backing up onto the next disk.

CAUTION   **Store the backup copies of your Quicken files in a safe place.**
Don't keep all your backup copies in the same place in case of fire or burglary. Store at least one copy at a location other than your home or business.

Restoring your files

I really hope that you never have to restore a Quicken file because you've lost the original one. Even though you know you have a backup copy, losing data can still make your heart stop for a moment.

If you do need to restore a file from a backup copy, here's what you do. First, open the file that you want to restore. Even though you may have lost data from the file, it should still be in your list of Quicken files. After you've opened the file, choose File, Restore to open the Restore Quicken File dialog box. Then select the drive where your backup copy is stored and the backup filename. Click OK. Quicken cautions you that restoring the backup file to the current file will overwrite any existing data. Select OK to tell Quicken to go ahead. When Quicken's finished restoring the data, you'll see a message that the file was restored successfully.

CAUTION **If disaster befalls a Quicken file that you didn't back up recently,** you may have to reenter transactions that transpired from the time you backed up to the day you lost your data. Hopefully, you have an up-to-date printed copy of your registers that you can use to enter these transactions. If you don't, however, you'll have to go back to the original source documents—checks, deposit slips, receipts, and so on—to re-create the lost transactions.

It's the end of the year

If you've got more than one year's worth of transactions in your Quicken file, you may want to archive the transactions from prior years for safekeeping. When you archive a file, Quicken makes a copy of transactions from previous years and stores them in a separate file. Your current file isn't changed; it still includes transactions from the current year and previous years.

Did you know that you can store as many as 65,534 transactions in a single Quicken file? But even though you have the space to store all of these transactions, you probably don't want to work with that many transactions in your Quicken registers. At the beginning of a new year, you can start a new file that contains only the new year's data. Starting a new year's file helps to curtail the growth of your Quicken file.

Should I archive my file data?

Archiving the data in your file simply means that you copy old transactions (those from previous years) into a separate file. This file becomes your archive file.

Select File, File Operations, Year-End Copy when you're ready to archive your data. Quicken displays the Year-End Copy dialog box as shown in Figure 23.6. Select the Archive option and click OK to display the Archive File dialog box that you see in Figure 23.7. By default, Quicken assigns the archive file the current filename followed by the preceding year and stores the file in the directory where the program files are stored. The transactions that Quicken includes in the archive file are any that precede the current year. Change any or all of this information, if you want, and click OK to begin archiving old data.

Fig. 23.6

If you want to copy (archive) old transactions to a separate file, select the Archive option.

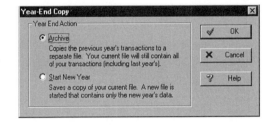

Fig. 23.7

Fill in the Archive File dialog box and click OK to begin archiving old data to a separate file.

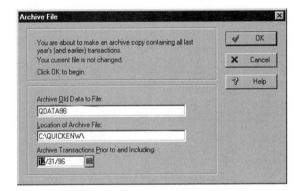

Is this the right time to start a new file?

The best time to start a new file is not necessarily on January 1. It's better to wait until after you've completed your income tax return and any end-of-year reports. When you start a new file, Quicken copies the current file and then creates a new file with only those transactions from the current year.

Start a new year's file by choosing File, File Operations, Year-End Copy to open the Year-End Copy dialog box (refer to Figure 23.6). Then, select the Start New Year option and click OK. What you see next is the Start New Year dialog box shown in Figure 23.8. Enter a name for your new year's file and make sure the correct transactions (based on the date) are going to be deleted. Then, tell Quicken where to store your new file and click OK.

Fig. 23.8
Just assign a name to the file for your new year's transactions and Quicken sets up the new file for you.

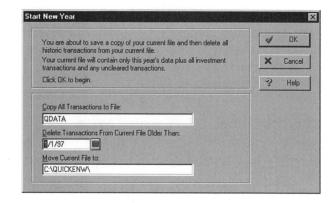

Passwords are important

I don't have to tell you how confidential your financial data is. What you've got stored in Quicken right now is information that you don't want just anyone to access or modify. Using passwords in Quicken helps to maintain the integrity of your data and keep unauthorized users out.

Assigning passwords

There are two kinds of passwords that you can use: file passwords and transaction passwords. A **file password** prevents unauthorized users from accessing your Quicken file. Quicken requires the password before opening a file. A **transaction password** restricts users from adding, changing, or deleting transactions before the date that you specify. So without a transaction password, a user cannot modify your data.

Setting up a file password

To keep unauthorized users out of your Quicken files, set up a file password. Choose File, Passwords, File to open the Set Up Password dialog box (see Figure 23.9). In the Password text box, type the combination of letters and numbers you want to use as a password (using as many as 16 characters). Quicken doesn't distinguish between the use of upper- and lowercase letters in your password, so the password **ABC** is also recognized if you enter **abc**.

As you type your password, you won't see the characters on your screen. Instead Quicken displays asterisks (*) so that others can't see your password. Press Tab to confirm your password. Type the same characters again and click OK to save your password.

Fig. 23.9
Set up a file password
so that unauthorized
users can't get into
your Quicken files.

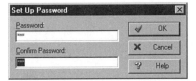

Quicken won't activate your file password until you close the file or exit the
program. When you try to open the file the next time, though, you'll have to
enter the correct password first.

Setting up a transaction password

To keep others from modifying your transactions, set up a transaction
password. Choose File, Passwords, Transaction to open the Password to
Modify Existing Transactions dialog box (see Figure 23.10). In the Password
text box, type the combination of letters and numbers you want to use as a
password (using as many as 16 characters) and press Tab. Then confirm your
password by typing it again in the Confirm Password text box.

Next, select the date before which a password will be required to change a
transaction. For example, if you don't want anyone to touch transactions
dated prior to 12/31/96, select this date. Now, click OK to save the transaction
password and immediately activate it.

Fig. 23.10
If you don't want users
to modify your
transactions, set up a
transaction password
and specify which
transactions are
restricted.

You can always change or eliminate passwords

If you know the password, you can change it or eliminate it altogether.
Choose File, Passwords and either File or Transaction (dependent on which
password you're changing). Quicken displays the Change Password dialog
box like the one you see in Figure 23.11. Regardless of whether you're
changing or eliminating a password, enter the old password first.

If you're changing the password, type the new password and then confirm it. (For transaction passwords, you can also change the date for transactions that require a password). If you're eliminating a password, leave both the New Password and Confirm Password text boxes blank. Click OK to save your password changes.

Fig. 23.11

If you're eliminating a password, leave the New Password and Confirm Password text boxes blank.

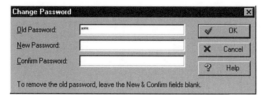

24

Making Quicken Work the Way You Want It To

● **In this chapter:**

- **The kinds of things you can customize in Quicken**

- **How to customize your Quicken program**

- **Changing the iconbar**

Who's the master here, you or your computer? Teach Quicken to behave the way you want it to! . . . . ➤

I n the early days of computer programs (oh, maybe eight or nine years ago), the thought of being able to change the appearance or the performance of a program to fit the needs of the user was ludicrous. Now, a program that can't be customized in some way doesn't seem to have a chance of lasting in the marketplace. My how times have changed!

When you start using Quicken, certain assumptions have already been made for you. For example, you see your registers displayed with two lines for every transaction, and the transactions appear in a particular typeface that has been chosen for you. Also, certain icons have been placed on the Quicken iconbar—these may or may not be icons you need. These assumptions, called defaults in some computer programs, are referred to as options in Quicken. You have the right to change the options in your own program.

How do I customize Quicken?

You can gain access to Quicken's options, the changeable, customizable features in Quicken, by choosing Edit, Options. Now you see the Options submenu with all the areas of the program that you can customize (see Figure 24.1).

Fig. 24.1
Pick your area of customization from the Options submenu.

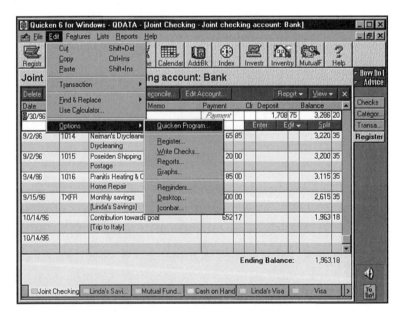

- **Quicken Program.** Controls the way your Quicken program works, in general. You can determine what's shown on your screen (QuickTabs, Activity Bar, flyover help, and so forth), color schemes, which prompts you get from Quicken, your working calendar, and other general program options. Quicken Program options are covered in this chapter.

- **Register.** Controls the way in which information is entered in the registers, how the registers are displayed, and how QuickFill works. Register options are covered in this chapter.

- **Write Checks.** Controls the information that prints on checks and gives you warnings when entering possible errors in checks. Also controls how the QuickFill feature works when writing checks. Write Checks options are discussed in this chapter.

- **Reports.** Controls the way reports are created and displayed. Reports options are covered in this chapter.

- **Graphs.** Controls the way graphs are created in Quicken. Graphs options are covered in Chapter 19, "Looking at Data Through Graphs."

- **Reminders.** Turns on the Reminder and Billminder features and sets the number of days in advance you're reminded of upcoming transactions or notes. Reminder options are covered in Chapter 10, "Scheduling Future Transactions."

- **Desktop.** Saves the open windows in Quicken when you exit the program. Desktop options are discussed in this chapter.

- **Iconbar.** Controls the icons that are displayed in the iconbar. Learn about iconbar options in this chapter.

Click any of the items in the Options submenu to open a dialog box that gives you access to the particular type of options you have selected.

Changing Quicken Program options

Quicken Program options control the way your Quicken program works. Setting Quicken Program options allows you to determine what's shown on-screen, the working calendar you'll use, the color schemes used, and so forth. To change a Quicken Program option, choose Edit, Options, Quicken Program to open the General Options dialog box (see Figure 24.2). Then, click one of the tabs at the top of the General Options dialog box to display QuickTabs, General, or Settings options. In Figure 24.2, you see the QuickTabs options that you can change. Figure 24.3 shows you the General options and the Settings tab; Figure 24.4 gives you the opportunity to set keyboard mapping and working calendar options.

Fig. 24.2
You can change what's shown in Quicken windows and dialog boxes by choosing from several QuickTabs options.

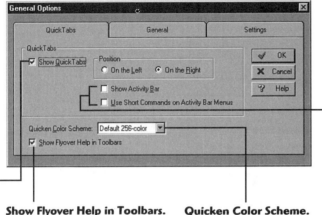

Activity Bar.
In Quicken 6, there's a new Activity Bar at the bottom of the Quicken screen. The Activity Bar includes icons that allow you to access the most common tasks in Quicken. If you don't want to use the Activity Bar, turn it off here. Or, if you want to use the Activity Bar but would like to see less text in the command lines, select this option.

QuickTabs.
QuickTabs appear along the right side of your Quicken screen each time you open a new window. You won't see QuickTabs if the Show QuickTabs option is not selected. Change QuickTabs to the left side by selecting the On the Left option.

Show Flyover Help in Toolbars.
If you let you mouse pointer hover over one of the icons in Quicken's iconbar, the Activity bar, or other command buttons, a little yellow box appears and a description of what task that icon or button performs appears on the screen. This is on by default when you start Quicken. If you prefer not to use it, you can turn it off.

Quicken Color Scheme.
Change the color scheme that you see in Quicken windows. Click the drop-down list to select a new color scheme.

Fig. 24.3
Change some Quicken settings in this dialog box.

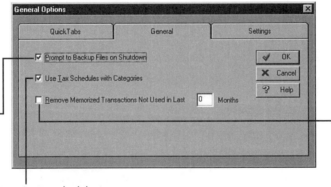

Select this option to be reminded to back up your Quicken file before you exit.

If you want to assign tax schedules to categories, make sure this option is selected. If not, you won't have the option of assigning a tax schedule when you add or edit a category.

If you want Quicken to get rid of memorized transactions that you haven't used in a certain number of months (fill in the blank), select this option. If you don't select this option, Quicken will keep all memorized transactions until you actually delete it from the Memorized Transaction List.

Fig. 24.4
Change some Quicken settings in this dialog box.

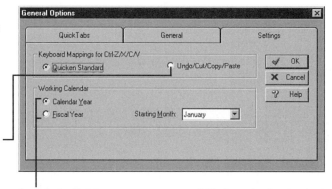

Quicken has its own uses for the key combinations Ctrl+Z, Ctrl+X, Ctrl+C, and Ctrl+V, which override standard Windows uses for these keys. If you normally use these key combinations select Undo/Cut/Copy/Paste.

By default, Quicken assumes you use a 365-day calendar that begins on January 1 and ends on December 31. Doesn't everybody? Actually, everybody doesn't. Occasionally businesses operate on a fiscal year, a year that for financial accounting purposes begins in a month other than January and proceeds for 12 months hence (April to March, for example). If you need Quicken to keep track of you records on a fiscal calendar, you can specify that calendar here.

Customize Your Quicken Register

Quicken has made an assumption about the way in which you want your register displayed on the screen: there are two lines for each entry, there is a description bar at the top of the register showing you what type of information goes in each section, the date precedes the Num field, and the category field precedes the memo field. All of these options can be changed in if you choose Register from the Options submenu to open the Register Options dialog box (see Figure 24.5). Figure 24.5 shows the available Display options.

Fig. 24.5
Change the appearance of your registers from this dialog box.

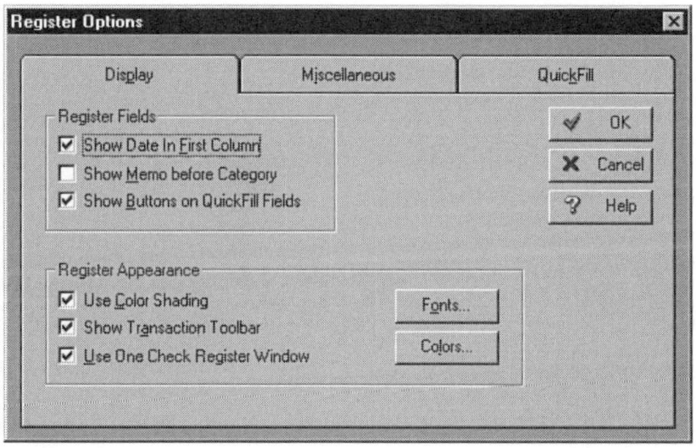

TIP **When you're working in a Quicken register, you can change** register options by clicking the Ｖiew button in the register button bar and then selecting Ｒegister Options to open the same Register Options dialog box that you see in Figure 24.5.

Customizing Checks

You can control the way checks are entered and the information that prints on your checks with the Write Checks options. Choose Ｗrite Checks from the Ｏptions submenu to open the Check Options dialog box (see Figure 24.6). You have a number of choices for making your checks look the way you want them to.

Fig. 24.6
Customize display and printing options for writing checks in this dialog box.

Click on any of the options that you want to activate, remembering that any selections you make can later be changed by opening this dialog box again.

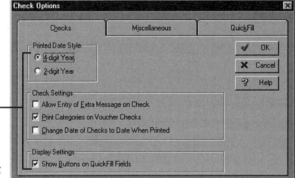

TIP **When you're writing checks in the Write Checks window, you can** change check options by clicking the Ｏptions button in the button bar to open the same Check Options dialog box that you see in Figure 24.6.

Change some things about reports, too

Just like most everything else in Quicken, some things about reports also can be changed. Maybe you'd like to see a category's description in a report rather than the category name. Or, perhaps you want to change the default report range from Year to date to Quarter to date. You can change these options, and more, in the Report Options dialog box that you see in Figure 24.7. Open the Report Options dialog box by selecting Reports from the Options submenu.

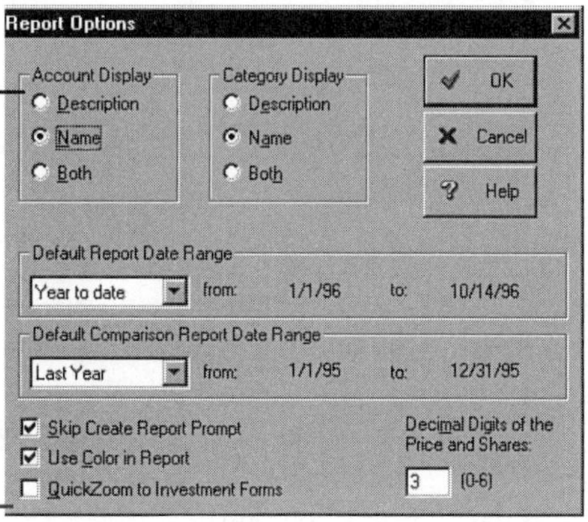

Fig. 24.7
Here's where you tell Quicken how you want reports to appear.

Select any of these report options to change the way reports are created and appear on-screen.

[Report Options dialog box]

Account Display
- Description
- Name
- Both

Category Display
- Description
- Name
- Both

OK | Cancel | Help

Default Report Date Range
Year to date from: 1/1/96 to: 10/14/96

Default Comparison Report Date Range
Last Year from: 1/1/95 to: 12/31/95

☑ Skip Create Report Prompt
☑ Use Color in Report
☐ QuickZoom to Investment Forms

Decimal Digits of the Price and Shares:
3 (0-6)

TIP **When you've got a report displayed on your screen, you can** change any report option by clicking the Options button in the button bar to open the same Report Options dialog box that you see in Figure 24.7.

Save your desktop

Did you know that you can save certain windows that you have open so that they open up again the next time you start Quicken? Well, you can by saving your current "desktop." Your desktop refers to the windows that you have open in Quicken at any given time.

By default, when you start Quicken, the windows that were open the previous time you used the program are opened again. But, if there are certain windows that you always want to open when you start Quicken, you can open those windows and select one of the desktop options that saves the current desktop.

To set desktop settings, choose Desktop from the Options submenu to open the Save Desktop dialog box (see Figure 24.8). Then, select the Save Current Desktop option. Now, the next time you start Quicken, the windows that you currently have open will open on startup.

Fig. 24.8
If you want to save certain windows so that they open when you restart Quicken, select the *Save Current Desktop* option in this dialog box.

I don't like what's in the iconbar!

The icons in the iconbar are shortcuts, placed there by Quicken to make your life easier. If you don't use some of those icons though, they aren't doing you any good.

You can rearrange the order of icons on the iconbar by merely pointing to the icon you want to move, holding down your left mouse button, and dragging the icon to a new location on the bar. Presto!

And if you think that happened quickly, just try removing an icon from the iconbar. Don't think you want an icon anymore? Hold down the Shift key and click the icon. Poof! It's gone!

You can replace icons in the iconbar with icons for tasks you like to perform, you can edit existing icons, and you can just clean house by removing the icons you don't ever use.

To change the iconbar, follow these steps:

1 Choose Iconbar from the Options submenu (as shown earlier in Figure 24.1) to open the Customize Iconbar dialog box (see Figure 24.9).

Fig. 24.9
Fill your iconbar with icons that fit your needs!

2 Notice in the Customize Iconbar dialog box that both the Show Icons and Show Text boxes are checked. This means that the icons you see on your screen have both a picture and a one-word text description displayed in the iconbar. You can select just Show Icons to display only the picture or select just Show Text to show only the word. Uncheck both of these boxes if you don't want to have icons displayed on your screen at all.

3 You can change an existing icon by clicking the icon in the Current iconbar display of the Customize Iconbar dialog box. Both the Edit and Delete buttons become accessible to you when you click an icon. Remove an icon from the bar entirely by clicking on the icon you no longer need, then clicking the Delete button. Replace an icon on the bar with an icon that performs a different task by selecting the icon you no longer need and clicking the Edit button. A list appears of all the available Quicken commands that can be assigned to icons. Select the item you want from the list, then click OK to replace the old icon with your new, hand-picked icon.

4 Change the picture used for an icon by selecting the icon in the Current iconbar display, clicking on the Edit button, and then clicking on the Change button. Pick from among a multitude of Quicken pictures for the new look for your icon.

One other neat iconbar trick you can perform is to place an icon in the iconbar that will open an account. Say you have your personal finances tucked away in Quicken and also have a separate register for a business account. Switch back and forth easily between accounts by using the iconbar.

To place an access to an account button on the iconbar, follow these steps:

1 From the Customize Iconbar dialog box (refer to Figure 24.9), click New to open the Add Action to Iconbar dialog box in Figure 24.10.

Fig. 24.10
Select an action that you'd like to add to the iconbar.

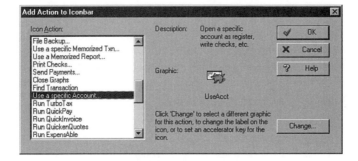

2 In the list of available actions you can add to your iconbar, scroll down the list and select Use a specific Account. Click OK and the Assign Account to Icon dialog box appears (see Figure 24.11).

Fig. 24.11
Choose the account you want to access from the iconbar.

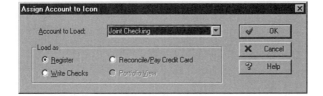

3 Select the account you want the Use Account icon to open. Choose whether you want this account to open as a register, a reconciliation or a credit card account, a portfolio view, or if you want to be able to write checks when the account opens. Then click OK.

4 Back in the Add Action to Iconbar dialog box, you can select this new icon, click the Change button, and not only select an appropriate graphics image for the icon but also change the text to read, for example, the name of your account.

From this point forward, when you click the icon for your account on the iconbar, Quicken opens the account you assigned to this icon.

Part VII: Using Quicken's Online Features

25

Making Online Payments

● **In this chapter:**

- **Set up your bank account for online payments**

- **You don't have to rely on the postal service for timely payment**

- **Get your bills ready for payment**

- **Send your payments hurtling into space**

- **Stop payment on a bill**

You now can send money from the comfort of your living room by simply clicking a few buttons! . . . .

I 've been dreaming of online bill paying for years. It seems I frequently wait to open my bills on the day they are due—sometimes even later—then I have to run out to make payments in person instead of relying on the "comfortable pace" at which our mail service moves. Sometimes I even have to make some phone calls explaining why my payment may be a couple of days late.

But now in the days of automatic teller machines and banking by phone, you can pay bills and send money in the comfort of your living room. Welcome to the 1990s!

Setting up Quicken for online bill payment

Wouldn't it be nice if you could just snap your fingers and tell Quicken, "Pay my bills electronically; I'm going on vacation." With online payments, that concept is closer than you think.

Quicken offers a service called Online Payments, which is an electronic bill-paying service. To use this service, you must have a modem, and you must sign up with your financial institution. If your financial institution doesn't offer online payment services, you can apply through the Intuit Services Corporation (ISC), which acts as a payment center to administer online payments. After you enroll in Intuit's Online Services, just set up your Quicken account for online services and you're ready to go.

 Q&A *I've used the CheckFree service before with Quicken. Is it still available?*

Yes. If you used CheckFree in previous versions of Quicken, you can continue to use it in Quicken 6. However, if you set up a new service in Quicken 6, you'll use that service instead of CheckFree.

First, set up your modem

 Setting up your modem is no big deal anymore because Quicken does all the work for you. Just choose Features, Online, Modem SetUp to open the Set Up Modem window and then click the Find Modem button. Quicken searches the recesses of your computer and the plug-in ports until it finds something resembling a modem. If Quicken finds more than one modem, you see them listed, by communications port, in the Select a Modem dialog box (see Figure 25.1). Just choose the modem that you want to use with Quicken and click OK. Quicken checks your modem configurations settings and enters them in the Set Up Modem window. If you need to make any changes, do so now. Click OK and, voilà, your modem is set up for use in Quicken.

Fig. 25.1
If Quicken finds more than one modem, select which one you want to use for online bill paying.

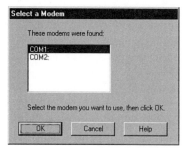

> ❝ *Plain English, please!*
>
> A **modem** is a piece of equipment you add to your computer that allows you to communicate with the world via your telephone line. ❞

 TIP **Test your modem by registering your software online with Intuit** (the folks that make Quicken). Select Register Quicken from the <u>H</u>elp menu in Quicken. Note that if this Register Quicken is not available in the <u>H</u>elp menu, then you've already registered your software.

Next, apply to use the online payment service

If your financial institution currently supports Intuit's Online Services, then the fastest, easiest way to apply for online services is to use your modem and apply directly from your computer. Choose Fe<u>a</u>tures, <u>O</u>nline, Online Banking Setup, <u>G</u>et Started to open the Get Started with Online Banking & Investment window that you see in Figure 25.2. Click the Apply for Online Services button to begin the application process. When your information is complete, send the application to Intuit through your modem.

Fig. 25.2
Get a quick and easy start to online services by applying directly from your computer.

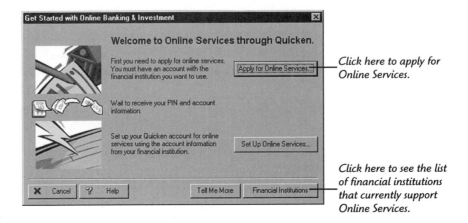

Click here to apply for Online Services.

Click here to see the list of financial institutions that currently support Online Services.

If your financial institution does not support Online Services, you can still use the service through your financial institution; you just need to complete the Intuit Services Corporation application form included in your Quicken 6 for Windows package, include a voided check from your checking account, and mail it to the address on the form.

In either case, before you can begin using Intuit's Online Services for bill paying, you must wait to receive your account information and PIN (personal identificiation number). This number is like a password that gives you access to your bank account information. You need this information before you can set up your Quicken account(s) for online bill paying.

 CAUTION   **If you have more than one bank account that you want to use for online bill paying, you have to complete the application process for each account. Each account that you enroll in Intuit's Online Services has its own PIN and account information.**

Now, set up a Quicken account for online bill paying

After you've applied (either online or through the mail) for online services, you will receive an Online Services Account Information Sheet that confirms that Online Services has been activated and is ready for your use. This sheet contains your 4-digit personal identification number (PIN) for each account for which you have applied for Online Services. Also included in the Online Services Account Information Sheet is the 9-digit routing number for each online account, as well as your monthly base service fee charged by your financial institution for online bill paying. This fee is determined by the financial institution and will vary.

To set up your Quicken account(s) for online bill paying through your bank, choose Features, Online, Online Banking Setup, Get Started to open the Get Started with Online Banking & Investment window as shown in Figure 25.2. Then click the Set Up Online Services button to see the Online Account Setup dialog box shown in Figure 25.3. If the account that you'll be using for online bill paying is not already set up in Quicken, select the Create New Quicken Account option. If the account is already set up in Quicken, select the Edit Existing Quicken Account option and choose the account from the Account Name list. Quicken then leads you through the steps necessary to enter your bank account number, the bank's routing number, and your PIN.

Fig. 25.3

Create a new account in Quicken to use for online bill paying, or designate an existing account as an online bill paying account.

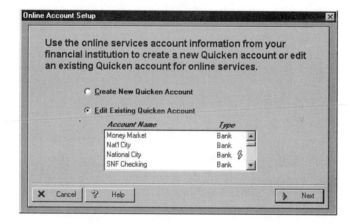

When you receive your Online Services Account Information Sheet, you will get a PIN assigned to you. When you set up online services, you are asked for this PIN, then you are asked to replace that number with one of your own choosing. Verify your new PIN by typing it again, right under the first place where you typed it. Remember your new PIN—this is the number you must type every time you want to pay a bill or send information to Intuit online.

Q&A *How do I know that my online finances are secure and confidential?*

Intuit and your financial institution ensure the confidentiality of your financial information. Your information travels through a private network, not the Internet, with a password issued and stored by Intuit. Your PIN, known only by you, must be entered each time you go online. And, your financial information is protected by the use of high-level, state-of-the-art encryption.

TIP **A number of financial institutions support Intuit's Online Services.** To view the names of these financial institutions, read a little about the services they offer, and get their phone numbers, click the Financial Institutions button from the Get Started with Online Banking & Investment Center (refer to Figure 25.2). Then just click the name of the financial institution from which you want more information.

Chapter 26, "Doing Your Banking Online," gives more detail about online banking, whereas this chapter is more concerned with online bill paying. You don't have to bank online to pay bills online.

Tell Quicken whom you want to pay

So, you've got your Quicken account(s) set up for online bill paying. Now you're ready to set up your online payees. Select Online Payees from the Lists menu to open the Online Payee List shown in Figure 25.4.

Fig. 25.4
Here's the list of payees that are set up in Quicken for online payment.

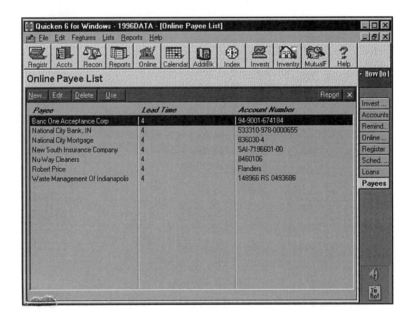

Next follow these steps:

1 Click New in the Online Payee List to display the Set Up Online Payee dialog box shown in Figure 25.5.

2 In the Set Up Online Payee dialog box, begin typing the name of one of your payees (see Figure 25.5), or click the Name drop-down list arrow to see a list of your QuickFill payees. When you begin typing one of your payees, Quicken fills in the rest of the name for you.

Fig. 25.5
Begin typing a payee's name and Quicken fills in the rest of the name for you.

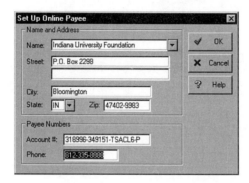

3 Type the address, city, state, and ZIP code for your payee.

4 Fill in the account number—this is your personal account number with that payee. You should be able to find this on a copy of a bill from that payee. If you have no account number, you may leave this blank, or type your name in the space for account number.

5 Type the payee's telephone number. This is the number you call if you have a question about your bill. Be sure to include the area code.

6 Click OK to record the payee in the Online Payee List.

I'm ready to pay a bill

The bills are approaching their due dates; it's time to try paying someone online. To set up a new online payment, follow these steps:

1 Click the Online icon in the iconbar. Quicken opens the Online Banking & Investment Center window that you see in Figure 25.6.

Fig. 25.6
Enter all of your online payments and send e-mail from the Online Banking & Investment Center.

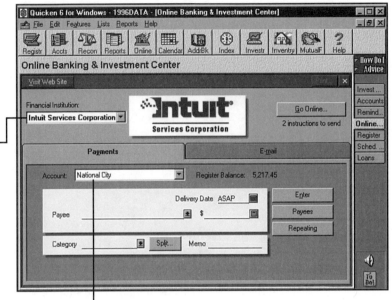

The name of the financial institution providing your Online Services should appear here.

Select the bank account you want to use for the payment.

2 Click the Payments tab.

3 Make sure that the financial institution to which you applied for Online Services appears in the Financial Institution drop-down list box at the top of the Online Banking & Investment Center window. If not, click the down arrow to select the correct financial institution.

4 Next, in the Account drop-down list, select the Quicken bank account from which you want to make the online payment.

5 Then enter the online payment just as you would if you were writing a check: Enter the delivery date, select the online payee, fill in the amount, assign a category (or split the online transaction to assign more than one category), and enter an optional memo.

TIP **To ensure that your online payment is made on time, schedule the** payment to occur at least four business days in advance of the payment due date. This allows enough time for the payee to receive payment if Online Service sends a printed check versus an electronic funds transfer.

6 Click the Enter button to record the online payment instruction.

7 Repeat steps 5 and 6 for each online payment that you want to make.

8 Now, click the Go Online button to open the Instructions to Send dialog box (see Figure 25.7). Any payment instructions or e-mail that you've entered will be listed in this window. Click on each payment instruction that you want to send now.

9 Enter your 4-digit PIN and click the Send button to download your payment instructions to your financial institution.

10 After the payment instruction is transmitted, Quicken displays a summary of your online transactions. Print a copy of the Online Payment Summary by clicking the Print button and then click OK. This serves as your confirmation that the payment instruction was received and the transaction will occur on the specified date.

Fig. 25.7
When you're ready to transmit your payment instructions, click the Send button in the Instructions to Send dialog box.

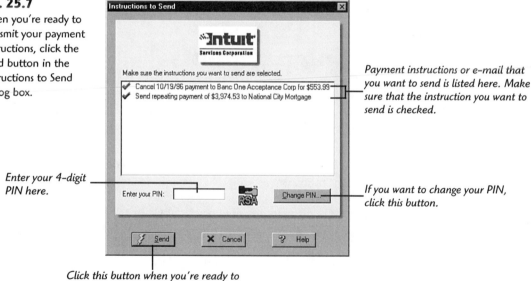

Payment instructions or e-mail that you want to send is listed here. Make sure that the instruction you want to send is checked.

Enter your 4-digit PIN here.

If you want to change your PIN, click this button.

Click this button when you're ready to transmit your payment instructions.

✓ **TIP** **You can also enter an online payment directly into the register** for your online account. Enter the date, payee, amount, category, and memo as usual. In the Num field, however, select Send Online Payment. Quicken enters the word "Send" here. Record the transaction and then go online, as explained in the previous steps, to send your payment instruction.

Your financial institution determines if a payee is able to receive electronic fund transfers. If that is possible, the funds can be received by the payee within 24 hours. If the funds cannot be sent electronically, your bank will issue a check and mail it to the payee, using the mailing address you entered when you set up the payee as an online payee. Typically there is no additional charge for this mailing service.

CAUTION **Online bill payment is convenient and efficient, but don't think** that you can wait until the last minute to send a payment instruction and the payment will arrive on time. Remember, there are two types of payments that Online Service processes: EFTs (electronic funds transfers) and printed checks. If a payee is set up to receive EFTs, Online Services initiates a funds transfer directly from your bank account to your payee. This takes about two days. If a payee is not set up to receive EFTs, a check is printed by Online Services (drawn on your bank account) and mailed to your payee. This type of payment usually takes four days.

Entering repeating payments

For those payments that are to the same payee, for the same amount each period, like your mortgage payment, insurance premium, auto lease payment, and so forth, you can enter a repeating payment. When you enter a repeating payment, you send the payment instruction once, and your financial institution automatically makes the payment each period. To set up a repeating online payment, follow these steps:

1 From the Online Banking & Investment Center window, click the Payments tab. Make sure that the correct financial institution and Quicken account are selected.

2 Click the Repeating button to open the Scheduled Transaction List. Notice that the Online Repeating tab is already selected. This is where Quicken stores all repeating transactions that you set up to be paid online.

TIP **You must be using an account that is registered as a member of** Quicken's online services to have the option to make online repeating payments. This registration process is described earlier in this chapter.

3 Click the New button to open the Create Repeating Online Payment dialog box (see Figure 25.8). Enter the date of the first payment, the online payee, memo, category, and amount—just as you would for setting up any new Scheduled Transaction (as described in Chapter 10, "Scheduling Future Transactions").

Fig. 25.8

The Create Repeating Online Payment dialog box opens when you select New from the Scheduled Transaction List.

4 If the payee you enter is not already set up as an online payee, Quicken gives you a message indicating the payee is "not found." To set up this payee for online payment, click the Set Up button and enter the address and account number information for this payee in the window provided; then click OK to add the payee to your online payee list.

5 Select the payment frequency and duration. You can also set the "Prompt To Go Online x Days Before Due Date," filling in a number for the "x." If you have Reminders turned on, Quicken will remind you in advance of impending payments.

6 Click Authorize to record the repeating online payment in the Scheduled Transaction List.

7 You're not finished yet. Now, you need to follow steps 8 through 10 in the previous section, "I'm ready to pay a bill," to go online and send your instructions for the repeating payment.

TIP **You can change a regularly scheduled transaction to a repeating** online payment by selecting the scheduled transaction in the Scheduled Transaction List and then clicking the Edit button. From the Edit Scheduled Transaction dialog box, in the Type of Transaction drop-down list box, select Online Pmt. Then click OK.

TIP **If you're planning a vacation and have bills you need to pay while** you're away, set them up as online transactions. You can send the online payment instructions before you leave but the payments won't actually be made by your financial institution until the designated due date (taking into account the requested lead time).

 Plain English, please!

Lead time is the amount of time in advance of the due date of a payment that you want your financial institution to begin the transfer of funds. If you want to make sure a payment gets where it's going two days early, request a lead time of three days—two days of lead time plus one day of transferring the funds from your account to that of the payee. Quicken omits holidays and weekends when figuring lead time; only regular business days are counted. **"**

Help! I need to stop payment on a check

If a payment instruction has been sent but the payment has not yet actually been made, you can transmit a stop payment order. To stop a single payment, follow these steps:

1 Click the transaction you want to stop in your register.

2 Make sure your modem is hooked up and your phone line is free.

3 Choose Edit, Transaction, Cancel Payment.

4 If your cancel payment request is made with enough time in advance, Quicken displays a confirmation dialog box to cancel the payment. Click Yes to create a cancel payment instruction. Quicken enters a Stop sign symbol next to the transaction in your register.

5 Next, you need to Go Online from the Online Banking & Investment Center and send the instruction to cancel the payment. Follow steps 8 through 10 in the section "I'm ready to pay a bill" earlier in this chapter to learn how to go online to send instructions.

Making payment inquiries

You can check the status of a payment at any time. When you send an online payment instruction, Quicken logs information about when that payment occurs. You can see this information at any time by clicking the payment you are concerned with in your register, and then choosing E̲dit from the transaction button bar and then selecting Payment Inquiry.

Quicken opens the Payment Inquiry dialog box (see Figure 25.9) that tells you the check number, payee, amount of the payment, and the date that the payment was made or will be made. Select the U̲pdate Status option to create an inquiry instruction in the Instructions to Send dialog box. Select E-mail M̲essage to create a text inquiry. Click OK. Then select G̲o Online from the Online Banking & Investment Center to send your status request or e-mail message.

Fig. 25.9
Quicken tells you the status of an online payment.

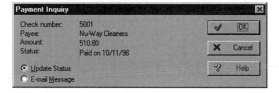

26

Doing Your Banking Online

⬤ **In this chapter:**

- **Getting started with online banking**

- **Setting up an account for online banking**

- **You can suck information from the bank's computer**

- **Getting online information for your Quicken credit card**

- **How to transfer funds among accounts**

Forget the lines and the hassles—I'm banking from the comfort of home! . . . .

I
magine a world in which you don't have to spend your lunch hour waiting in line at the bank, only to have the teller stick the "Next Teller Please" sign in your face as you finally make it to the front of the line. Things like direct deposit of paychecks and automatic teller machines have done a lot to alleviate the teller lines. Now there's a new way to relieve banking frustration: online banking.

You can use your computer to perform several banking functions that once were reserved for the teller lines—find out if checks have cleared, compare bank records to your own, and update your register with the latest transactions from your bank account. Best of all, you can perform these actions day or night, 24-hours a day.

The incentives for online banking are enormous: save time by not having to make a trip to the bank, save aggravation by not having to remember what days and hours the bank is open, and you don't even have to wait in line until it's your turn.

 Now, with Quicken 6, you can send instructions to your financial institution to download transactions, transfer money, and pay bills, all from the new Online Banking & Investment Center window with just a *single* phone call! In this chapter, you learn all about online banking from the Online Banking & Investment Center window. In the previous chapter, "Making Online Payments," I told you how to pay your bills online from the same window.

I'm convinced! Sign me up

Signing up for Online Services is easy. And guess what? You can even sign up when you are online. Or, you can fill out the Online Service enrollment form that came with your Quicken software, send it to your bank, and your bank will return to you a Welcome Kit, introducing the online features. Included with the Welcome Kit are two numbers that you need: a 7-digit bank routing number, and a Personal Identification Number (PIN).

When you receive your Welcome Kit, you are ready to begin banking online. Make sure your modem is set up correctly (see Chapter 25, "Making Online Payments" for specific information regarding setting up your modem and getting hooked up with your bank).

Q&A ***How do I find out if my bank is a participant in Quicken's online banking service?***
Click the Online icon in the Activity Bar and then select Get Started with Online Banking & Investment to open a window where you can apply for and set up online services. Now, click the Financial Institutions button to see the directory of financial institutions that participate in Quicken's online banking service.

Setting up accounts for online banking

To get your Quicken account ready for online banking, follow these steps:

1 Click the Accts icon from the iconbar to display the Account List.

2 Select the account you plan to use with online banking (this will be a checking or savings account at that bank). Click the Edit button to open the Edit Bank Account dialog box (see Figure 26.1).

Fig. 26.1
Click the Enable Online Banking option to tell Quicken you plan to implement the Online Banking feature with this account.

3 Click the Enable Online Banking check box.

4 Click the Next button.

5 In the next Edit Bank Account dialog box, shown in Figure 26.2, enter the name of your bank, the routing number, your bank account number, the type of account you are using, and your Social Security number. You cannot proceed beyond this screen without filling in the requested information.

6 Click Done to indicate you have finished entering your bank information.

On the Account list you now see a bolt of lightning next to your account name indicating that your account is available for online banking.

Fig. 26.2
Enter the name of your bank, routing number, account number, type of account, and your Social Security number in this dialog box. You should have received the bank routing number in your Welcome Kit that came from the bank.

I want to download my bank transactions—NOW!

All right, all right, don't be so impatient! You've gotten yourself set up with the bank and you're ready to communicate. One of the joys of doing online banking is that your bank is now open 24 hours a day. So when you want information, you don't have to wait until the tellers get there in the morning.

To access the online banking services through Quicken, follow these steps:

1 Make sure your modem is hooked up and your phone line is free.

2 Click My Accounts in the Activity Bar and then select Download Online Transactions. Quicken opens the Online Banking & Investment Center window that you see in Figure 26.3.

3 If you have more than one online service, select the appropriate financial institution from the Financial Institution drop-down list in the Online Banking & Investment Center window (see Figure 26.3).

4 Click the Transactions tab and select the account you want to access in the Account list. In Figure 26.3, the account I'm using is the Checking Account.

Fig. 26.3
Open the Online Banking & Investment Center window and open up a world of armchair banking opportunities.

Click here to display a list of the institutions with whom you have online accounts.

A list of all your accounts with this financial institution appears here.

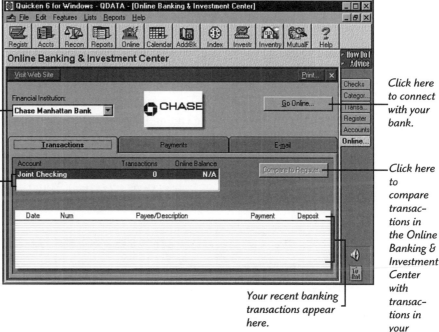

Click here to connect with your bank.

Click here to compare transactions in the Online Banking & Investment Center with transactions in your register.

Your recent banking transactions appear here.

5 Click the Go Online button to connect with your financial institution. Quicken displays the Instructions to Send dialog box with a list of instructions.

6 Make sure that the instruction to download transactions is checked. Then click the Send button.

7 You are then prompted to enter your Personal Identification Number (PIN). Enter your PIN and then click OK. Quicken dials the bank's number and collects data for all of your accounts at that bank.

Now that you're connected to your bank, what's the next step? You can review your transactions, update your register, and get information about your credit card; you can even transfer funds if you have more than one account at that financial institution.

Q&A *How long am I online when I download transactions from my financial institution?*

Don't worry. You're only online for a short time. As soon as your instructions are transmitted and your transactions are downloaded, Quicken disconnects.

Take a look at your account transactions

When you connect with your bank, Quicken grabs the transactions from your account. Now you need to look at those transactions. Click the Compare to Register button in the Online Banking & Investment Center window and Quicken opens your register along with the Online Balance dialog box displaying the transactions you just downloaded.

You can review your transactions on-screen. Your transactions are sorted by date.

Can I update my register with these new transactions?

Don't be satisfied with just looking at your transactions. Take advantage of the fact that you are viewing the real transactions as recorded at the bank. If you are viewing a checking account, what you see are the checks that have cleared your bank since your last statement.

- Quicken looks at the date, amount, and check number of each transaction in the bank's records and tries to match it up with one in your register.

- For transactions that match, Quicken fills in the payee and category information it gets from your register. The word "Match" is placed next to each bank transaction that matches the register transaction.

- If the bank's transaction doesn't match a transaction in your register, it is assumed the transaction is a new transaction. The word "New" is placed next to these transactions.

- If a transaction is a duplication of one already in your register, click on the extra, unneeded transaction and click the Delete button to remove it from the list.

- If you agree with a transaction that is matched to your register transaction, click the Accept button. If all of the bank transactions match your register transactions, click the Accept All button. For all matching transactions, Quicken marks your register with a c in the Clr column to indicate the transaction has cleared your bank (not to be confused with the R mark that signifies the transaction has been reconciled). For all new transactions, Quicken adds the transaction to your register and marks it with a c to indicate it has cleared.

- To choose only selected transactions for updating your register, click individual transactions, and then click the Mark button to mark the transactions you want to update. Click the Accept button to enter new transactions in your register and clear all marked transactions.

- When Quicken finishes, it automatically disconnects the modem link to your financial institution, clears the Online Balance dialog box, and returns your view to the register that you just updated.

Can I get data for my Quicken credit card?

You can get information about your Quicken Credit Card online from the Online Banking & Investment Center window. Begin in the same way that you did to get information about your checking account.

1 Make sure your modem is hooked up and your phone line is clear.

2 Click the My Accounts icon in the Activity Bar and then select Get My Transactions Online to open the Online Banking & Investment Center window (refer to Figure 26.3).

3 Select the appropriate financial institution from the Financial Institution drop-down list in the Online Banking & Investment Center window (refer to Figure 26.3).

4 Click the Transactions tab. In the list of accounts enabled for online banking, choose your Quicken credit card account.

5 Click the Go Online button. Quicken displays the Instructions to Send dialog box with a list of instructions. Make sure that the instruction to download your transactions from your credit card is checked.

6 Then click the Send button.

7 You are then prompted to enter your Personal Identification Number (PIN). Enter your PIN and then click OK. Quicken connects to the financial institution and gets the latest data regarding your credit card.

The techniques you just learned for comparing and updating information in your register with transactions from the online account apply to the Quicken Credit Card as well.

I want to transfer funds between accounts

You can use Quicken's Online Banking feature to transfer funds between two accounts at the same financial institution. Follow these steps to transfer funds online:

1 Make sure your modem is hooked up and your phone line is free.

2 Click the Online icon in the iconbar to open the Online Banking & Investment Center window (see Figure 26.4).

Fig. 26.4
Transfer money between two accounts that you have at the same financial institution.

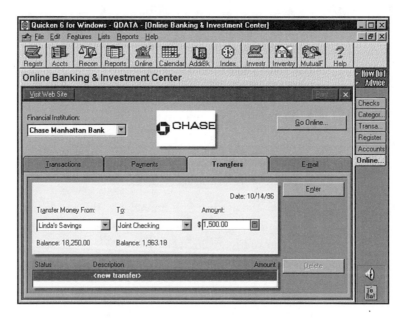

3 Choose the financial institution at which you bank from the drop-down list.

4 Click the Transfers Tab.

5 Choose the accounts in the Transfer Money From and To drop-down list boxes.

6 Enter the amount of the transfer in the Amount box and then click the Enter button.

7 Now, click the Go Online button to open the Send Instructions dialog box with a list of instructions. Make sure that the instruction to transfer funds is checked and then click the Send button.

8 You are then prompted to enter your Personal Identification Number (PIN). Enter your PIN and then click OK.

9 Quicken calls your bank and requests the funds transfer. The transfer occurs and a Transmission Summary dialog box appears. If you are satisfied with the information that appears in this dialog box summarizing the transaction, click OK.

Quicken disconnects the modem and you're finished.

Index

A

Accept All button, 391
accessing
  accounts, 368
  financial planners, 322
  online banking, 388-389
Account command
  Edit menu, 45
  Lists menu, 25
Account List, 45-50
  accessing, 26
  Balance Total, 46
  displaying, 27
  View Hidden Accounts
    checkbox, 48
Account menu commands,
  New, 45
Account Name box, 17
Account selection bar,
  49-50
accounts
  adding, 40-45
  asset, creating, 190-194
  balances
    entering, 18-19
    inserting, 42-43
    reviewing, 165-166
  balancing, 117-123,
    125-126
  cash, setting up, 184-186
  credit card, setting up,
    197-199
    see also credit cards
  debt reduction plan, 335
  defining, 38-39
  deleting, 27, 47-48
  displaying, 48
  editing, 27, 46, 76
  hiding, 48
  investments
    assigning names, 249
    comparing mutual
      funds, 253
    inserting transactions,
      254-259

    setting up, 248-252
  liabilities, 224-225
  listing, 45-46
  naming, 17-18, 42
  online banking, setting up,
    387-388
  online bill payments,
    374-376
    creating, 375
    setting up, 377-380
  reconciling, 26, 117-123
  savings
    entering contri-
      butions, 330
    monitoring, 331-332
    paying off debts,
      337-341
    Savings Goal Account,
      328-332
    tracking, 328-332
  securities
    buying, 255-256
    setting up, 251
  selecting, 49-50,
    117-118, 313
  setting up, 16-17, 40
  sorting, 49
  starting new, 27
  statements
    dates, 18-19
    inserting, 118-119
  transactions
    reviewing, 390
    updating, 390-393
  types of, 38-39
Accts icon, 25
activating reminder
  settings, 168
Activity Bar, 30-31, 40, 45
Add button, 58-59
Add Categories window, 58
adding, see inserting
Address Book, 26, 156,
  172, 179-180

addresses
  entering payee's, 102
  Financial Address Book,
    174, 177
    deleting, 176
    editing, 176
    inserting, 175-176
    personal names, 174
    printing, 178-180
    searching, 177-178
Adjust button, 86
adjusting, see editing
adjustment trans-
  actions, 124
Ads category, 53
Advanced button, 313
Advice button, 223
Align button, 109
Align Checks dialog
  box, 110
aligning
  checks, 108-111
  continuous-feed checks,
    109-110
amortized loans, 208
archiving
  data files, 353-355
  transactions, 353-355
armchair banking, 389
asset accounts, 38
  creating, 190-194
  transactions, entering,
    192-193
assets, defined, 184
Assign button, 237
assigning
  categories
    multiple, 84-88
    to transactions, 82-83
  checks
    categories, 103-104
    subcategories, 103